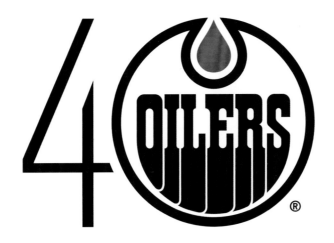

GRIT *AND* GLORY

CELEBRATING 40 YEARS OF
THE EDMONTON OILERS

LORNA SCHULTZ NICHOLSON

VIKING

VIKING

an imprint of Penguin Canada, a division of Penguin Random House Canada Limited

Canada • USA • UK • Ireland • Australia • New Zealand • India • South Africa • China

First published 2018

www.penguinrandomhouse.ca

LIBRARY AND ARCHIVES CANADA CATALOGUING IN PUBLICATION

Schultz Nicholson, Lorna, author
     Grit and glory : celebrating 40 years of the Edmonton Oilers / Lorna
Schultz Nicholson.

Issued in print and electronic formats.
ISBN 978-0-7352-3346-1 (hardcover).—ISBN 978-0-7352-3347-8 (electronic)

     1. Edmonton Oilers (Hockey team)--History. I. Title.

GV848.E35S38 2018   796.962'6409712334   C2018-900622-6
                                                       C2018-900623-4

Cover and interior design: Andrew Roberts
Cover image: (front cover) David E. Klutno / Contributor / Getty Images;
(back cover) Codie McLachlin / Stringer / Getty Images

Printed and bound in China

10 9 8 7 6 5 4 3 2 1

Penguin
Random House
VIKING CANADA

CONTENTS

Letter from Glen Sather . . . VI

Letter from Kevin Lowe . . . VII

Letter from Ryan Smyth . . . VIII

Letter from Connor McDavid . . . IX

Introduction by Wayne Gretzky . . . X

PART 1: BUILDING BLOCKS (1972–79) . . . 2

PART 2: BECOMING CHAMPIONS (1979–90) . . . 18

PART 3: AFTER THE DYNASTY (1990–1997) . . . 118

PART 4: EDMONTON'S TEAM (1997–2003) . . . 180

PART 5: EDMONTON FIRST (2003–2018) . . . 202

The People Who Keep the Machine Well Oiled . . . **299**

Past and Future . . . **303**

Bibliography and Works Cited . . . **305**

Image Credits . . . **306**

Acknowledgements . . . **307**

Index . . . **308**

Creating a winning team takes a lot of people, and I had many to help me along the way. I thank Barry Fraser for drafting the way he did and Peter Pocklington for letting me coach the team the way I wanted. And the city of Edmonton is just terrific. I was born in High River, Alberta, and grew up in Viking and Wainwright, Alberta. My first junior hockey game was played in the old Edmonton Gardens. Being in Edmonton for as long as I was suited me and my family just fine.

Now, about gelling a team. It all started when we got Wayne from Indianapolis and I knew we had to surround him with the right players. I watched these boys grow up and I knew right from the beginning I had a good group. They were humble and talented and that's quite the combination. But they were boys—kids really. I knew that was going to be a problem. So, I wanted to let them experience other things beside playing hockey and being celebrities and just going to bars. There was no shortage of bars for them to go to in Edmonton, so we made sure to do other things. We went fishing and target shooting and these were things some of them had never done before. These opportunities were good for them and they had a good time together. We also went snowmobiling—that might not have been the smartest thing to do. Snowmobiles can be dangerous. Pocklington got stuck in a tree hole once and we had to go back and dig him out. And Buchberger ran into a fence post. I had a lot of fun around the players and I really wanted to give them another interest in life. Kids need to have fun.

But I also had hockey players. They were fast and I always wanted them to be on the offence even when we were up by a lot of goals. I never felt that they were over-confident and I never told them to let up. The rule was to just keep going. My job was fairly easy because I had such good players. I didn't have to do some big pregame speech. Once they were ready in the dressing room, I always read the opposing team's line-up to them. Then one of the players (probably Essa or Kevin) would hit the back of our door with his stick and we would sit there and boo the opposing team. All I had to say was "kick the hell out of them." Then they would file out, because they knew what to do.

I had the best group of guys, who loved and appreciated each other. I had great captains in Wayne, Mark, and Kevin. And we had a city and an owner behind us. I'm lucky to have had such a great run in Edmonton.

—*Glen Sather*, President of the New York Rangers

I've been with the Oilers for most of my life and it has been quite the ride. I am blessed to have played and coached here, and have management roles. I've enjoyed the pinnacles of success, but seen my share of failures as well.

It's a very tough and often unforgiving business. Perhaps Mike Keenan, my coach when I played for the New York Rangers, put it most succinctly. He said, "There're only two things in hockey, winning and misery." I've experienced both. People see the glamorous side of the game, and that of course can be wonderful, but you have to be all in, all the time. I've always kept in mind something veteran teammate Pat Price said to me in my rookie season: "kid, if you want to stay sane in this game, don't let your highs take you too high or your lows take you too low." Great advice for longevity in the NHL.

As you might imagine, playing was the most rewarding job. When you're a player, you focus on getting ready for a game. If you're fortunate and win, you're in a relaxed mode until the next game. If you lose, you do your best to put it behind you. Either way, your focus is only on the next game.

As you go higher in the hockey world, those moments of peace grow shorter. A coach has to get everybody ready. When you win a game, you get a few moments to enjoy it, but you must quickly shift gears and prepare for the next. As a general manager, win or lose, there is no time to be satisfied; there's always something that needs to be done. When I was considering taking the GM position with the Oilers, Glen Sather sagely advised me that, from his personal experience, playing was the most fun, followed by coaching, and then managing. Ten years later and I knew what he was talking about. Managing a team is a difficult and thankless job. But that is the reality of being in a hockey market with the highest of expectations. And I wouldn't have it any other way. Those relationships with the team and the city are precious, and it's the most exciting place to be.

Now, the Edmonton Oilers have the expanding core of a very good hockey team, and with Connor McDavid as the leader, there is every good reason for optimism as the Oilers head toward success over the next decade. This book takes a look back, celebrating the stories of our past. As we enjoy them, I join you in looking ahead to the future.

—Kevin Lowe, Vice-Chairman of Oilers Entertainment Group

I'm an Alberta boy. When I was a kid growing up in Banff, I was a huge Oilers fan. So when I was

drafted by the Oilers I had to pinch myself; it was so surreal. It was like a dream come true. My parents had already moved from Banff to Red Deer for my brother's hockey and once I started playing for the Oilers they got to come to all the games. They already had Flames tickets and gave them up so they could come to the Oilers games. When we made it to the Stanley Cup Finals in 2005–06, it was like a dream. We took it to game 7 and I don't live in regret about that loss—not for a minute. Not winning that final game put a lot of things into perspective. I have a great family and I have won gold medals for Canada. Being with the Oilers allowed me to accomplish things along my journey. I owe Glen Sather a lot for drafting me and seeing me through.

Being traded to the Islanders was a blow and I think I was thankful we didn't come west while I was with them. Then I was signed as a free agent with Colorado. The first time I came back to Edmonton—this time as a visitor, and in an Avalanche sweater—I had to come out to the ice on the Zamboni side instead of through the Oilers tunnel. That's when it really hit home that I wasn't an Oiler. Then Don Metz (Aquila Productions) had a tribute for me before the game. This made me cry. I never wanted to leave and coming back was emotional. But in the end, leaving was something I had to do to appreciate my hockey career. I was able to see that the game of hockey was bigger than the team I had loved from the time I was little. I always felt alive on the ice whether it was in an Oiler or Avalanche uniform. But when I landed back in Edmonton at the end of my career, my family was thrilled. I spent my last years on the ice playing for my team. It was so humbling to receive a standing ovation on my retirement night, and to have my family at centre ice. It was a first class event and it was touching how the whole day went.

On February 12, 2018, I got to speak at the 1984–85 Greatest Team Ever Event. When my name was called to the stage I walked up there and looked around. I was eight years old when these players won the Stanley Cup and I was now on stage with them. I grew up watching them play! They were *my* team. I was so honoured. Edmonton is home. I love the community, the people, and I love the Oilers.

—*Ryan Smyth,* Retired player

It was low odds the Edmonton Oilers would win the draft lottery in 2015, so it was a big shock when they got the right to select first overall. When Bill Daly revealed the winning team, I was as surprised as anyone and it took a moment for it to sink in. There was no guarantee the Oilers would select me with their pick, but I couldn't help myself. I started to learn more about Edmonton and the Oilers—and I got even more excited.

After the entry draft, I visited the city and met the organization. It hit me that I was going to play for a team that had a lot of history. Learning more about all the accomplishments, and the amazing players that had worn the Oilers sweater, I felt honoured to join in that history.

Initially, there was definitely a sense of pressure. The city hadn't seen the playoffs in almost a decade—but it knew greatness. All I could think was that I wanted to bring it on, to try and make history again. I wanted to be part of the city and the organization more than ever.

In my second year with the team, I was named captain. It made me a little nervous at first, but I felt ready for it. To be a captain of an NHL team was something I had always wanted, but not something I ever saw for myself at nineteen. I wanted to learn from the guys in the dressing room, who were older and more experienced than me, and I wanted to be a good leader. It was an honour, especially following so many great Oiler captains.

The team really came together in the 2016–2017 season and when we made the playoffs, the fans were amazing—Edmonton fans are all in, and they know their hockey. Seeing our fans come together, and have our backs the way they did, and cheer so hard for us, is something I want to see again. The energy in Rogers Place was so crazy and I want to feel that again.

The expectations were high after having such a good playoff run in 2017. This year (2017–2018) has definitely been filled with ups and downs. We didn't get the winning start we wanted. But we have a strong nucleus of players from last year and the guys in this room are excited as ever to be part of the Oilers. We will figure it out and we will move forward. We want to bring the Stanley Cup back to Edmonton.

—*Connor McDavid, Oilers Captain*

Introduction by WAYNE GRETZKY

Even today, when I put on an Oilers jersey I'm proud to be wearing it, proud of the logo, proud of the city, and the fans behind the team. Edmonton has some of the best fans in the world, and it was both a privilege and an honour to be part of such an organization.

When I first arrived in Edmonton I was a young kid, 17 years old, and I had no idea what to expect. The WHA team was an old team age-wise and I was just this skinny kid who'd already been traded. Being so young, it was an adjustment for me to be moving again so soon, settling in with a new team, and living in another new city. Immediately, the people in Edmonton made me feel at home. I was lucky that the players accepted my arrival and many of them treated me like a son. Ace Bailey, Dave Dryden, Blair MacDonald, Ron Chipperfield, Eddie Mio, Colin Campbell—they all had their eye out for me. I'm pretty sure Glen Sather had instructed them to look after me.

For the first couple of months in Edmonton I lived with Anne and Glen Sather and their children. Right away, I felt as if I had a home and that was important to me and my parents. Glen knew exactly what to do to make a team, and if that meant taking in a naïve kid, then that's what he did. He took the pressure off me and didn't push me through media. In those days there wasn't a lot of press, especially playing in the WHA. Half the time, the games weren't even on television. So, the only press I really had to deal with was Rod Phillips and Jim Matheson and those guys were really good to me. So much was radio back then. From day one, I was accepted and I feel lucky that these older guys treated me so well.

When I got to Edmonton, I enrolled in school: Ross Sheppard High School. My dad had to sign my contract with the Oilers, to legalize my deal. And he told me I had to continue in school until I was 18. On my birthday I could make up my own mind on whether I wanted to go to school or not. With such a hectic hockey schedule, the day I turned 18 I made the decision to stop going. Back then, there was no online schooling or tutors who travelled with the team—if you wanted to graduate, you went to class. That was your only option. Playing professional hockey didn't give me that option. I was practising every morning, and we were the farthest west of any WHA team, so we spent a lot of time sitting on planes. It was too hard to maintain my school work and be a professional hockey player. In today's world, I would have graduated for sure.

I had a lot of mentors during my early years, and Garnett Ace Bailey stands out.

My relationship with Ace started in that first WHA year. I spent a lot of time with him and his wife Kathy, and they were like second parents to me. Ace had played with the Boston Bruins in Bobby Orr's early years so he knew what to do with a young kid like me. He'd seen a young Bobby deal with his career and he guided me with the media, the guys, our opponents, and also helped teach me what to do in the community. When it came time for the Oilers to be part of the NHL, Ace's career was kind of over—he had a bad knee and a bad shoulder. Glen saw the importance of our relationship, though, and moved him to the front office. He went on to scout with the Oilers for years. This was such a good move for me because I could relate to Ace, and I was able to sit down and talk to him at the arena or over dinner. It was different than talking to a coach.

In that first NHL year, we went from an older team to a very young team. In an inaugural year like that, you're not sure where you fit in and you just try and survive. You're always worried about keeping your spot on the team and on the roster. Kevin Lowe and I were both NHL rookies and we became friends and roommates. We rented an apartment in the Lord Nelson complex at 5125 Riverbend Road. Near our building was an outdoor hockey rink. Late in the afternoon, on days off from games, we would take our skates, sticks, pucks (even tennis balls) and head outside to jump on the rink with the other kids in our neighbourhood. My goodness, I probably did that a couple of times a week. I wasn't really well known yet in the city so I just had fun playing with the other neighbourhood kids. That tells you how young I still was. Playing outdoor hockey was so enjoyable, and we'd play for hours.

Right from the beginning, we thought we were going to win the Stanley Cup. I laugh about that now. It's funny that we thought like that, but that's a good thing, I guess. Because in the end we did win. Although we were a young team, Glen made sure we had some unselfish veterans on the roster. These players taught us young guys how to be good in the community: Colin Campbell, Blair Macdonald, Ron Chipperfield. I like to say these players were the ones who "ran through the knives" for the Oilers. They knew we were going to be something special and just wanted to be there, to help in any way with our growth and development. They were honest and hard working and felt a deep responsibility to the team and the game. With them, we learned how to be part of a community, and not just hockey players. They took us to visit hospitals and to places were we signed autographs. They taught us to be gracious, all the while knowing they might not even be on the bench to celebrate the end result, a Stanley Cup victory. I admire that. They just wanted to do their part to help. I believe it was these unselfish players who created the saying "Once an Oiler, Always an Oiler!"

I'm proud of that saying. I'll always be an Oiler first. I love Edmonton, and the people in Edmonton. Some of my greatest hockey memories are from playing for the Oilers.

PART I

1972–1979

BUILDING BLOCKS

To tell the story of the Oilers' 40 years in the NHL, we have to first

look back to where it all began—a unique group of players in Alberta,

and a remarkable hockey builder known as "Wild Bill" Hunter.

The Alberta Oilers

Year in and year out, no matter what the hockey season brings, the Oilers can count on a base of passionate fans in a city that loves them. Even though we're celebrating 40 years of the Edmonton Oilers in the National Hockey League, the team's history dates back to 1972, shortly after the World Hockey Association was founded. At the end of that league's seven-year run, the NHL agreed to admit four of its teams—the Hartford Whalers, Quebec Nordiques, Winnipeg Jets, and the Edmonton Oilers.

Four decades later, the Oilers are the only team of the four still playing in the same city as in 1979-80. Their highs have been very high, including five Stanley Cup championships, but the low points include a ten-year run of not making the playoffs. The team has almost been relocated to Houston, or Seattle, or Minnesota, or Hamilton. There have been ownership changes, and ultimately a move into a new arena with a brand-new look.

One man, a child of the prairies, was instrumental in the birth of the Oilers. His name was William Dickenson Hunter or, as most people knew him, "Wild Bill" Hunter. Born in Saskatoon, Saskatchewan, Hunter had spent countless hours in hockey arenas as a coach, manager and owner of hockey teams. He wore all three hats with the Edmonton Oil Kings when they won the Memorial Cup, Canada's national championship of junior hockey, in 1966. The same year, he helped create the Canadian Major Junior Hockey League, which evolved into the Western Hockey League. An entrepreneur, hard worker and visionary given to (some would say) crazy schemes, Hunter was determined to bring professional hockey to Alberta. He was always thinking bigger and broader.

In 1970, Hunter lobbied for an NHL team for his adopted home province. Being turned down only fired him up. Having already started one league, he figured it was more than possible to start another. As luck would have it,

Despite exciting hockey action, and boasting some of the biggest stars in the game, the WHA didn't last.

Hunter got a call from two American promoters, Gary Davidson and Dennis Murphy, who were trying to get a new professional hockey league started—one that would include franchises in markets the NHL had rejected as too small or remote for expansion teams. In 1967, Davidson and Murphy had launched the American Basketball Association, a league that was in direct competition with the National Basketball Association, and by 1971 they were seeking to do the same with hockey. Their brainchild was to be called the World Hockey Association. Hunter jumped at the chance to be involved. With great gusto, he travelled extensively, visiting arenas all over North America—sitting in stands, eating concession food, schmoozing in the press boxes, searching for suitable markets and ownership groups. Of course, Edmonton and Calgary were at the top of his wish list.

On November 1, 1971, the Edmonton Oilers became one of the 12 founding WHA franchises—the name had been an informal nickname for the Edmonton Oil Kings back in the 1950s. And a franchise called the Broncos was granted to Calgary. The makings of a highly anticipated rivalry seemed to be in place, but the Battle of Alberta would have to wait a few years to be waged. Before the season started, the Broncos franchise folded and its place was taken by the Cleveland Crusaders. This move occurred before the WHA's opening faceoff in October. The shift caused Hunter's team to be renamed the Alberta Oilers and a plan was put in place to split home games between Edmonton and Calgary.

Wild Bill Hunter had absolute faith that he could build a competitive pro team with players who had played junior in Edmonton or elsewhere in the province. True to his vision, the Oilers lineup had a distinctly homegrown flavour. Eleven players were born in Alberta, including defencemen Doug Barrie (Edmonton), Bob Falkenberg (Stettler), Steve Carlyle (Lacombe) and Derek Harker (Edmonton), and forwards Jim Harrison (Glendon), Ron Walters (Castor), Eddie Joyal (Edmonton), Val Fonteyne (Wetaskiwin), Brian Carlin (Calgary), Ron Anderson (Red Deer) and Dennis Kassian (Vegreville). Others, who weren't born in Alberta, were graduates of the Oil Kings. That was good enough for Hunter.

On October 11, 1972, the Oilers would win the first game in WHA history, beating the Ottawa Nationals 7–4 on the road. As the season continued, the arrangement that the team would play half of its home games in Calgary never did materialize. Instead, the Oilers played all of their home games in Edmonton. But that was Bill Hunter in a nutshell. He made up rules as he went along—some he kept, many he broke.

The Oilers played mediocre hockey all season, ending up with a record of 38–37–3 that left them tied with the Minnesota Fighting Saints for fourth place in the WHA's West Division. Alberta and Minnesota then had to meet in a one-game showdown to determine which of them would advance to the playoffs. The only remnant of the

Calgary plan was this tiebreaker game, played at the Stampede Corral. The Saints won the game 4–2, advancing to the playoffs against Winnipeg.

At the end of the season, the Alberta Oilers reverted to their original name, the Edmonton Oilers.

NORTHLANDS COLISEUM

Most of the Oilers' games in the first two WHA seasons were played in the 5,200-seat Edmonton Gardens. The Gardens had been hailed as a magnificent building when it opened way back in 1913, when any indoor rink was a marvellous luxury. Edmonton fans have always been supportive of their heroes on ice. Fan favourites during the WHA Oilers' early years included defenceman and team captain Al Hamilton, goaltender Dave Dryden and forwards Blair MacDonald and Bill "Cowboy" Flett.

But by 1972 the arena was already outdated and dilapidated—historic, perhaps, but definitely not suitable for professional hockey. Hunter, naturally, aimed high and envisioned a new arena worthy of a major-league operation. He and his Oiler co-owners, Dr. Charles Allard and Zane Feldman, hooked up with Northlands, the non-profit

organization that, among many ventures, promoted rodeos. Charles Allard was a surgeon at Edmonton General, and an entrepreneur. Although he was heavily involved in real estate, it was the automotive industry where he met Zane Feldman. They partnered up for business and a long term friendship. Wild Bill saw the many benefits of teaming up with them, and today all three are considered Oilers' founders. Their vision and tenacity kept professional hockey alive in Edmonton. They asked one another why couldn't a new arena be for both horses and hockey?

Of course, there were naysayers who didn't think a new arena in Edmonton was a good idea, and as with any structure of this kind, there was debate about who would pay for what, where the arena would be built, who would be allowed to use it, and so on. Feldman took over the role of getting this arena built. Ground

was broken at 118th Avenue and 73rd Street in November 1972, and despite delays and cost overruns, the building—to be called Northlands Coliseum—was ready to host its first Oilers game two years later, almost to the day.

Well, almost ready. The club's 1974-75 home opener was scheduled for November 9, but it had to be postponed because several thousand seats still needed to be installed. Workers hustled all night, and on November 10, the Edmonton Oilers took to the ice against the Cleveland Crusaders—even as 200 patrons had to bring seat cushions with them because the final batch of seats had not yet been delivered, much less bolted into place. The players had to dress at the Gardens and be bussed to the arena because their dressing room was still plywood. One of those players was Jacques Plante, who at the age of 45 was in net for Edmonton. Plante had retired

Bill Hunter never really liked to be called Wild Bill. "If to be passionate and emotional looks wild to some people, so be it. Other people call me an eternal optimist." Here, he works with his beloved Oil Kings.

from the game in 1965, after winning six Stanley Cups with the Montreal Canadiens, but was lured back to the NHL in 1968 to play for the St. Louis Blues. From there he went to the Toronto Maple Leafs and the Boston Bruins before he retired for a second time and joined the WHA as a coach and General Manager for the Quebec Nordiques for the 1973–74 season. The Oilers coaxed Plante to come out of retirement yet again to play in their new arena. In that first game at Northlands Coliseum, the Oilers beat the Crusaders 4–1 and the new building was off to a strong start.

Originally, the Coliseum seated 15,423, but over the years it was upgraded to a capacity of nearly 17,500. When the Oilers joined the NHL in 1979, it was one of the larger arenas in the league. In the 1990s, in response to the changing financial landscape of pro hockey, several hundred seats were removed to allow for the construction of luxury boxes and suites. By 2016, as the Oilers played their final games there, the capacity was 16,839.

Despite several rounds of renovations, the Coliseum was the last NHL arena to have the player benches on the same side of the ice as the platforms for the television cameras—a quirk that gave Oiler home games a distinctive appearance on TV.

Northlands Coliseum (also known at various times as the Edmonton Coliseum, Skyreach Centre, and Rexall Place) was an important, necessary factor in Edmonton becoming part of the National Hockey League.

NUMBER 3: AL HAMILTON

Born in Flin Flon, Manitoba, 26-year-old defenceman Al Hamilton became the team's first captain, a WHA all-star and the glue that held the Oilers together throughout their first seven years and into the NHL era. A product of the Edmonton Oil Kings, Hamilton broke into the NHL at the age of 19, playing four games for the New York Rangers in 1965–66. He finally caught on full time with the Rangers in 1969–70, and then was claimed by the Buffalo Sabres in the 1970 expansion draft. In February 1972, the Oilers claimed him in the WHA's General Player Draft.

A few months later, in May, Hamilton got a call from Wild Bill Hunter, whose Oil Kings were playing in the Memorial Cup tournament at the Ottawa Civic Centre. "Meet me in Ottawa," Hunter said. "I've got a deal for you."

"He was the ultimate promoter," said Hamilton. "I was intrigued."

The drive from Buffalo to Ottawa would take between five and six hours. Hamilton thought about the phone call, and a pang of homesickness flowed through him. During those junior years in Edmonton, he had come to think of the city as home. Maybe meeting Bill Hunter in Ottawa would be worth the drive.

So, he went. Face to face with Hunter, Hamilton was further swayed and he started to think this new league might just be OK. Plus, Hunter wanted him to be the first player to sign with the new franchise—and best of all to a five-year contract. By this time in his life, Hamilton was married with children, and he loved the city of Edmonton. He took the deal and never looked back.

Hamilton holds the distinction of being the only player to spend the WHA's seven years with the same team. There were others who stayed in the league for its duration, but never without being traded or being signed as a free agent. The difference is, Al Hamilton *wanted* to play in Edmonton. In a league where changes were happening every day, his stability proved to be a rare feat among the expansion and contraction, divisional realignments, franchise and player moves, and new arenas and ownership groups.

He did, however, play for many different coaches. In 1972, there was Ray Kinasewich, who had led the Oil Kings to their 1966 Memorial Cup championship. But, dissatisfied with his performance, Hunter took over for the rest of the season. Brian Shaw, another ex–Oil Kings coach, made it through 1973–74 and most of '74–75 before Hunter let him go and again stepped behind the bench.

Clare Drake, a longtime coach of the University of Alberta Golden Bears, took over the reins for the 1975–76 season. Drake was a forward thinker, but perhaps a little ahead of his time for Bill Hunter. Drake liked to record hits, face-offs, shots, and turnovers, and study where they happened on the ice. He was a student of the game and a master at teaching and sharing. Winning wasn't his only goal. The Oilers had a record of 18–28–2 when, for the third time in four years, Wild Bill fired a coach and took over. Ending up at 27–49–5, good for fourth in the Canadian Division, Edmonton

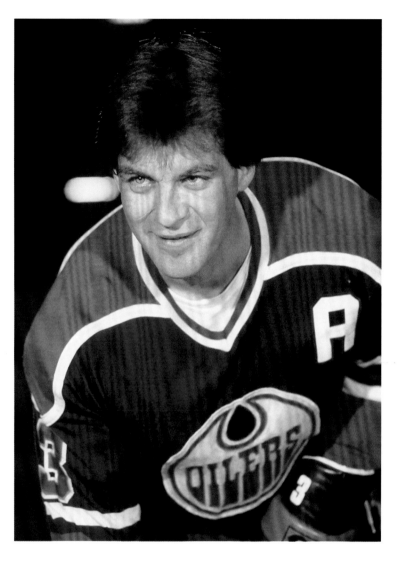

managed to make the playoffs, but the Winnipeg Jets had little trouble sweeping their best-of-seven series by scores of 7–3, 5–4, 3–2 and 7–2.

Despite the team's struggles on the ice, Hamilton enjoyed success on a personal level, leading the Oilers with 50 assists in 1972–73 (and a club-high 124 penalty minutes) and tying for the team lead with 45 a year later. In 1974, he was a second-team all-star and played for

Al Hamilton is the only player in the history of the WHA to spend seven years with the same team.

Team Canada in the series between WHA stars and the Soviet national team. A bad knee sidelined him for the bulk of the next two seasons.

The year 1976 marked a turning point for the Oilers in many ways. During the summer, Wild Bill Hunter stepped aside as general manager, his place taken by Bep Guidolin. Control of the team passed to Allard, who quickly sold a majority stake to Nelson Skalbania. Soon afterward, Peter Pocklington purchased a share of the team. The Oilers would show a steady improvement over the next three seasons, culminating in a first-place finish and an appearance in the Avco Cup final in 1979. Al Hamilton would be part of that transition. In 1977–78, despite more injuries, he earned a spot on the WHA's first all-star team after scoring 54 points in 59 games.

Hamilton retired after the 1979–80 NHL season, and on October 10, 1980, the Oilers raised his number to the rafters, the first sweater the team had ever taken out of circulation—a fitting honour for the original Edmonton Oiler.

ENTER PLAYER-COACH GLEN SATHER

When general manager Bep Guidolin signed Glen Sather in September 1976, the energy of the Edmonton Oilers changed and a sliver of hope emerged. Sather was a hard-working, gritty winger with a decade of NHL experience. What no one could have known at the time was how important signing him would prove to be for the future.

Sather was born in High River, Alberta, and had played junior hockey for the Oil Kings, winning a Memorial Cup championship with them in 1963. In 1964, the Detroit Red Wings assigned him to Memphis of the Central Professional Hockey League, where he began his pro career. He gained a reputation as a reliable role player, becoming a full-time NHLer in 1967–68, but he moved around a lot: from Memphis to Oklahoma City, Boston, Pittsburgh, New York, St. Louis, Montreal and Minnesota. In three years, he had played for four teams. So when Guidolin offered him a two-year contract, Sather knew he had to sign. He had a family and he just wanted to be in one spot.

There was an added bonus: he was to be the captain of the Oilers. This may have caused tension in the beginning, but Al Hamilton (who was then wearing the C) quickly realized that Sather had a vision. Right from day one, Sather helped run the Oilers practices. His years of running summer hockey schools came in handy. Since 1969, Sather had run the *Holiday Hockey* camp in Banff, Alberta, and he was always searching for new drills. When he took over the Oilers practices, he held innovative, European-inspired drills designed to make the team faster and more skilled. The WHA had already opened its doors to European players, who brought with them a new skill set and approach to the game, which intrigued Sather. He had spent countless hours watching the Winnipeg Jets, the 1976 Avco Cup champions whose lineup included Swedish forwards Anders Hedberg, Willy Lindstrom and Ulf Nilsson and defencemen Thommie Bergman and Lars-Erik Sjoberg.

With the 1976–1977 season over, Sather was once again called into Pocklington's office. This time, co-owner Nelson Skalbania joined them. Skalbania asked Sather what he thought about the season. Sather answered that he thought the team had potential. Then a zinger was thrown out: What did he think about taking on the role of head coach full time? And, further, how would he like to be in charge of player personnel? The idea was that Larry Gordon would handle the business side, Brian Conacher would become GM, and Sather would coach and also help with the selection process. Again, Sather agreed. He was more than ready for the challenge and for his family to remain in Edmonton.

As Sather was adjusting to the idea of becoming head coach, he got a call telling him that since the Oilers were out of the playoffs, he should go over to Prague, Czechoslovakia, to scout at the International Ice Hockey Federation (IIHF) World Championships. He was to leave as soon as possible. Just one problem, though: the banks wouldn't be open before he was scheduled to depart, and he had no foreign money. What would happen if he got over to Europe and the Oilers couldn't (or wouldn't) send any money to him? Would he have to buck up for his trip? He wasn't sure yet how they operated from the business side. This trip, for Sather, became a test of trust. With little money in his pocket, he boarded the plane. Once overseas, he met with Skalbania, who gave him the funds he needed up front. "That started it all," said Sather.

OWNERSHIP

In 1975, the trio of Charles Allard, Zane Feldman, and Wild Bill Hunter sold the Edmonton Oilers to Vancouver businessman Nelson Skalbania. Soon after, Skalbania took on a partner named Peter Pocklington. There's a story behind how that transaction came to be. Pocklington and his wife, Eva, were having a quiet dinner at the Steak Loft on Jasper Avenue in Edmonton when Skalbania walked in with an entourage of at least 20 people. Pocklington got up to say hello and to ask what was going on. Skalbania answered that he'd just bought the Edmonton Oilers. Pocklington took a few seconds to think about this before he asked if Skalbania might want a partner. Why not? With Skalbania in agreement, Pocklington took Eva's diamond ring and, right there in the restaurant, gave it to Skalbania as a down payment. They drew up an agreement on a paper napkin. Also included in the sale was a vintage 1928 Rolls-Royce Phantom that was used in the Robert Redford film *The Great Gatsby*. Skalbania drove the car back to Vancouver, grinding the stiff gears and squeaking the rusty brakes. Pocklington never got the car or the ring back, and Skalbania ended up giving both to his ex-wife in a divorce settlement, much to Pocklington's dismay. Pocklington replaced the car with other models, and bought Eva a sparkling new diamond.

The partnership lasted six months before Pocklington bought out Skalbania, giving him full ownership of the Edmonton Oilers. The team at this point was floundering and losing money,

Young Wayne Gretzky played eight games for the Indianapolis Racers before being traded to the WHA Edmonton Oilers.

but Pocklington agreed to assume the debt. He liked the high profile that owning the Oilers gave him in Edmonton, and thought the publicity would be good for his car dealership businesses. Skalbania, not yet finished with professional hockey, turned around and bought the Indianapolis Racers of the WHA. While in Indianapolis, he acquired the rights to a 17-year-old phenom from Ontario named Wayne Gretzky.

YOUNG WAYNE GRETZKY

When Pocklington approached Sather in 1978 with the name of a young player on the Indianapolis Racers who might be a good fit for the Oilers, Sather

agreed to have a look. Pocklington already knew about Wayne Gretzky, having read about him in the *Star Weekly* years prior. Sather also remembered the article. It ran under the headline "Little No. 9 with Big 9 Aspirations" and described a 10-year-old boy from Brantford, Ontario, who wanted to be the next Gordie Howe. The article captured the attention of *Hockey Night in Canada* and prompted a meeting between young Wayne Gretzky and his hero, Mr. Hockey, Gordie Howe.

Sather looked at the teen's stats. They were good—certainly good enough, seeing as the kid was only 17. One night when the Oilers were in Indianapolis to play the Racers, Sather went to the home team's practice and sat in the stands. He stared at the ice, at all the players. Where was this Wayne Gretzky? All he could see was a skinny kid on the ice who looked like he "was one of the player's kids out for a skate."

When he found out that kid *was* Gretzky, he watched him but didn't really see anything special. He shrugged and headed back to the Oilers dressing room. They had a game to prepare for.

When the game got underway, Sather changed his mind about the boy. The kid had intelligence, smarts with the puck and an uncanny sense of vision uncommon in other players his age—or even other players, period. Sure, he wasn't big, but there was something there. He's going to be great, thought Sather.

Later that evening, after the game, Sather met with Pocklington and they talked about Gretzky. The decision was made: "If you can get him, get him."

WAYNE GRETZKY FLIES TO EDMONTON

The story has circulated for years that the Oilers obtained Wayne Gretzky, possibly the best hockey player ever, by winning a backgammon game. According to Gretzky and Pocklington, there isn't any truth to it. Pocklington and Nelson Skalbania were friends, and they did make a lot of wagers while playing backgammon, but they didn't make any bets over a player, especially not Wayne Gretzky.

In 1978, at the age of 17, Gretzky had played just eight games with the Indianapolis Racers. Gretzky was not yet old enough to be drafted by an NHL team, so Skalbania had signed the young player as a free agent—after he had played just one season of major junior with the Sault Ste. Marie Greyhounds in Ontario—thinking he could turn his franchise around with a star player in the lineup. Ticket sales didn't take off, perhaps because Gretzky wasn't yet ready to be that hero. In need of cash to keep his team operating, Skalbania sought to sell the contract of his young star-to-be.

When Gretzky arrived in Indianapolis, his father, Walter Gretzky, had said he wanted his son to live with a family—as he would have done in junior—and take some high school courses towards his diploma. Unbeknownst to either Wayne or Walter, Skalbania was looking to sell him and a few others on the team. In a conversation that must have seemed to come out of the blue, Skalbania told him he was going to be traded. But the owner gave the youngster a choice, telling him he could be traded to either Winnipeg or Edmonton. Gretzky had no idea how to answer this question. He remembers thinking that he was only eight games into his professional hockey career, and already he was being traded. Confused, he called his agent and manager at the time, Gus Badali, and asked what to do.

"Edmonton has a 16,000-seat arena," said Gus. "They have a better chance of getting into the NHL. Tell them you want to go to Edmonton."

Michael Gobuty was a part owner of the Winnipeg Jets at the time, and he likes to say that the standard operating procedure in the WHA was different—they just made "I need your guy, you need my guy" deals. "We knew nothing about hockey, but we had camaraderie like you would not believe. We just had the most amazing time. The WHA was just fun. And the business was just a sidetrack for all of us because we were all independent and wealthy. It was just a toy; the NHL was business."

Gobuty flew to Indianapolis to watch Gretzky play and have dinner with him afterward. (Gretzky couldn't have a beer because he was too young.) Even after watching him score two goals, he still wasn't sure about acquiring Gretzky. Upon returning to Winnipeg, Gobuty talked to his general manager, Rudy Pilous, a longtime scout, coach and manager. He said, "No, Gretzky's too skinny. They'll kill him."

Gobuty broke the news to Skalbania one evening after a game in Winnipeg. Skalbania phoned Pocklington from the Winnipeg airport and asked if he wanted Gretzky. Without hesitating, Pocklington said yes.

Then the dealing started. Pocklington was to cover the cost of Gretzky's original WHA contract, which was worth $250,000. Then he was to provide a $200,000 down payment for the rights to Gretzky, goaltender Eddie Mio and left winger Peter Driscoll. At first, Pocklington also agreed that Skalbania could buy back 50 percent of the team at a time of his choosing—a month later, Skalbania waived this right in exchange for a further $200,000 from Pocklington.

The story goes that Gretzky, Mio and Driscoll were called into Nelson Skalbania's office one morning after their skate and were told they had been traded. To whom, though? the boys asked, but the answer apparently wasn't settled yet: it was still either Winnipeg or Edmonton. They were told to bring their belongings to the airport and board a private jet that was scheduled to take off at two o'clock that afternoon. The boys went back to their dressing room, gathered their equipment and threw it in their hockey bags. With bags slung over their shoulders, they said goodbye and split up, each heading to his respective home to pick up personal items. They arrived at the airport to find a Learjet waiting for them. They seriously thought they'd hit the big time. Cargo space was tight in the small plane, so they ended up putting most of their bags on the seats. Of the seven seats, four were occupied by hockey gear and luggage. Before the plane taxied down the runway for takeoff, the pilot asked them who was paying for the flight.

Who *was* paying? The boys tried to convince the pilot that the team was paying. The pilot said he needed the money up front or else he couldn't leave the ground. The boys looked at each other in confusion and shock. Gretzky didn't own a credit card, nor did he have more than a few twenties in his wallet. Peter Driscoll didn't have any money either. Eddie had a credit card—with a limit of $500. He stepped forward and offered it to the pilot, who took it and said it would do until they landed.

The plane took off and the three men glanced out the tiny windows. Eddie looked at Gretzky, his face white, his legs jiggling. Gretzky felt sick because he was a nervous flier anyway, and the uncertainty surrounding his career wasn't helping. The plane touched down in Minneapolis, and it was there that the pilot told them that they were going to Edmonton.

Just 17 games after the trade that took Gretzky, Driscoll and Mio to Edmonton, the Indianapolis Racers folded.

Once they arrived in Edmonton, Sather could see how young this Gretzky kid was, so he took him under his wing—so much so, in fact, that Gretzky lived with Sather and his wife, Anne, for the rest of that first year. "He spent more time in the basement playing with our kids," Sather said. Heeding his father's wishes, Gretzky also enrolled in Ross Sheppard High School. Mio kept an eye out for Gretzky, sometimes catching up with him while he was at school or with friends. He would get out of his Pontiac Trans Am, see Gretzky sitting with his high school friends and ask, "You okay, kid?"

Gretzky would give him a wave and tell him he was doing great.

And so began the career of the young WHA Oiler who would become the Great One.

THE ENFORCER

Everyone writes and talks about Wayne Gretzky being the building block for the dynasty years of the Edmonton Oilers, but one player liked to joke about how he was there first. With a grin bigger than an arena, Dave Semenko would say, "I was there before Wayne. I like to say they built the team around me." Of course, he'd chuckle as he said this.

At the age of 17, Dave Semenko had never been in a fight—not even as a boy in the schoolyard. His very first fight was in training camp for the Brandon Wheat Kings of the Western Hockey League, when a player with a five o'clock shadow came at him. So he threw some punches. The player went down, and suddenly everyone was talking about the big boy who could fight. Immediately, Semenko had a reputation, and the gentle giant was awakened. One day, many years later, he even went head to head with Muhammad Ali for a fundraising event (Ali was over 40 at the time).

Semenko joined the Oilers in the fall of 1977, having begun the season with Brandon. He had spent the previous two seasons—plus part of a third—with the Wheaties, scoring 27 goals and spending 265 minutes in the penalty box in 1976-77. The Minnesota North Stars selected him in the NHL Amateur Draft, while the Houston Aeros did the same in the WHA draft. By now, he was a 20-year-old overage junior. Sather liked how he fought and how he crushed players into the boards; he wanted him in an Edmonton jersey. Having been granted permission by the Aeros, Sather approached Semenko and told him that if he came to Edmonton, he would play— and perhaps more importantly, he wouldn't be sent down to the minors as he would if he signed with Minnesota, who had also made an offer. Sather was persuasive, so in late October Semenko arrived in Edmonton.

He was met at the Edmonton airport by Oilers scout Bob Freeman. On the drive into the city, Freeman asked Semenko why he had made the decision to play in Edmonton. Semenko replied that Sather had promised him he wouldn't be sent down. Freeman shook his head and told him there was nowhere *to* send him from Edmonton—the Oilers had no farm team. "Sather had a way of twisting words," said Semenko, laughing as he remembered the story. Sather hadn't lied to Semenko in his bid to sign the tough guy, but neither had he told the entire truth.

Semenko was there when Gretzky arrived in Edmonton. Years later, looking back, Semenko said, "Celine Dion had more meat on her bones than he did."

LAST DAYS OF THE WHA

The 1978-79 edition of the Oilers showed a marked improvement, thanks in no small part to the addition of the young players from Indianapolis. On January 26, Wayne Gretzky turned 18. The Oilers had a home game scheduled that night, and before the opening faceoff, Gretzky went to centre ice with his parents, Walter and Phyllis, who had flown in from Ontario. Right there on the ice he signed a 21-year personal-services contract with Pocklington. (Although Gretzky does admit the contract was signed formally before the big show on the ice.) Many had advised him not to sign, but Walter gave him the go-ahead.

After the game, there was a cake waiting for him in the dressing room with a big number 99 iced on the top. He never got to eat his cake, though, because before he got to the dressing room, someone had sat on it. "Probably Semenko," said Gretzky.

The Oilers finished first in the WHA in the 1978–79 season with 98 points, winning 48 games. Despite his lack of size and pro experience, Gretzky led the team with 43 goals and 61 assists for 104 points in 72 regular-season games. Including his stats with Indianapolis, he tied for third in the league with 46 goals, and his 110 points were third best in the league. In the semifinals, Edmonton beat the New England Whalers four games to three, sending the Oilers to the Avco Cup finals against third-place Winnipeg.

The Jets, who were the defending champions, took an early lead in the series, and after four games they were up 3–1. The Oilers fought back in Game 5, beating Winnipeg by a score of 10–2. But in the next game, played on May 20—in what would turn out to be the last WHA game ever played—the Oilers lost 7–3 and the Jets claimed the Avco World Trophy for the third time in seven years. The final goal in the history of the "rebel league" was scored by Dave Semenko, from Ron Chipperfield and Risto Siltanen, with 12 seconds left in the third period.

As far as the team had come, the loss was still disappointing for the Oilers. With the season over, players and management prepared to enter uncharted territory. The team would be playing in the NHL—that much was certain. What remained to be seen was whether Edmonton would be able to maintain the upward momentum it had generated over the past few seasons.

The WHA was known for its scrappy fights, and the Oilers, even in their early days, were gritty to the core.

PART 2

1979–1990

BECOMING CHAMPIONS

When a team joins the NHL, expectations for the new club are usually low.

But Edmonton fans knew what this young group were capable of, and a bold

prediction by owner Peter Pocklington was going to be proven right—and then some.

Joining the National Hockey League

Over the summer of 1979, the four WHA teams that had been admitted into the National Hockey League for the 1979–80 season—the Oilers, Hartford (formerly New England) Whalers, Quebec Nordiques and Winnipeg Jets—prepared for the upcoming season. There would be an expansion draft in June, and the amateur draft, now renamed the entry draft, had been pushed back to August.

As a precursor to the expansion draft, the 17 established NHL teams were allowed to "reclaim" any players on the four new teams whose rights they still owned. For instance, the Chicago Blackhawks reclaimed Bobby Hull, the superstar who had left them to sign with Winnipeg in 1972. Among Oilers, the Minnesota North Stars reclaimed Dave Semenko. However, the four incoming clubs could name two goalies and two skaters as "priority selections," in effect cancelling out any NHL claims. In the end, 42 players were reclaimed, of whom 12 were clawed back as priority selec-

tions. (Through side deals, including trades for draft picks, a few more players were able to remain with their former WHA teams or were dealt back. For instance, Glen Sather traded his second- and third-round picks in the upcoming entry draft to reacquire Semenko.)

Wayne Gretzky represented a special case in this process. No NHL team held his NHL rights as he had signed with Skalbania's Racers before he was old enough for the NHL amateur draft. He was old enough in 1979, and under ordinary circumstances he would have been placed into the pool for the NHL Entry Draft (as future Oiler Mark Messier, who had spent 1978–79 with the Indianapolis Racers and Cincinnati Stingers, was). However, there was a wrinkle. At that pregame ceremony in January, Peter Pocklington had signed him to a *personal-services* contract, not a standard player's contract. This meant he could work for Pocklington in any capacity—as a personal assistant, say, or doing

When the WHA folded, the Edmonton Oilers were one of four teams picked to enter the NHL for the 1979-80 season. The beginning of 40 years.

Pocklington's laundry. That contract would prove to be a blessing for the Edmonton Oilers. Had Gretzky decided to void the deal, he would likely have been drafted first overall by the Colorado Rockies. The league deliberated about how to address the situation and ultimately ruled that the Oilers could protect Gretzky as one of their priority selections. Thus, Wayne Gretzky became an NHL player without ever having been drafted.

The Oilers also named goalies Dave Dryden and Eddie Mio as priority selections. But they got stung on the fourth member of their priority quartet: right winger Bengt-Ake Gustafsson. The Oilers had signed him in March 1979 and brought him over from Sweden. There were some delays in processing his paperwork, but he managed to make it into two playoff games. Glen Sather liked what he had seen of the 21-year-old, enough to deem him worth keeping. But NHL president John Ziegler ruled that the Oilers had violated WHA rules by bringing Gustafsson to North America after the trade deadline and therefore had no claim on him. The Washington Capitals, who had drafted him in the fourth round in 1978, were awarded his rights and the Oilers lost a priority selection. He went on to play 629 games over nine seasons for Washington, scoring 196 goals and 555 points. Even now, Glen Sather says, "Can you imagine if we would have had Gustafsson?" Every team has a player that gets away.

Now it was time for the expansion draft. Each established NHL team was allowed to protect 15 skaters and two goalies, which didn't leave much for the four new teams to pick from. Among the Oilers' haul were a number of players destined to retire or play out the string in the minor leagues, although they did land three defencemen who had been first-round picks in the NHL draft: Pat Price, Doug Hicks and Lee Fogolin. Fogolin, a 24-year-old ex–Buffalo Sabre, would spend seven and a half seasons in Edmonton and would wear the C for the Oilers in 1983, when they made their first trip to the Stanley Cup final.

THE FIRST ENTRY DRAFT: BUILDING A DYNASTY

If the expansion draft didn't yield many building blocks for the newly minted NHL franchise, the entry draft was another story. Called the NHL Amateur Draft since its inception in 1963, the name was changed this year to the NHL Entry Draft because a number of eligible players had already appeared in the World Hockey Association. Another difference was that the draft age was lowered by one year, allowing players who would only turn 19 during the season to be drafted (in past years, age 20 had been the rule). Again, the WHA was responsible and several players, including future Oiler Mark Napier, had challenged the established order by signing with teams in the rival league as teenagers. And in 1977, nineteen-year-old Ken Linseman sued the WHA when it ruled that he was too young to play in the league. A case had been made that players as young as 18 had a legal right to play professional hockey, and in 1980 the NHL draft age would be lowered yet again, to 18. For these and a variety of other reasons, the 1979 draft is considered the richest in history in terms of the talent level as better than 80 percent of those drafted appeared in at least one NHL game.

Another difference with the 1979 draft was that it was held in August, rather than June. And this year, there were only six rounds; in previous years, there had been upwards of 20.

The NHL didn't do the four former WHA teams any favours, assigning them the final four picks in each round. In previous expansion years (1970, 1972 and 1974) the new teams had been given the top picks. The Oilers' first pick didn't come until the end of the first round: 21st overall. The name they called when it was finally their turn was that of Kevin Lowe of the Quebec Remparts, a big, stay-at-home defence-man from the Montreal area. Sather liked Lowe's fierce, edgy game and the fact that he showed his opponents no mercy. (Later in his NHL career, he was given the nickname "Vicious.") Plus, he was putting up offensive numbers in Quebec: in 68 games in 1978–79, he accumulated 26 goals and 60 assists for 86 points, to go with 120 penalty minutes. He had also been the captain of the Remparts that season, becoming the first English-speaking captain of a team in the Quebec Major Junior Hockey League. Leadership skills, scoring ability and size were the reasons the Oilers wanted him as their first-round pick. "He was heads and tails above everyone in maturity," said Sather.

When Lowe arrived in Edmonton, he'd never been further west than London, Ontario. In training camp, like most rookies, he was nervous about being sent to the minors. He did, however, move from rookie camp to main camp. Wayne Gretzky hadn't been at the rookie camp, so Lowe didn't meet him until the main training camp. Within a week, Gretzky had approached Lowe and asked if he wanted to be his roommate. Lowe's response was, "If I make the team. Sure." Gretzky responded by saying, "Don't worry, you'll make it."

A bond was cemented between the two young players, and for three years they roomed together. They rented a two-bedroom apartment in a brand-new building. When Kevin showed up with his things, Gretzky told him to "take the master bedroom." Lowe could hardly believe that Gretzky, who was already on his way to being a star, had offered up the bigger room. Even at this early point, the Great One was showing leadership skills off the ice as well as on it.

The Oilers didn't have a pick in the second round, having traded it to Minnesota, but they did have one early in the third round, at 48th overall, and they selected another fierce competitor: Mark Messier. A local boy from St. Albert, Messier had played with the St. Albert Saints in the Tier II Alberta Junior Hockey League, as well as a few games at the major junior level with the Portland Winter Hawks during the 1978 Western Hockey League playoffs. In November 1978—a few days after Gretzky was traded to Edmonton, in fact—he signed with the Indianapolis

Racers, and when the Racers folded, he caught on with the Cincinnati Stingers. In 52 WHA games, he managed a lone goal and 10 assists.

When the Oilers' rookie camp opened, Messier was nowhere to be found. Having not yet come to terms on a contract, he didn't report to camp. Lowe remembers not being able to figure out why Messier was holding out when he'd only scored one goal the year before. Who was this guy? Kevin thought. He must have a lot of guts.

Sather recognized Messier's potential, in terms of both grit and skill, but he also knew that, like any young player, he just needed to mature. And Sather wasn't known as a coach who babied his players. In late October, Messier missed a team flight. He was living at home at the time, and his mother was driving him to the airport. In Edmonton, there were two airports: Edmonton Municipal and Edmonton International. Somehow, Messier got confused and had his mother drive him to the wrong one. When he got to the municipal airport, he knew something was wrong because he couldn't see any of his teammates. He phoned the Oilers office and was told the team was leaving from the *international* airport and that Sather had left him a boarding pass there.

Embarrassed to be missing the team flight, but feeling a sense of relief that he could get on another one, Messier made his way to the international airport. When he looked at the boarding pass, however, it said Houston, Texas. Sather had brought the hammer down and sent the kid to Edmonton's farm team, the Houston Apollos. Messier played four games with the Apollos before he was brought back to the Oilers. During his time in the minors, he earned three assists—and learned a lesson. In the rest of his 26-year pro career, he never played another game in the minors.

The Oilers weren't done drafting. In the fourth round, at 69th overall, they found another player who would have a huge influence in the dynasty years: Glenn Anderson of the University of Denver. Enthusiastic and a free thinker on the ice, Anderson wouldn't make his debut for another year, splitting 1979–80 between the Canadian national team and the Seattle Breakers of the WHL. Sather and his scouting director, Barry Fraser, knew the boy didn't know how good he could be. For a full year, they watched him play with the Olympic team, liking what they saw.

With their first three picks, the Oilers had uncovered three players who would be instrumental in the years to come.

1979–1980

MEET THE OILERS

For their inaugural NHL season, the Edmonton Oilers iced a team of new draft picks, NHLers picked up via the expansion draft, and members of the WHA Oilers.

This was the team that was presented in the media guide at the beginning of the season.

GOALIES

Number 28: At age 38, **Dave Dryden** (older brother of the Montreal Canadiens' Ken) was returning to the NHL after five years in the WHA—the last four with Edmonton. His best season had been in 1978–79, when he was given the WHA's MVP award—the Gordie Howe Trophy—and the Ben Hatskin Trophy as best goaltender, and was named to the first all-star team. Dryden spent countless hours working with children and attending dozens of charity events. Glen Sather asked Dryden to help the team by mentoring and coaching Eddie Mio, Hannu Kamppuri, Pete LoPresti and all the other goalies in the Oilers system.

Number 31: A skilled baseball player who was offered a tryout with the Pittsburgh Pirates, **Ed Mio** chose hockey as his career. Known for his agility, quickness and fast arm movements, Mio showed up at training camp in top shape. He definitely had a different style than Dave Dryden, who was much more technical, but Sather knew they would work well together and possibly learn from each other.

Number 1: When Glen Sather saw that **Pete LoPresti** was still available in the sixth round of the NHL expansion draft, he quickly picked him up. LoPresti hadn't just lost his job as the Minnesota North Stars' Number 1 goalie in 1978–79, but he had dropped to third on the depth chart, appearing in just seven games. Still, the Oilers thought the 25-year-old LoPresti still had some good hockey left in him. "Pete's still a young man," said Sather. "And we're a young organization."

DEFENCE

Number 2: After the Oilers secured defenceman **Lee Fogolin** in the expansion

The 1979-80 Oilers NHL debut team was composed of veterans and young players.

draft, other teams came knocking on their door, asking about his availability. Sather was adamant that there was to be no deal. A first-round pick in 1974, Fogolin had played with the Buffalo Sabres for the past five seasons. He moved the puck quickly, which gave goalies extra confidence. During training camp, he used his experience to help the rookies settle down, including first-round draft pick Kevin Lowe. Lowe and Fogolin became a defensive pair in the first game of the 1979 season. They were nicknamed "the Pros-qui-toe Brothers" because that is how Kevin pronounced the name of the Italian meat prosciutto. Lee, who was of Italian

heritage, laughed hysterically at that. Players often earn nicknames for the oddest reasons.

Number 3: The oldest defender on the Edmonton Oilers, 33-year-old **Al Hamilton** wanted one more chance, maybe one more year, to play in the NHL. For seven seasons, Hamilton had established himself as an Oiler, and he was a veteran who had a bum knee and a bad eye and who understood his role on the team. He had a house and a family and lived outside of town on an acreage, and he often had his young teammates over for team get-togethers, to play pool and "drink beverages." To

Al, the young guys were "filled with piss and vinegar." Sometimes they called him up and said, "We're coming over."

Number 6: The entire Oilers organization agreed that **Colin Campbell** was obtained for his experience—five years in the NHL and one in the WHA. He had a stocky build, which he used aggressively on the ice. His game was consistent and stable. When he arrived in Edmonton in the summer for a charity ball game, he toured Northlands Coliseum and was impressed. "I remember playing in the old place [Edmonton Gardens] across the road," he said. "It wasn't a great place to play, but I bet this will be."

Number 8: A stocky, five-foot, eight-inch Finn, **Risto Siltanen** was given the nickname "the Littlest Hulk" by his Oilers teammates. Siltanen had played in 20 games for the Oilers in 1978–79, but prior to the expansion draft he was reclaimed by St. Louis. Some fans were a bit shocked when the Oilers traded Joe Micheletti, a popular defenceman, for Siltanen and Tom Roulston. "There was never any doubt we would make the deal if we could," said Bruce MacGregor. "We were sure Risto would improve."

Number 22: **Doug Hicks** had been the Minnesota North Stars' first draft pick in the 1974 Amateur Draft, going 11th overall. Things didn't pan out for him in Minnesota; he didn't produce the numbers they thought he would. Hicks thought that perhaps he was too young to be the star of an NHL team. After a few years they traded him to the Chicago Blackhawks, but Chicago sent him down to the Dallas Blackhawks of the Central Hockey League. Arriving in Edmonton was a bonus for Doug. "We've got a good organization and a good nucleus. I think there is enough talent at this camp to surprise a lot of teams."

Number 26: The Oilers picked **Pat Price** in the third round of the 1979 expansion draft. In 1974, when he was recognized as the best defenceman in all of Canadian junior hockey, the Vancouver Blazers of the WHA drafted Price as an underage junior and signed him for $1.3 million over five years, the biggest rookie contract at that time in professional hockey. This made him a bit of a veteran when he showed up at the Oilers' training camp, even though he was only 24 years old. Sather said, "He's a big talent."

FORWARDS

Number 7: The captain of the team at the beginning of the inaugural season was **Ron Chipperfield**, a player who had been with the Oilers for two years, putting up back-to-back 30-goal seasons. Sather liked him because he was a leader. "People realize how good he is," said Sather, "but many don't realize that he's a leader off the ice, too. We need all the leadership we can get this year." Chipper was known for his unselfishness, and as a centre was often teamed with various wingers. "Sometimes you might have to give up good chances of your own to make sure the wingers keep going," he said.

Ron Chipperfield was the first player to wear the C for the Oilers in their inaugural season with the NHL.

Number 12: **Dave Hunter** was a fan favourite from the 1978–79 Oilers. When the WHA folded and it became known that NHL teams could reclaim players, fans were worried that Dave Hunter would be returned to the Montreal Canadiens, who had drafted him in the first round in 1977. Sather wasn't about to let him go, so he negotiated a deal allowing Edmonton to keep him. What was so special about him? He'd only scored seven goals in his rookie season. But Hunter impressed with his hard work, raw talent and crushing checks. His defensive style of play was successful because of his skating and strength. Chief scout Barry Fraser was the key to him getting to Edmonton. "Even when David didn't score too much, I wasn't worried," said Fraser. "He's got too much raw talent to be held down for long. I think he'll be a star for years."

Number 14: **Blair MacDonald** started his professional career with the Oilers in 1973. After a few seasons he was traded to the Indianapolis Racers. Within two seasons he returned to the Oilers to play two more years in the WHA, and the fans loved having him back. In fact, in the 1978–79 season the fans named him as Edmonton's player of the year, even though there were other stars on that team, including young Wayne Gretzky. Blair always deflected his popularity by giving the credit to his linemates, Brett Callighen and Wayne Gretzky. Sather worked hard to keep MacDonald through the expansion process because he wanted to keep his best line intact.

Number 15: Although he had missed 40 games the previous season, due to a broken back from surfing, the Oilers were happy that **Wayne Bianchin** had been left exposed in the expansion draft by the Pittsburgh Penguins. He had a good touch around the net and that impressed the Oilers; plus, like a lot of Sather's picks, he was a hard worker. "I like to play it physically," he said when he arrived in Edmonton. "That's my game; I don't crunch people but I'm comfortable in the corners."

Number 16: As both a player and a coach, Sather had watched **Cam Connor** when he was with the Winnipeg Jets and Houston Aeros. "He skates, shoots and works—besides, he's tough," said Glen. All of these attributes convinced Sather to work out a pre-draft deal with the Montreal Canadiens, who had drafted Connor fifth overall in 1974. Sather agreed to leave other players with more star power alone if he could get Cam Connor. Unfortunately, Connor missed training camp due to a back injury.

Number 17: In 1978–79, left winger **Garnet "Ace" Bailey** saw more of the press box than he did the ice. Many considered him to be washed up. At the end of the season, he said he would come to training camp even if he didn't have a contract. His determination was his biggest asset, and at camp he showed up lighter, and faster. "All I wanted was a chance to prove to myself whether I could still play," he said in the fall. "I didn't learn anything about myself last year." His quicker skating made Sather take a second look. Being a longtime Edmonton resident, Bailey had played hockey for the Oil Kings from 1964 to 1967, winning the Memorial Cup in 1966. He was known at that time as one of the best Oil Kings ever. Ace Bailey, being a little older, had taken Wayne Gretzky under his wing and they became close friends. Even though Bailey didn't see any ice time in that inaugural NHL year with the Oilers, he still became a mentor to Gretzky—a big brother, almost a father figure.

Number 18: **Brett Callighen** played four years in the WHA, including one with the New England Whalers and three with the Oilers. He was the kind of player who steamrolled his way into corners, not caring about the size of the opposition. His hustle was probably his greatest attribute as a player, and he had speed and second effort. When it came time for the Oilers to move to the NHL, he had the skating and hitting ability to make waves in the established league.

Number 19: **Bill "Cowboy" Flett** played for the Oilers for three WHA seasons, and over the 1979 off-season he was given a choice to either look for another place to play, or report to training camp without a contract. The decision was in his hands. And it was his hands that won him a spot on that inaugural team. (Well, that and the fact that he was decidedly a fan favourite, even at the age of 35.) In training camp, Sather was impressed with his skill around the net as well as the fact he had shown up in great shape. "He's a top scorer," said Sather. "It seems that whenever we need a goal late in the game, I can send the Cowboy out to get it for me. He doesn't always score, of course, but he always does something. It's possible to teach skating and shooting and puck handling, but you can't teach magic." Cowboy had won a Stanley Cup with the Philadelphia Flyers in 1973–74, so he had experience that he could impart to the younger players. Flett got his nickname simply because he wore cowboy boots—all the time. A true Alberta boy, he'd been in his fair share of rodeos, and cowboy boots and hats were part of his wardrobe—as were cowboy boots with spikes for the golf course. He even had skates with spurs, which he wore to charity events.

Number 20: Twenty-five-year-old **Dave Lumley** had played two years in the American Hockey League and two games in the NHL before attending the Edmonton Oilers camp. At first, he was disappointed to be told that he had to show up at the preliminary camp,

feeling that it was a bit of a punch in the gut. After skating with the rookies and feeling the burn in his legs from their speed, he came to believe he'd gained a bit of an edge as he headed into the main camp. The extra skating helped Lumley play aggressive hockey, winning the coaches over. His 160 penalty minutes from the previous year, with the Nova Scotia Voyageurs of the AHL, helped the coaches make their decision. Lumley talked to the media during camp. "The Oilers have a lot of good forwards," he said. "Maybe some of the players aren't well known yet—but I'm sure they will be."

Number 21: Born in Ponoka, Alberta, **Stan Weir** played six years in the NHL, for the California Golden Seals and Toronto Maple Leafs, before making his way back to Edmonton. Weir was also one of the first graduates of Sather's hockey school in Banff to have a professional career. Coach Sather knew Weir well, so when he became a free agent after his time with the Maple Leafs, Sather made an offer.

Number 25: **Doug Patey** was the Edmonton Oilers' sleeper—a young player with pro experience but who hadn't achieved his full potential. Patey showed up to camp in top physical condition, impressing the Oilers with his shot and ability to get open for a pass. Plus, he did what Sather liked, and that was to head into the corners without hesitation. It was assistant coach Bryan Watson who encouraged Sather to take Patey in the 15th round of the expan-

sion draft in June. "We'll never be sorry," said Watson. "He's young and he wants to play in the biggest league." But after all that, Patey never even played for the Oilers.

Number 27: At the age of 22, **Dave Semenko** was already known to his teammates as "Cement." He had established his reputation as a fighter and as the team policeman, but he also spent time working on his skating. After almost every Oilers practice at home, he stuck around to work some more. "Semenko has improved more than most people realize since he's been with the Oilers," said Sather. "His fighting ability is not why he's on this hockey club and it's not why we got him back from Minnesota after the expansion draft. He has a great raw talent and I'm counting on him to use it as he gains confidence in all areas of his game."

Number 99: After leading the team in scoring in 1978–79, **Wayne Gretzky** was fast becoming popular with teammates, fans and coaches. Sather summed it up at the beginning of the 1979–80 season: "I can hardly wait to see what happens when the big guys in the NHL see him. They'll think he's unbelievable, just as we do." Right from his first few days in Edmonton, Gretzky had a willingness to work hard off the ice, and not just physically. He always made himself available to the community, attending functions for children and adults, and was always willing to lend a hand.

Bill "Cowboy" Flett was a fan favourite. How he loved his cowboy boots!

At the end of the guide, there was a section on players who were "In the System." Those projected to be on their way, but not yet ready for the roster. These players included Kevin Lowe, Mark Messier, Max Kostovich, Mike Toal and Mike Forbes. Kostovich never played a game, Toal played just three and Forbes appeared twice that season and 16 times in 1981–82. However, both Lowe and Messier became key players in their rookie years with the Oilers.

THE INAUGURAL SEASON

Of course, as with most new hockey teams, trades were frequent, injuries happened, players that the coaching and scouting staff thought would be huge assets didn't pan out—and then there were the surprises. Sather and his staff were trying to put together a puzzle.

Just before the end of the season, on March 11, after 67 games had been played, Oilers captain Ron Chipperfield was traded to the Quebec Nordiques for goalie Ron Low. Low was from western Manitoba and had broken into the NHL with the Toronto Maple Leafs in 1972–73. In 1978–79, playing with the Kansas City Red Wings of the Central Hockey League, he had won the MVP award and been named to the CHL's first all-star team. With Chipperfield leaving, Blair MacDonald took over as captain for the remainder of the regular season.

The Edmonton Oilers ended up with a record of 28–39–13 for just 69 points. That result left them fourth in the Smythe Division and in 16th place overall, but because all but five of the

21 teams qualified for the playoffs, the Oilers were about to get their first taste of NHL postseason play. Their opponents were the Philadelphia Flyers, whose 116 points led the entire league. The Flyers swept the best-of-five preliminary-round series, but the Oilers put up a fight, holding a 3–2 lead late in Game 1 before losing 4–3 in overtime. Don Murdoch opened the scoring in Game 2, but it was all Philadelphia the rest of the way, ending in a 5–1 defeat. Game 3, played on April 11, 1980, was the first Stanley Cup playoff game ever to be played in Edmonton. The Oilers took a 2–0 lead into the first intermission, on goals by Wayne Gretzky and Mark Messier, but lost 3–2 on a Flyer goal by Ken Linseman just under four minutes into the second overtime period. At the end of this series, former Flyers captain Bobby Clarke remarked that Gretzky was going to be great, but that everyone should also look out for that Mark Messier kid, because he was going to be a player. The Oilers' first playoff appearance reaffirmed what the coaching and management staff knew about their team: there was a lot of raw potential in their young players. But perhaps the roster needed more size.

Gretzky, now 19, proved he was not only ready to play in the NHL, but to be a dominant offensive force. He racked up 137 points—the same number as Marcel Dionne of the Los Angeles Kings, who won the scoring championship because his 53 goals edged out Gretzky's 51. The league ruled that, because he had played in the WHA the year before, he was not eligible for the Calder Memorial Trophy, presented to the

Tough as he was, behind the bench Sather allowed his young players to be creative.

Sather's Rules

Glen Sather was a no-nonsense coach. He had to be, with so many young players in his lineup who were not only short on hockey experience but maturity and sophistication. When he first started coaching, some members of the team were in the habit of wearing headbands and showing up to games casually dressed. As far as Sather was concerned, if the Oilers were going to play in the NHL, that was not going to continue on his watch. He wanted them to dress like professionals and look respectable, as he believed it would translate into a professional approach on the ice. Sather was also a stickler for punctuality, and he would fine players for such infractions as missing the bus, missing practice, or being late to practice. At the end of the year, however, Sather would return the fines he'd collected. Although Sather was tough, he also knew his charges needed to have some fun, so he organized team-building events, including fishing, trap shooting, and even snowmobiling. The boys loved the trips. Looking back on the snowmobiling event, Sather said, "Maybe that wasn't such a good idea. It was a bit of a high risk outing." Fortunately, no one was injured.

NHL's rookie of the year, but he did win the Hart Memorial Trophy as the player judged most valuable to his team, as well as the Lady Byng Memorial Trophy for excellence and sportsmanship.

The season was a last hurrah for Oiler veterans Dave Dryden, Bill Flett and Al Hamilton, all of whom retired. The 1980–81 edition of the team would almost certainly be younger. But would team management be able to fit more pieces into the puzzle?

Right out of the gate, the Edmonton Oilers were making their mark.

1980–1981

MORE GEMS IN THE DRAFT

During the 1979–80 season, chief scout Barry Fraser paid particular attention to a defenceman from the Toronto area who'd been traded from the Sault Ste. Marie Greyhounds to the Kitchener Rangers. The kid could skate. He'd also recorded 102 points in 75 games. With the sixth pick in the 1980 NHL Entry Draft, the only question was whether he'd still be available when the Oilers' turn came around. The Montreal Canadiens picked Doug Wickenheiser, a centre out of Regina. Winnipeg took a defenceman—Wayne Babych. Another centre, Denis Savard, went to Chicago. Then two more blueliners—Larry Murphy to Los Angeles and Darren Veitch to Washington. So with the sixth pick, Edmonton selected Paul Coffey.

Coffey lacked a little confidence and swagger. He attended the Oilers' rookie camp that fall, often keeping to himself, and made it to the main camp, held in Jasper, Alberta, in the heart of the Rocky Mountains. In an effort to fit in, after an ice session Paul made his way into the bar to hang out with some of the guys. Maybe even order a beer.

As he sat there, not saying a word, Dave Semenko said, "Who is our first pick again? I didn't see anyone who had anything special out there."

Coffey slunk down in his seat, but he did hold up a finger. "Ummm, that would be me," he said.

Oddly enough, Paul Coffey's hockey path had paralleled that of Wayne Gretzky, whom he'd known since the age of 14. Gretzky had left Brantford to play Junior B with the Toronto Nationals. A year later, in 1976–77, the team changed its name to the Seneca Nationals, and Coffey got called up to play a few games for them. In 1977–78, Gretzky moved up to the Sault Ste. Marie Greyhounds of the Ontario Major Junior Hockey League, putting up 70 goals and 112 assists for 182 points in 64 games. Coffey followed him to the Soo, the year after Gretzky left to play in the WHA.

Coffey's agent, Gus Badali (whom Gretzky had relied on in his early years) had been in talks with the Oilers, so was aware of their interest. The defenceman figured if he did end up in Edmonton,

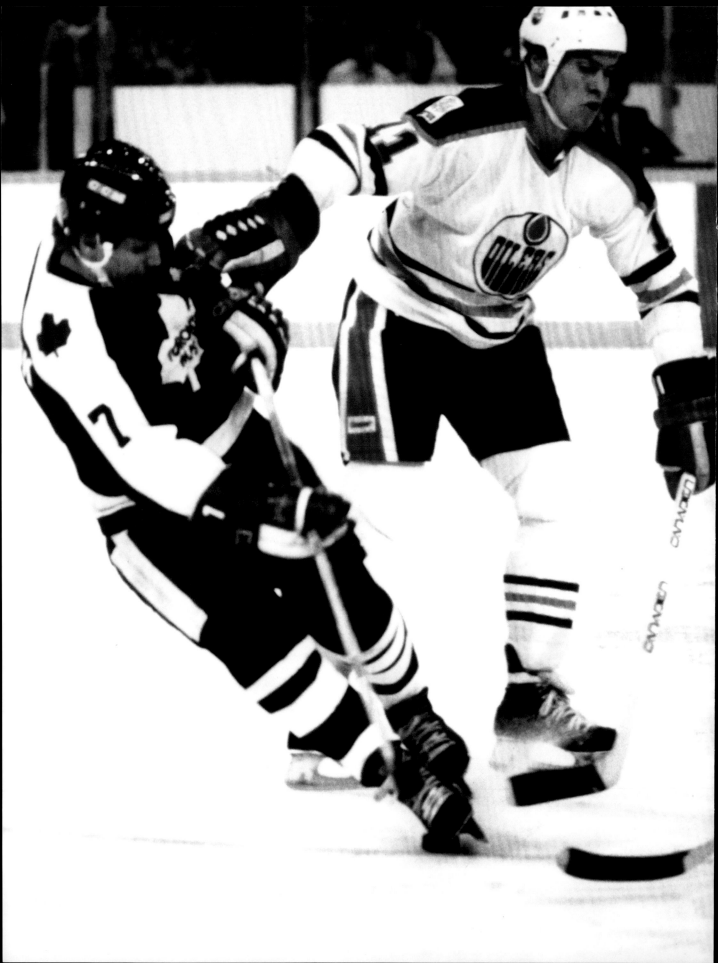

at least he would know one person. That is, if Wayne Gretzky remembered him.

Before the draft, Coffey went to watch the Toronto Maple Leafs play the Oilers at Maple Leaf Gardens with Badali. He stared, eyes wide, when he saw that all the Oilers players wore cowboy boots with their suits, plus hats and fur coats. Badali took him down to the Oilers dressing room after the game because Barry Fraser wanted to show him around. When Sather walked past young Paul, he said, "Hey, kid. I hear you're pretty good. I guess if you're still around when it's our turn, we'll draft you." That was it. That's all he said as he swished by.

After being drafted by the Oilers, Coffey arrived in Edmonton with the feeling that if he had been selected by any other team, he would be sent back to the junior ranks. But the Oilers needed players, especially defencemen, so he had a shot. Coffey was told he had ten games to show he belonged with the team. He phoned home, as most teens do when they are nervous, and his dad told him he needed confidence and to get out there and play with authority. Coffey took "authority" to mean playing a more physical game, so he tried to change his style. After a road game in Colorado, he was in the hotel lobby when Fraser came up and told him to just relax, play his game and stop trying to be who he wasn't. Fraser patted him on the back and told him it was all but certain he was going to stay with the big club, but he had to start using his speed and skating ability, because those were the reasons he was drafted. This was all Coffey needed to hear. In the very next

game, he started skating the way that only he could.

Coffey wasn't the only key player to come to the Oilers via that 1980 entry draft. In the fourth round, 69th overall, they chose winger Jari Kurri from Jokerit in Helsinki, Finland. For the past two seasons, he had been playing with Jokerit's senior squad. He had also been amassing international experience. In 1978, Kurri helped Finland win the European under-18 championship by scoring in double overtime of the gold-medal game against the Soviet Union. In 1980, he had an amazing run at the World Junior Championship, tying Vladimir Krutov for the tournament lead in points (11) and helping Finland win a silver medal, the country's first medal in an official World Junior Championship. His success in this tournament earned him a spot on Finland's 1980 Olympic team.

After hearing he'd been drafted, Kurri wasn't sure he wanted to move so far from home. His English was minimal and Canada was far away. Two other Finnish players, Matti Hagman and Risto Siltanen, were already on the Oilers roster, and they convinced the 20-year-old to make the leap. Reluctantly, Kurri got on the plane and arrived in Edmonton, but he said he would only stay for one year. His season started off slowly, but on November 26, 1980, in a 10–3 victory over the Chicago Blackhawks, Jari scored a hat trick in front of a Northlands crowd of 17,283. (It was the Oilers' second hat trick of the season; the first was scored by Dave Semenko on October 19, against the New York Rangers.) Sather loved Kurri's quick release, and after the game he said, "Jari

Messier showed his toughness from day one. Here he is giving Leafs Rocky Saganiuk a healthy shove.

Fast wheeling Paul Coffey being interviewed in the dressing room after a game.

really zips the shots." In the dressing room, with Siltanen as his interpreter, Kurri said, "He [Gretzky] gets me a lot of chances. When he is at the blue line, it seems everybody follows him."

In the seventh round, with the 132nd pick of the draft, the Oilers selected Andy Moog of the Billings Bighorns of the WHL. The guys nicknamed him "the Penticton Peach," although many, Gretzky included, weren't sure why. He suggested it might've been because the goaltender was still shaving peach fuzz

off his face, or maybe because of his build.

The truth was, Moog was born and raised in Penticton, British Columbia, a quaint little city nestled between two lakes in the Okanagan Valley. Known as the Peach City, Penticton is home to the annual Peachfest, and boasts a giant peach near the beach. One night in the stands in Edmonton, someone had a sign that said, "Penticton sent us a real peach." Paul Coffey knew Andy was from Penticton, so he was the one who started calling

Al Hamilton has his #3 jersey retired. His was the first in the rafters.

him the Peach. When Gretzky asked why he called Moog that, Coffey asked him if he'd seen the sign. Gretzky said no. Coffey grinned and told him, "Really? You should skate with your head up."

In his early days with Edmonton, Moog found the style of stick that he would use for his entire career. Late in that first season, on March 23, 1981, the Oilers called him up from Wichita to play a game against the Bruins in Boston. Unfortunately, Moog didn't have

a great game and the Oilers lost 7–2. After the game, Bruins coach Gerry Cheevers saw Glen Sather in the belly of the arena. Cheevers gave his former teammate—the two had played for Boston in the late '60s—a goalie stick and told him to give it to his young goalie to try out. He had seen something in Moog's game that he liked, and he thought the blade pattern on the stick would help the kid out. Sather handed the stick to Moog and, although it was

The First Banner

Before the Oilers' home opener (a 7–4 loss to the Quebec Nordiques), the team retired Al Hamilton's Number 3 jersey. Hamilton was driven onto the ice in a car, like visiting royalty. Then he stood and addressed the crowd, telling them that the reason he was in Edmonton for such a wonderful ceremony was Wild Bill Hunter, who had recruited him back in 1972 to play for the WHA Oilers. Hamilton may not have been a top scorer, nor was he the fastest skater to grace the ice for the Oilers, but he was a vital part of the team's history. "I know why they retired the number," he said at the ceremony. "They wanted to make sure nobody wore it again—because that number is injury prone. I was worried I would trip up the stairs, wearing the sweater when I left the ice."

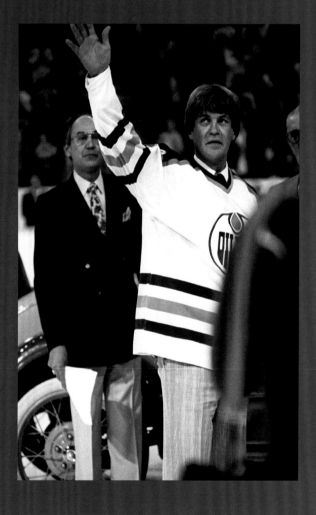

Boys and their Pranks

Practical jokes are part of any hockey dressing room, and Edmonton was no exception. Even Glen Sather was known to pull the occasional prank on his players, who in turn targeted one another, especially on road trips.

In February 1981, the Oilers travelled to Hartford. When they stayed in hotels, Kevin Lowe and Lee Fogolin loved to take the mattresses off the beds of unsuspecting teammates and put them in the stairwells. Just for fun. While in Hartford, Dave Semenko and Curt Brackenbury (who roomed together on the road) stayed out a bit later after the game than they should have. When they came back to their room and opened their door, they saw that their mattresses were gone. Figuring they knew who had done it, they knocked on the door of Lee Fogolin's room. Sporting bed head and yawning, Fogolin opened the door. He shook his head and told them, "It wasn't us." Then he pointed down the hall to a door on the right.

Dave and Curt devised a plan. They went to the front desk and got a key to the room, but when they got back, the key wouldn't work—whoever was on the other side had messed with the lock, knowing that Semenko and Brackenbury would come knocking.

Then Semenko saw the fire hose.

Without thinking of the consequences, he grabbed the hose and shoved it under the door of the room, and they turned on the water. The room flooded, enraging the hotel staff. At the next practice, Sather skated up to Semenko and waved his finger at him, telling him he knew he had been involved. But nothing was ever proven, so the boys weren't fined.

heavier than anything he would've picked out for himself, Moog knew he had to give it a shot, if only because goaltending legend Gerry Cheevers had given it to him. For the rest of his career, Moog ordered the same type of stick.

"OK, YOU'RE IN"

The Oilers' second season showed a slight improvement, their record of 29–35–16 giving them 74 points, five more than in 1979–80. Wayne Gretzky led both the Oilers and the entire NHL with 164 points—29 more than runner-up Marcel Dionne, and 12 more than the previous all-time high, set by Phil Esposito in 1970–71. His 109 assists broke the league record of 102, set by Bobby Orr in 1970–71. As a rookie, Jari Kurri scored an impressive 32 goals and

75 points, followed by Mark Messier with 63 points, Brett Callighen with 60, and Glenn Anderson, Matti Hagman and Risto Siltanen with 53 each.

As league scoring champion, Gretzky won the Art Ross Trophy he had fallen just short of claiming the year before. He also won his second Hart Trophy as most valuable player and was named to the first all-star team.

Fans in Edmonton were growing ever more excited about NHL hockey, and their team in particular. The Oilers' average attendance of 17,436 per game was the highest in the league. Virtually every home game was played to a sold-out arena.

For the second year in a row, the Oilers traded a captain. Blair MacDonald was sent to Vancouver at the March trading deadline. MacDonald had first suited up

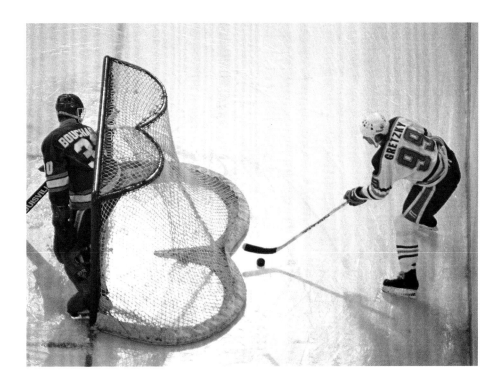

Gretzky hanging out in his office, ready to make his next move.

with Edmonton in 1973, and after a trade to Indianapolis in December 1976 was reacquired for the 1977–78 season. Upon his departure, Lee Fogolin was given the C.

On February 2, the Oilers landed Gary Edwards in a trade with the Minnesota North Stars, adding goal-tending depth. They would need it as the regular season drew to a close. Late in the season, both Eddie Mio and Ron Low broke their hands. Suddenly, Andy Moog—who had started the season at Number 4 on the depth chart—was being called up from the minors, starting three of Edmonton's last seven games (including that loss in Boston where Gerry Cheevers gave him a new goal stick).

Heading into the playoffs, the Oilers were seeded 14th—two spots higher than in 1979–80—but that didn't make their task in the postseason any easier. Their opponents in the preliminary round were the Montreal Canadiens, who had led the Prince of Wales Conference with 103 points. Adding to the difficulty, their two top goaltenders were still unavailable. For Glen Sather, the choice came down to Gary Edwards, an 11-year veteran who had posted a 5–3–4 record since the trade, and Moog, the rookie who had only played seven games in the NHL.

On the day of the first game at the Montreal Forum, Sather skated up to Moog in practice.

"How you feeling?" he asked.

Having no idea what to expect, and still being young and very naive, Andy replied, "Good."

"Okay," said Sather. "You're in."

There was no pat on the back, no words of encouragement, no tips on how to play a better game or deal with the likes of Guy Lafleur, Larry Robinson and Steve Shutt. Just a simple statement, telling a goalie with next-to-no big-league experience that he was going to play the first playoff game. Sather skated off to tend to something else and, happy that he was going to play, Moog went to his crease to practise.

In those days, the young Oilers loved to play music in their dressing room— rock and roll by performers like Bruce Springsteen and Billy Joel. Some of the players had been to see a Billy Joel concert prior to the first game, so his music was blasting from the speakers. The Oilers stepped onto the ice without much sense of what lay ahead—and quite possibly a bit too much bravado. Verbal jabs were slung back and forth between the teams, one coming from Canadiens goalie Richard Sevigny, who said Lafleur would "put Gretzky in his back pocket."

Twenty minutes into Game 1, the Oilers had a 3–1 lead. Gretzky had assisted on all three goals, while Kurri had scored two of them. The third was scored by Glenn Anderson. Gretzky would assist on two more Edmonton goals, giving him five in all, as the Oilers won the game 6–3. For his part, Moog stopped 28 of 31 shots. In the second period, Mark Messier decided to get into a scrap with Larry Robinson, at one point starting to swing his stick around, threatening to spear Robinson. At the age of 20, the gritty, fierce side of Mark Messier was starting to show.

Lee Fogolin, the third captain of the Oilers, leads the post-game handshake line. ▶

In Montreal, the game was written off as a blip—a mistake—by fans and media who were certain their team would come back and take the series in four games. But the next night, Paul Coffey scored the first goal and the Oilers bore down against the Canadiens, coming away with a 3–1 victory and a 2–0 lead in the series. Moog stood on his head, stopping 40 of 41 shots as the Habs threw everything they had at the novice in net. On April 11, in Edmonton, the Oilers wowed their fans with a 6–2 win to sweep the series. Gretzky scored his third goal of the night against Sevigny with just seven seconds left on the clock, giving him a total of 11 points in just three games.

For the first time, the Edmonton Oilers had won a playoff series, which meant a quarter-final matchup against the defending Stanley Cup champions, the New York Islanders. The first two games, on Long Island, ended in losses of 8–2 and 6–3. Back home for Game 3, the Oilers dug in and won 5–2. Edmonton grabbed a 2–0 lead early in Game 4, and a third-period goal forced it into overtime, but the Islanders took the game 5–4. In Game 5, the Oilers held on and came away with a 4–3 road victory. This comeback made the 5–2 loss in Game 6 that much harder. The Oilers were devastated, but also encouraged. They'd lost the series 4–2, but it was a well-fought battle. They'd won one playoff series, so now they had a new target. Next year, they would win two.

According to Glenn Anderson, "although we had lost, we didn't lose the lesson." They hadn't bowed down and been swept by the powerful Islanders.

The coaching staff was similarly encouraged. Perhaps what they had was raw still, but there was progress.

Many of the players were still very young, and sometimes it showed. Anderson remembers being on the bench during that series as they were all chanting, "Let's go, Oilers!" Then they would tap their sticks. "It was like we were cheerleaders," laughed Anderson. At first, the Islanders, a team loaded with veterans, looked over in disbelief. Were these guys really so immature that they were chanting like fans on their own bench?

The truth is, they were. While in New York, they had all bought Walkmans off the street in front of the hotel. As Messier went through airport security, actually wearing his headphones, he was asked if he had anything to declare and he said no. Then he was asked if he had just bought the Walkman and said yes. Security took them away on the spot, from all the players. They even marched up to Kevin Lowe, who was sitting by the gate where the Oilers' plane was due to board, and took *his* away from him.

Still, the brash youngsters were undeniably good hockey players, and veterans knew that about them. There was something intimidating about their naïveté.

Owner Peter Pocklington and coach Glen Sather believed that, given time, this Oiler team could win the Stanley Cup—a belief they preached over and over to the young squad. Pocklington was even brazen enough to stand up in front of the media and say that his franchise would win the Cup within five years. No expansion team had ever accomplished that, and most assumed it was impossible.

1981–1982

TIME FOR ANOTHER GOALIE

Though Andy Moog had proven himself during the playoffs, and Ron Low was playing well, Oilers management set their sights on adding another goaltender in the 1981 entry draft, to be held at the Montreal Forum on June 10 (for the first time ever, the doors were opened to the public). And this year, there happened to be a very good one, who also had a local connection.

When the time came for Edmonton to announce its first pick of the day, eighth overall, they chose goalie Grant Fuhr, an 18-year-old from Spruce Grove, Alberta. Fuhr had played with the Victoria Cougars of the WHL for two years, and in both he was a first-team all star. He seemed especially well suited to the Oilers' run-and-gun style of play, the skaters often leaving the goalie alone.

Over the years, Fuhr and Moog would split the regular-season games fairly evenly, but once the playoffs started, Sather leaned on Fuhr. Although Fuhr became the Number 1 goalie in the post-season, Sather made him work for his time in net. To keep him in top shape and keep his reflexes sharp, Sather set up a tennis-ball machine in the belly of the arena, and Fuhr would have to stop the balls served at him in quick succession.

BREAKING RECORDS

The Oilers' third season was one of broken records. Wayne Gretzky exploded, scoring 92 goals—16 more than Phil Esposito had scored in 1970–71. His 120 assists and 212 total points eclipsed his own marks of 109 and 164, set just the year before. In the race for the Art Ross Trophy, he finished 65 points ahead of Mike Bossy of the Islanders—the largest-ever margin of victory. Gretzky played in all 80 games, and there were only eight in which he didn't appear on the score sheet.

Ever since Maurice "Rocket" Richard scored 50 goals in 50 games in 1944–45, the feat had been the gold standard for individual offensive prowess. No one repeated it until Mike Bossy in 1980–81. Then, on December 30, 1981, in his *39th* game of the season, Gretzky scored his 50th goal of the season.

He wasn't the only one scoring goals, either. The Oilers' 417 regular-season

Alberta boy Grant Fuhr had a snappy right glove hand, amazing reflexes, and a competitive but relaxed spirit.

goals broke the record of 399 set by the 1970–71 Boston Bruins. Glenn Anderson had 105 points, while Paul Coffey had 89 points (the most for an Oiler defenceman so far). Mark Messier scored 50 goals and 88 points, and Jari Kurri had 86 points. In goal, Grant Fuhr's 28 victories were the most by an Edmonton netminder since the team joined the NHL.

Edmonton won the Smythe Division with a record of 48–17–15 and 111 points, second only to the New York Islanders.

ON THE WRONG SIDE OF A MIRACLE

On the strength of the Oilers' season and their surprising run the previous spring, expectations were high as the 1982 play-offs got underway. The NHL introduced a new format wherein the top four teams in each division qualified for the postseason, which began with a best-of-five division semifinal series. The winners would progress to the division final, the conference final, and ultimately the Stanley Cup final. Edmonton had a favourable matchup in the Smythe Division semi-finals: the fourth-place Los Angeles Kings had the weakest record (24–41–15 for 63 points) of the 16 playoff qualifiers, and the Oilers had gone 5–1–2 in head-to-head contests.

But the Kings took Game 1, in Edmonton, in a wild match—the final score was 10–8. The Oilers came back in the second game, winning in overtime by a score of 3–2, with Gretzky scoring the overtime winner. Things were looking good for the Oilers on April 10, as they took a 5–0 lead into the second intermission of Game 3 at the Great Western Forum on West Manchester Boulevard, in the Los Angeles suburb of Inglewood.

This game has since become known as the "Miracle on Manchester." The Kings were embarrassed and came out for the third period just wanting to make a good showing, and maybe get on the scoreboard. Glen Sather was smirking behind the visitors' bench. The Oilers were not ready for what happened next. The Kings scored twice in the early going, and the momentum shifted. Shortly after Los Angeles scored a third goal, Garry Unger drew a five-minute major for high sticking. He sat in the box, watching the Kings add two more goals to tie the game and force it into overtime. The Oilers had their chances in that third period, with open nets and breakaways, but it was as if their scoring power had been snipped with a pair of sharp scissors. They just couldn't seem to put the puck in the net, which was their forte. In the extra period, it looked as if the Oilers would win when Mark Messier had a wide-open net, but he shot the puck high. The Kings picked up the loose puck, skated down the ice, and Daryl Evans blasted a shot past Grant Fuhr. The Kings won 6–5. The Oilers battled back in Game 4, winning 3–2, but Los Angeles ultimately won the series with a decisive 7–4 win in Game 5.

This was a devastating loss for the Oilers. Over the summer, Edmonton's coaches and management looked hard at the series. So did the players. As disheartening as the upset was, when Glenn Anderson looked back on it, he said, "Losing was always our best lesson on winning."

This young team was invested in the full sixty minutes of each game, even from the bench.

Creative Discipline

Although Glen Sather liked his players to have fun and he wanted to keep them loose, he also applied discipline to make them work hard, especially in the early seasons. In addition to fines for lateness, not working hard or missing the bus, he sometimes got creative with his punishments. At one morning skate, he noticed that four players were missing: Kevin Lowe, Mark Messier, Dave Semenko and Curt Brackenbury.

First, Sather called Lowe and asked, "Were you thinking of coming to practice?" Lowe and Messier were rarely late, so they raced to the rink, flew into the dressing room and started to put on their hockey gear. Semenko and Brackenbury then arrived and started hustling to get their equipment on. When they saw that Lowe and Messier were also late, they concluded there was power in numbers. Plus, Lowe and Messier were stars.

The four stragglers got dressed and headed to the ice. Sather took one look at them and told them each to go to a corner of the rink and sit in the top row of the stands. Lowe looked at Messier and shrugged. Dave grinned, because he didn't have to practise. Each took a corner and hiked up the concrete stairs, skates scraping on the hard surface, blades dulling with every step. Once at the top, they sat down and watched Sather put their teammates through their paces. The latecomers actually sort of liked the seated position and the rest time. But just as they were getting comfortable, or as comfortable as one can be sitting in full equipment in the stands, Sather blew his whistle and called them down.

One more trip down the same concrete stairs did nothing for the sharpness of their skate blades. Sather told them to get on the ice. Then he told all the other players to sit on the players' bench. With their teammates lined up watching, Sather bag-skated the four—in their dull skates—until the sweat poured. The other boys watched and learned the lesson to never be late.

Gourmet cooking for the young Oilers. Kurri and Coffey making KD, their meal of choice. In the 1980s, guidelines for training and nutrition were looser.

1982—1983

A WINGER FOR GRETZKY?

Selecting 20th this year, the Oilers didn't have the advantage that an early slot had offered them in the previous two years' drafts. The best Edmonton pick in 1982 turned out to be a 31-year-old from Motor Ceske Budejovice in Czechoslovakia. Jaroslav Pouzar went in the fourth round at number 83 overall.

In Europe, he'd been a skill player with great hands. Head Scout Barry Fraser asked Pouzar to come to Edmonton and he agreed with no idea where he was going. He spoke little English and didn't know much about the NHL. Even so, he packed two bags and away he went. The Oilers put him on a line with Wayne Gretzky and Jari Kurri in the hopes that the left winger would

"From Gretzky to Kurri… he shoots, he scores!" Wayne Gretzky and Jari Kurri made magic.

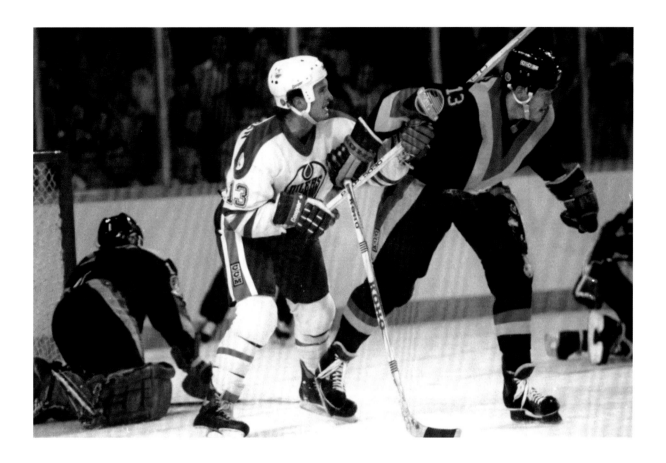

Oilers Ken Linseman would take on anyone, no matter the size. Here, he battles with Lars Lindgren of the Canucks.

complement this high-scoring pair. He played a tough game and was like a brick wall on the ice, but despite his skill, he struggled to keep up with Gretzky and Kurri, as well as to adapt to Edmonton's style of sending in two forecheckers with the third forward moving to the slot.

OILERS WELCOME THE PERFECT PEST

In August, the Oilers traded defenceman Risto Siltanen and the pro rights to winger Brent Loney, who was playing with the Cornwall Royals of the major junior Ontario Hockey League, to the Hartford Whalers for centremen Ken Linseman and Don Nachbaur. With

Linseman, another key ingredient had been added to the mix.

Linseman, known as "The Rat," was the type of player an NHLer would rather play with than against. His new teammates had seen him in action when they played the Philadelphia Flyers in the first round of the 1980 playoffs. At that time, Sather had told Gretzky to stay away from him at all costs if they were both on the ice. He was a pest, and he loved to use his stick to jab, spear and cross-check. Chirping constantly, he often drew penalties because players, unable to stand him anymore, would take a swipe at him.

On top of that, however, he brought a

SMYTHE DIVISION *Championship* OILERS **1982-83**

CAMPBELL CONFERENCE *Championship* OILERS **1982-83**

'99 IN THUMPER'S EYES OILERS YOUR 9 NO.

CONGRADULATIONS in your wedding and Good Luck in the Finals From your FANS!

CFAC Radio CALGARY AND ITS LISTENERS.... WISH THE BEST TO THE Oilers Bring THE STANLEY CUP TO ALBERTA

There's work to be done off the ice, too. Here, the team exercises in the dressing room in their short shorts and Nike shirts.

Heading into the Stanley Cup Finals with good luck cards and the successes of the season on full display for motivation.

bit of a scoring touch and postseason experience—the Flyers had gone to the Stanley Cup finals in 1980.

During his first season, Sather put Linseman together with Mark Messier and Glenn Anderson. He thrived by doggedly digging the puck out of the corners, but also showing an uncanny ability to find holes in opposing defences. Linseman had starred in junior hockey in his hometown of Kingston, Ontario, and was drafted by the Birmingham Bulls of the WHA as a 19-year-old in 1977. The WHA tried to prevent him from signing as an underage player, and Linseman turned to the courts, obtaining

an injunction that allowed him to play as a pro. His case changed pro hockey forever. The WHA started signing teenagers as young as 17, and by 1980 the NHL had lowered its draft age to 18.

SEMENKO'S TEAM BUILDING

Whenever the Oilers flew east for games, they often had to catch connecting flights in Toronto—usually on smaller aircraft that weren't as comfortable as the airliners that served larger metropolitan cities. On one such trip during the 1982–83 season, they were on a small plane and encountered some particularly rough turbulence.

The players had basically split into two groups—some at the rear of the plane, and others up front in what was known as the "nerd" section. Wayne Gretzky wasn't a great flyer, and his face was the colour of chalk.

Dave Semenko decided to loosen everyone up, employing teamwork and Glen Sather's pressure-relieving tactics to the tense situation. He took a survey, asking each player at the back of the plane: If the plane crashed, who would they eat first? The answer was unanimous. Dave called out to Andy Moog, who was sitting up front, and when Andy heard his name, he turned around. Then he thought, "Am I being called back to hang out with the cool guys?" His heart jumped a few beats. Since the turbulence had subsided a little, he got out of his seat and headed to the back of the plane. When he got there, Semenko said, "If we crash, we're eating you first." Laughter erupted, even from Moog.

CUP DREAMS SLASHED BY SAMURAI BILLY

The sting of losing to the Kings in the first round was still fresh in everybody's minds when the Oilers got off to a slow start this year. In their first 17 games, their record was just 6–7–4. Sather came into the dressing room one day and asked the team, "Are you having fun?"

The players looked at each other.

"Get out and have some fun," he said.

Once their wheels starting moving, they were like a loose train speeding down the track. With a record of 47–21–12 and 106 points, they easily won the division, leading second-place Calgary by 28 points, and had the third-best record in the entire NHL. For the second straight year, they scored a record number of goals: 424 this time, seven more than in 1981–82. Wayne Gretzky didn't quite reach the 200-point plateau again—he fell four points short—but his 125 assists were five more than he'd had the year before and established a new high. In all, four Oilers had at least 100 points: Gretzky (196), Mark Messier (106), Glenn Anderson (104) and Jari Kurri (104). Each of the four scored more than 40 goals: Gretzky with 71, Messier and Anderson with 48 and Kurri with 45.

Andy Moog was Sather's first choice in goal during the regular season, making 50 appearances, while Fuhr got into 32 games. Ron Low, who had been acquired during the Oilers' first NHL season was traded to New Jersey with minor-league defenceman Jim McTaggart for goalie Lindsay Middlebrook and minor-league forward Paul Miller.

On March 7, a more significant deal was made. Scrappy young centre Laurie Boschman was traded to Winnipeg for a veteran winger, Willy Lindstrom. Originally from Sweden, Lindstrom had been a goal scorer for Winnipeg ever since he joined the Jets in 1975–76. He stepped up to the plate in Edmonton, accumulating 11 points in the Oilers' last 10 games.

A month later, the Oilers and Jets faced off in the Smythe Division semifinals. There would be no repeat of the playoff misstep against Los Angeles, as Edmonton swept the series in three straight. Next up were the Calgary Flames, with whom the Oilers had little trouble as they took the series 4–1. The Chicago Blackhawks, who provided the competition in the Campbell Conference final, had put up 104 points in the regular season, suggesting that they might give the Oilers a run for their money. Instead, Edmonton took the first two games by scores of 8–4 and 8–2, for a four-game sweep. Through three rounds, the Oilers' record was 11–1. Averaging over

six goals a game, the Oilers had outscored their opponents 74–33. They set 16 scoring records in those three rounds. Among them, Gretzky set a new NHL record on May 12 for most assists in playoffs. Before that, on April 17, he'd tied the NHL record for most short-handed goals in playoffs. That same night, he also set the record for most playoffs goals for the Oilers on the road (at the Saddledome). On April 14, Messier had taken the same honour in Edmonton—most playoff goals in a home game—in the same series against the Flames, scoring four in front of the fans.

For the first time since 1923, a team from Edmonton was playing a series with the Stanley Cup on the line. (The Edmonton Eskimos, after winning the WCHL title in 1923, had moved on to the Stanley Cup finals.) And best of all, the Oilers were getting their long-held wish: they were pitted against the mighty New York Islanders, who had won three straight Stanley Cups since the last playoff meeting between the two teams. The Islanders, however, were bruised and battered from playing so far into the spring for the past three years. On top of 80-game regular seasons, they had played 21, 18 and 19 playoff games, and this year had already played 16. They were also a veteran team with eleven players who were at least 28 years old, and five were past 30. Could this group successfully match up against the youthful energy of the Oilers? The scoring machines? Nobody could deny that, just two years earlier, a younger, less explosive Oilers team had pushed the Isles to Game 6 of a playoff round.

When the media suggested that New York wasn't going to be able to keep pace

with the speedy Edmonton team, some of the Islanders spoke up. "We want to beat [the Oilers] more than anything," Clark Gillies said before the series. "They think they're the greatest thing since the invention of sliced bread." Bob Bourne added, "The Oilers are so damn cocky. Edmonton doesn't respect anyone. There isn't any one team we want to beat more."

After finishing first overall for two years, the 1982–83 edition of the Islanders had placed sixth, with 96 points. Was this a team in decline, or had the players conserved their energy for the postseason? Adding to the uncertainty, the news broke just before Game 1 that Islanders superstar Mike Bossy would be scratched from the lineup due to an illness.

Duane Sutter's goal at 5:36 of the first period was the only scoring until Ken Morrow put the puck into an empty net with 12 seconds on the clock. The final score: 2–0 for the Islanders. The Long Island defence was stifling—as soon as Gretzky stepped onto the ice and got the puck, he was swarmed. Islanders goalie Billy Smith stopped 35 Edmonton shots, while dishing out a few shots of his own— defending his crease, often with the aid of his stick, as aggressively as ever. When he slashed Glenn Anderson in the knee, preventing the winger from practising the next morning, Sather was furious. He demanded that the NHL give Smith a match penalty for attempting to injure Anderson, but was unsuccessful. So Sather went to the media, hinting that the Oilers might deliver payback if necessary. Having none of it, Smith responded, "Let's face it. If Semenko runs at me and hurts me, anything could happen, and the victim could be Gretzky."

After missing Game 1, Mike Bossy returned to the lineup. In the next two games, the Islander offence opened up while the defence remained as tight as ever, resulting in victories of 6–3 and 5–1. Smith had an agenda: he dished out slashes and then drew retaliation penal-

away and tired himself out. The Islanders remained patient, aiming primarily to keep the Oilers from scoring by only allowing them shots from poor angles. Plus, they were quick to clear rebounds. The Sutter brothers, Duane and Brent, were a force. At 12:39 of the first period, Bossy scored his second Stanley Cup–winning goal. In their first trip to the final, the Oilers were limited to just six goals in four games. Gretzky failed to score, but managed four assists.

> "The Oilers were a scoring team with high speed and lots of skill. We had to find ways to slow them down individually and as a team." —Duane Sutter

ties, tactics that successfully frustrated the Oilers' players and coaches, as well as the hometown media. In one headline, the *Edmonton Journal* labelled Smith "Public Enemy No. 1." They also called him "Samurai Billy," "Jack the Ripper" and "Mr. Obnoxious."

Game 4, at the Nassau Veterans Memorial Coliseum, was heated. In the third period, with the Islanders up 3–2, Smith performed a spectacular dive, saddling Glenn Anderson with a five-minute penalty for slashing. Sportswriters said New York held the Oilers off by playing a "rope-a-dope" style—a reference to Muhammad Ali's strategy in his 1974 heavyweight championship bout against George Foreman, in which he rested against the ropes in a defensive stance while Foreman flailed

After that fourth game, some of the Oilers walked by the Islanders dressing room. They expected to see the victors drinking champagne from the Stanley Cup, but instead saw the players icing their wounds. The boys were shocked, thinking it should be all fun and games after winning a Cup. This made them reconsider how they had played. Perhaps they hadn't sacrificed enough. Perhaps they needed to go one step further and get a little bloody, form a few scars. Next year, they resolved, they would need more ice packs when it was all said and done.

Paul Coffey remembers being in the dressing room after that final game and hearing Wayne Gretzky, who had scored nearly 200 points that season, say, "I'm never going to be a good player unless I win the Stanley Cup."

1983–1984

DRAFTING A BIG BODY

The spotlight at the 1983 draft was on a group of high-profile juniors, including Pat LaFontaine, drafted third by the New York Islanders, and Steve Yzerman, taken fourth by Detroit. Drafting 19th, the Edmonton Oilers elected to take a player who would still benefit from some seasoning. Jeff Beukeboom had all the size he needed to move opponents off the puck, but he also had the ability to move the puck. When he parked himself in front of the net, he won battles and showed the ability to clear the puck from the goalmouth. He would spend the next two years with the Sault Ste. Marie Greyhounds of the Ontario Hockey League, along with a full season with the Oilers' American Hockey League farm team in Halifax.

In the fourth round, at number 80 overall, Edmonton unearthed another key player who was still a couple of years away from taking the ice at the Coliseum. Left winger Esa Tikkanen had played with Jokerit's junior club in Finland before moving to Canada to play for the Regina Pats of the Saskatchewan Junior Hockey

League. In 1982, he returned to Finland to play for HIFK Helsinki, with whom he would spend 1983–84 and '84–85 regular season. He did come back to Edmonton during the '84–85 playoff run, and even graced the Oilers score sheet.

HANDING OVER THE LEADERSHIP

Four days into training camp, equipment manager Barrie Stafford told Wayne Gretzky that Glen Sather wanted to see him. Gretzky headed to Sather's office to find Lee Fogolin also sitting there. After telling Gretzky to close the door, Sather said, "I told you when you arrived here that you would be captain one day. Lee came in the other day and wants you to be captain."

Gretzky was stunned. The first thing he said was, "I don't want to steal the captaincy." He respected Fogolin, who was like a godfather to the players. The defenceman had taught him how to get ready, how to practise and how to treat teammates. He was always the guy who put the team first.

Fogolin looked at Gretzky and was adamant when he said, "It's time for you to take over."

The Oilers get another chance to face the Islanders for the Stanley Cup.

Both Gretzky and Fogolin went back to the dressing room and asked everyone except the players to leave. They stood before their teammates, and in an emotional moment, Fogolin broke the news that Gretzky was going to be the captain from now on.

ADDING A TOUGH GUY

On December 5, the Oilers made a trade that paid significant dividends, sending centreman Tom Roulston to Pittsburgh for winger Kevin McClelland.

McClelland was fearless, loved to dish out hits and didn't mind dropping his gloves to get into a scrap. He was an important addition to the Oilers' checking line, a role he was more than willing to play, and his energy and work ethic made him a natural leader no matter which line he played on. On top of all that, later in the year, McClelland would score one of the most important goals in Oilers history.

THE BIRTH OF THE BATTLE OF ALBERTA

Having made it to the final in just their fourth year, there was only one piece of new business on the agenda for the 1983–84 season: win the Stanley Cup. From the first game of the regular season, it was clear that the Edmonton Oilers meant business. They pushed, they shoved and they scored goal after goal, the only lapse in momentum coming in February, when they lost five

in a row, including a stinging 11–0 defeat to Hartford. After that embarrassment they went 18–4 the rest of the way, finishing first overall with a record of 57–18–5 for 119 points, 15 ahead of the Boston Bruins and New York Islanders. In what was becoming an annual occurrence, the Oilers again broke the NHL goal-scoring record, this time with 446. Paul Coffey became only the second defenceman in history to score 40 goals, and his 126 points were second only to Gretzky's 205 among all NHL skaters. Grant Fuhr's 30 wins were the most among goaltenders; Andy Moog (27) was close behind.

The Edmonton Oilers were primed for the playoffs, steamrolling the Winnipeg Jets in three straight in the division semifinals. Next came the Calgary Flames, who despite finishing with a winning record (34–32–14), weren't really supposed to pose a threat. In the fall of 1983, the Flames had moved into their brand new arena, the Saddledome (so called because its roof was designed to look like a horse's saddle). The Oilers had beaten them in all four of their regular-season meetings in the new digs, including the Saddledome's opening night on October 15. The Flames' fortunes weren't better at the Coliseum, where they had last won a game on December 20, 1981—since then, they had lost 10 and tied three.

This woeful streak included the February 3 matchup in Edmonton that saw superstars Gretzky, Messier and

One of the first dust-ups in what became the Battle of Alberta.

Kurri all wearing suits instead of hockey gear. Both Gretzky and Kurri were nursing wounds, while Messier was finishing off a suspension. The Flames arrived in Edmonton riding a nine-game unbeaten streak and talked to the press about how the Oilers were doomed without their three stars. Then along came Pat Hughes, a role player who had his name engraved on the Stanley Cup as a part-time member of the 1978–79 Montreal Canadiens. On this night, he scored five goals (including a hat trick in the first period) to help the Oilers trounce the Flames 10–5. Kevin McClelland and Dave Hunter fought in the corners, and Lee Fogolin fought with his fists. But this night will always be known as the "night Pat Hughes scored five goals." Of the night, Hughes said, "It was one of those freak nights, I guess. You're Gretzky for a day.... I'll call it all lucky, and I'll leave it at that, because I don't think anybody who played with me or against me would have ever expected anything like that to happen."

The playoff series opened in Edmonton, and the Flames scored first, a shorthanded goal by Mike Eaves. It was a huge wakeup call for the Oilers. In each of their regular-season games, the Oilers had been on the board first. Edmonton still won the game 5–2, but the Flames had played well and there was a feeling that they weren't going to roll over easily.

Glen Sather woke up on the morning of the second game, a Friday the 13th, and had a weird feeling in his gut that something was off. That night, the Oilers took a 4–1 lead and thought for sure they had the game in hand. Then the pesky Flames came back, taking a 5–4 lead into the final minute. Gretzky tied it with 45 seconds left, forcing overtime. When Carey Wilson scored for the Flames (his second of the night) at 3:42 of the extra period, the Oilers were shocked. Afterward, Messier said, "We didn't have the killer instinct."

That Friday the 13th was a lucky one for the Flames, breaking their 13-game winless streak on Northlands Coliseum ice. But Games 3 and 4 were in Calgary, in an arena where the Oilers had had no problem making themselves at home.

The 3–2 and 5–4 Oiler wins, giving them a 3–1 series lead, weren't pretty. The Flames attacked, over and over again, specifically targeting Gretzky, Kurri and Anderson. Gretzky claimed after the fourth game that he'd been "cranked at least eight or nine times." The Flames were coached by "Badger Bob" Johnson, and barbs were launched back and forth between Sather and him after Game 4. Sather claimed Gretzky had been "maimed." Badger Bob pulled out the rule book and asked, "Where does it say you can't hit Wayne Gretzky?"

Lanny McDonald was playing for the Flames at that time, and he was also quick to tell the media that "it ain't over 'til it's over." The Flames drove north to Edmonton for Game 5 and won 5–4, showing that Friday the 13th hadn't been a fluke. Game 6 in Calgary turned into another Alberta barnburner. The Oilers were down 4–3 when Mark Messier scored in the third period to tie the game. When the final buzzer sounded, the score was still tied and the

Family Values

Glen Sather espoused family values. In this playoff run, the players took the concept a step further.

Andy Moog's wife, Karla, was due to give birth to the couple's second baby. Sather told Moog that she had better have the baby in between series, because he wasn't getting any time off. Every time the players saw Karla, they told her she should name the baby Stanley if it was a boy, because they were going to win the Cup. The thing was, Karla—who, deep down, didn't like the idea—had told Andy he could name the baby. So the players started working on their goalie, telling him to name the baby Stanley. Naturally, it became a running joke.

In between the first and second playoff rounds, Karla went into labour while Andy was at practice. Karla Moog was thrilled and relieved when they had a girl, whom they named Arielle.

game went into overtime. It was McDonald who scored in that extra frame, just 64 seconds in, tying the series. The seventh and final game would be in Edmonton.

The media now agreed with Messier's earlier assessment that the Oilers might suffer from a "lack of killer instinct."

In a surprise move, Glen Sather decided to put Andy Moog in net for Game 7, even though Fuhr had played all six games in the series. In the dressing room before this crucial match, the Oilers thought about what they had to do—what they *wanted* to do. They also knew what they didn't want, and that was a summer of wondering what had gone wrong. "We sat in the dressing room before the game," said Wayne Gretzky, "and told ourselves that the 440 goals and 119 points in the standings wouldn't mean anything. We sat there and said, 'We're a good team. Let's prove it.'"

Partway through the game, Moog gave up a goal on a three-on-one rush, and Sather yanked him and put Fuhr in. Tensions were running high, the energy of the team sparking in all different directions. But the hometown fans weren't disappointed at the end of the night. The Oilers had developed into a strong team—not only capable of unprecedented scoring power, but able to come together and focus on their shared goal. Edmonton rallied and won by a resounding 7–4 score, ending the series and claiming the first victory in the Battle of Alberta. With this, the Oilers advanced to the next round, against Minnesota.

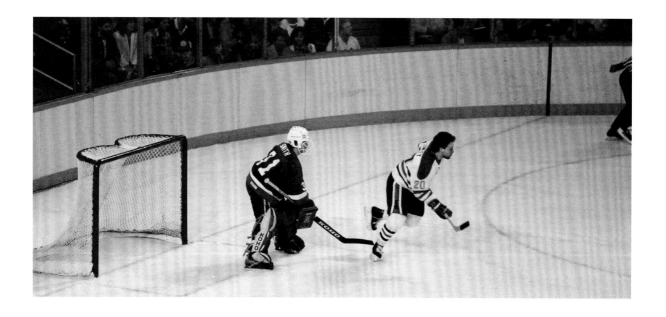

REMATCH

After beating out the Flames, the Oilers pushed on, physically bruised from the intense and long series. Their next matchup was against the Minnesota North Stars, and even though they swept the series, it was fraught with a few wacky games.

For Game 1, Sather put Fuhr back in net and they won easily, 7–1. The second game was more of a struggle, a seesaw battle that ended 4–3. Fuhr had to leave with a hyperextended elbow and was relieved by Moog, early in the third period.

However, it was in Game 3 that things really started to go sideways. The Oilers took the ice at the Met Center in Bloomington, Minnesota, with Moog in net and the players eager to make it a 3–0 series. Dave Lumley and Wayne Gretzky popped in a couple early, giving Edmonton a 2–0 lead. Eight minutes into the second period, with the score now 2–1, Lumley took a major penalty for spearing. He made his way to the penalty box and could do nothing but drink water as he watched Minnesota score three goals during the power play, making it 4–2 North Stars. Seconds after he got out of the box, Minnesota scored to make it 5–2.

This turn of events could easily have taken the air out of the Oilers' game, but instead they went on a tear, getting goals from Coffey, Kurri, Anderson, Linseman, Messier and Gretzky, with Gretzky's goal coming off a penalty shot. The game ended 8–5. Although Minnesota put forth a tremendous effort in Game 4, the Oilers won the game 3–1 to complete the sweep.

The stage was set for a rematch with the New York Islanders. Because of the sweep, the Oilers had a nine-day break between series. Sather was always thinking ahead, looking for an edge. Over the course of the season, Roger Neilson had

Samurai Billy takes a swing at Dave Lumley.

been let go by the Vancouver Canucks and Los Angeles Kings, so Sather gave him a call, asking him to help as a video coach. Both Neilson and Sather went over the Islander tapes and noticed that New York collapsed into the slot on defence. All five players would circle the middle and protect the net, forcing their opponents to hug the perimeter, making them take long shots, often at bad angles. So the Oilers came up with a new game plan. Forget the beautiful plays in front of the net, the players were told. The coaches wanted them to go wide, fool the Islanders, and then crash the net and get the dirty goal in front.

In the first game of this series there was just one goal. It came after the Oilers lost a faceoff, but Dave Hunter dug deep and rushed to the corner. Fighting hard to gain possession, he freed up the puck. Pat Hughes hovered nearby, nabbed the puck and rifled it off to Kevin McClelland. McClelland used his quick release to whistle it past goalie Billy Smith. After losing four straight games to the Islanders the previous year, the Oilers finally won a game in the Stanley Cup final.

McClelland's goal was one of the most important in the team's history so far, and to this day it remains one of the most significant in the franchise's 40 years. To make things even sweeter, Fuhr stopped 34 shots for the club's first Stanley Cup finals shutout since joining the NHL.

The team was in good spirits heading into Game 2, but that feeling was short-lived. The Islanders walloped them 6–1. The teams headed west for the next three games of the series. The Islanders weren't happy to be in Edmonton for three games. "That was ridiculous," Denis Potvin said. "We had to spend eight days in Edmonton. [The fans] circled our hotel with pick-up trucks . . . day in and day out."

Back in Edmonton, the Oilers had a favourite watering hole, the Grande Hotel, built in 1904—but despite its name, it wasn't known for its elegance or its upkeep. None of that mattered to the Oilers. "It was a place we went when we were losing," said Paul Coffey. Being back in Edmonton, the Oilers met for lunch at the Grande. "You could feel the intensity," Gretzky said. "We wanted to win."

"I started coaching junior in Kamloops and at the break at Christmas I would go to Edmonton and I would watch all their practices, their pre-game skates and games. Every day. The precision and execution were so pristine. If you loved the game in those early '80s, you had to watch the Oilers." —Ken Hitchcock

Although Gretzky was the Oilers' scoring machine, Mark Messier was no slouch. The Oilers were trailing 2–1 midway through Game 3 when Messier grabbed the puck, flew down the wing, pulled a few moves to deke the defence and beat Smith on his stick side. The bench erupted, as did the fans. Edmonton scored five more unanswered goals to win 7–2. There was a tense moment with eight minutes left, when Fuhr and Pat LaFontaine collided and Fuhr went down. Moog took his place in the crease and faced only one shot the rest of the way.

"I've never heard a crowd like this for a constant 60 minutes," said Messier after the game, in which he scored two goals.

For Game 4, the Oiler coaches kept the media in the dark about which goalie would play. In the dressing room, the players decided to be cagey as well. There were some things the reporters just didn't need to know right away. For the players' part, they focused on the game ahead, having lost enough to know how to win.

It was a solid game all around for the Oilers. Gretzky broke his 10-game scoring slump, Messier kept up his playoff pace and Moog picked up the win in net, stopping 19 of 21 shots. The result was a duplicate of Game 3: a 7–2 win. Here were the Oilers, in just their fifth year in the league, and they were heading into Game 5 of the Stanley Cup final with a 3–1 lead in the series.

The date was May 19, 1984. As captain, Wayne Gretzky stood up before the game and said, "All the individual awards I've won could never compare to winning the Stanley Cup."

It was all he needed to say to get his team fired up. Everything else had been said, practising had been done, coaches' orders had been given. Now it was time. The Oilers stepped on the ice, and the fans' cheers echoed off the arena walls. Even the sound of the puck smacking against the boards during the warm-up couldn't be heard.

The game stayed scoreless for 12 minutes, until Kurri passed to Gretzky, who raced down the right side and popped it past Smith. The announcer said the phrase, heard so many times before: "From Kurri to Gretzky . . . and he shoots, he scores!" The fans went absolutely wild. At 17:26 of the period, Kurri again passed to Gretzky, who drove home his second goal of the night. The Oilers headed to their dressing room leading 2–0. They had posted little signs bearing messages of affirmation all over the room—with slogans like "The Drive for Five Is No Longer Alive" (referring to the Islanders playing for their fifth consecutive Cup) and "The Thirst for First Shall Be Quenched Tonight"—and as they sat there between periods, they read the notes and talked about how they could win.

Thirty-eight seconds into the second period, Ken Linseman scored a power-play goal to put the Oilers up by three. The fourth goal came on another power play, this time from Kurri. In the third period, the Oilers got a bit of a scare when LaFontaine scored a pair of goals just 22 seconds apart, bringing the Islanders to within two with 19 minutes to go. Regrouping on the bench, the boys dug deep. As the end of the period

The first Oilers Stanley Cup Victory! Everyone was allowed on the ice to celebrate with the team.

drew near, the Islanders, desperate for a couple of goals, pulled their goalie. The fans were now standing, cheering nonstop. Dave Lumley, a role player who had been with the Oilers since 1979-80, ended up on the ice for the final couple of minutes. Lumley described how that came to be, and laughs when he thinks about it now. "So when they pulled their goalie and Slats is looking around on who to go on, I stood up, rattled the gate, looked at him and he looked at me. 'Lummer, you're on the ice.'"

He raced out, and the puck got loose and ended up on his stick. Lumley took a shot, firing the puck towards the empty net. When it hit the mesh, the fans went crazy. To this day, Lumley says, "My favourite memory is the empty-net goal that clinched the first Cup."

Willy Lindstrom and Glenn Anderson enjoying a taste of the Stanley Cup.

The roar of the crowd almost blew the roof off Northlands Coliseum. The Oilers had delivered on Pocklington's Stanley Cup pledge, right on schedule. People screamed until their voices were hoarse. They threw orange and blue balloons and sent streamers dancing through the air, all of them landing on the white ice. They watched as the team swarmed the Cup, and their cheering intensified when the captain, Wayne Gretzky, hoisted that Stanley Cup over his head. (He almost dropped it, too, because he didn't realize how heavy it would be.) Mark Messier accepted the Conn Smythe Trophy as playoff MVP, swiping his eyes to bat away his tears. The noise seemed to penetrate every centimetre of the Coliseum. Players hugged—they had all played their part. Strong play, a tremendous work ethic and timely contributions from Don Jackson, Dave Lumley, Charlie Huddy, Pat Hughes, Randy Gregg, Rick Chartraw and Pat Conacher all culminated in this moment.

Broadcast crews dragged camera and microphone cords everywhere. Family members embraced. The players skated around with the Cup, trying to touch it over and over. They took turns holding the precious Cup, the one they'd fought so hard for. When the festivities on the ice were over, the Oilers went back to the dressing room and the party continued, with Randy Gregg drenching everyone with champagne and Messier still crying.

When the fans had finally left the building, the players remained in the dressing room with Sather, the rest of the coaching and management staff and the Stanley Cup.

The boys pointed to the Cup.

"What do we do with it?" they asked.

Sather shrugged. "You won it. You take it."

The fans in Edmonton turned up in droves for the victory Parade down Jasper Avenue.

City Pride

"This is the most incredible high I've ever experienced in my life. When I said we'd win the Stanley Cup in five years the day we got into this league, I said it because I was a naive fool. But that's what I believed." —Peter Pocklington

"Edmonton had tasted winning before, but never like this. The Grey Cups were great. But uh-uh. No way. Not even close. That was the greatest single sports experience this unbelievably fortunate city—Canada's City of champions—has ever seen." —Terry Jones, *Edmonton Journal*

The celebrations didn't end that night. Once the evening ticked away, plans went into motion for the team to have a parade. On May 22, more than 100,000 fans lined the sides of the streets. The players sat in convertibles (even a Rolls-Royce convertible), waving, whistling, pumping their fists and dressed up in their best '80s garb. Fans tried to mob the vehicles, and cops even surrounded the car holding the Cup. Wayne Gretzky needed a police escort to get to the podium at City Hall.

Edmonton had indeed become, as Terry Jones said, a "city of champions."

1984–1985

CANADA CUP 1984

A month after the Oilers won the Stanley Cup, Glen Sather was named coach and general manager of Canada's team in the forthcoming Canada Cup tournament. Sather brought with him his assistant coaches, John Muckler and Ted Green, and to avenge the country's defeat at the hands of the Soviet Union in the 1981 tournament, he drew heavily from his own roster—a move that critics had a field day with. In all, eight Oilers were named to the 31-player training squad: goalie Grant Fuhr; defencemen Paul Coffey, Randy Gregg, Charlie Huddy and Kevin Lowe; and forwards Glenn Anderson, Mark Messier and Wayne Gretzky. Five members of the New York Islanders were named—Mike Bossy, Bob Bourne, Denis Potvin, John Tonelli and Bryan Trottier. Brent Sutter was also added when arm surgery side-lined Barry Pederson of the Boston Bruins. But Trottier, who had played for Canada in the 1981 Canada Cup, elected to play for Team USA instead, and Potvin had to sit this one out because of hypertension.

Despite being called on to play for their country, the rivalry between the Oilers and Islanders hadn't cooled off by the time the players came together. Glenn Anderson remembers a divided dressing room, the Oilers sitting on one side and the Islanders on the other. Snide comments were thrown around. When some of the Oilers would walk past the trainer's room and see Mike Bossy on the table, getting his back worked on, they would say he had "no guts."

Despite opening with a 7–2 victory over West Germany, the team started off poorly. There was just too much animosity on the team. Then, "to his credit," according to Glenn Anderson, "Bob Bourne changed where we sat in the dressing room and put an Oiler beside an Islander. There was also a meeting where we talked about putting our differences aside." It helped, although Canada closed out the round robin with a 6–3 loss to the Soviet Union, leaving the team an embarrassing fourth in the standings and setting up a rematch against the Soviets in the semifinal game. Late in the third period, with Canada trailing 2–1, Doug

Kevin Lowe hoists the 1985 Stanley Cup.

Wilson of the Chicago Blackhawks scored to tie the game. In overtime, Paul Coffey—the only man back—made an unbelievable defensive play to break up a Soviet two-on-one. He poked the puck away from the puck carrier, creating a turnover, and then skated it up ice. His shot from the point was deflected into the net by Bossy.

With that goal, the Canadians advanced to the best-of-three final against Sweden. Canada cruised to a 5–2 victory in Game 1, played at the Saddledome in Calgary, and jumped to a 5–1 lead in the first period of Game 2, played at Northlands. Sweden battled back, and the score was 6–4 after 40 minutes. The Swedes managed to score once more in the third, but the Canadians were able to hold on and claim the Canada Cup, giving Edmonton fans a chance to watch "their own" win for a second championship. Tonelli of the Islanders was named the tournament MVP, while Coffey and Gretzky made the Canada Cup all-star team.

THE NEW FACES OF 1984-85

Despite the Stanley Cup championship, Glen Sather was still searching for an effective winger to skate with Wayne Gretzky and Jari Kurri. So it was that, on June 21, just a month after the final was over, Ken Linseman was traded to the Boston Bruins for Mike Krushelnyski. The Oilers would miss Linseman, who was a key role player and a tough guy on the ice. Krushelnyski offered size, a long reach, good stick-handling and playmaking skills, and

Glen Sather assessing from behind the bench.

goal-scoring ability. He was coming off a 25-goal year with Boston.

Assistant coach John Muckler spoke to the difficulty of finding a player who could keep up with Edmonton's two most skilled forwards. "There are psychological problems involved in working with Gretzky. You have to do things on blind faith, assuming he'll get the puck to you, and that's hard to do."

Krushelnyski put up good numbers in 1984–85, with 43 goals and 45 assists, his 88 points ranking fourth on the team and earning him a trip to the NHL All-Star Game in Calgary. But the coaching staff concluded that he would

Mark Napier was a solid contributor to the Oilers.

ultimately be better-suited to a defensive role on the third line, and they encouraged him to focus on his two-way play.

In the waiver draft on October 9, the Oilers picked up a couple of role players: 28-year-old winger Terry Martin of the Toronto Maple Leafs and 25-year-old centreman Billy Carroll of the New York Islanders. This was the first trade where the Oilers saw an Islander enter their dressing room. Martin's skating and versatility impressed Sather, while Carroll was seen as a hard worker with an aggressive streak who had had his name engraved on the Stanley Cup three times. The Oilers were surprised, however, to

lose 30-year-old winger Dave Lumley, who was claimed by the Hartford Whalers. He took with him the satisfaction of scoring the empty-net goal that sealed the Stanley Cup in the spring. Still, Sather valued Lumley enough that, when the Whalers put him on waivers on February 6, he jumped at the chance to grab Lumley back. He made it back to Alberta in time to appear in 12 regular-season games, and eight more in the playoffs.

On January 24, the Oilers shipped Martin and rookie winger Gord Sherven to Minnesota for right winger Mark Napier. The 28-year-old Napier, a 40-goal scorer with Montreal as recently as 1982–83, was tagged to play on the Gretzky line, where his speed and offensive ability would fit right in. In 33 regular-season games he totalled 35 points, and then went on to earn 10 more in 18 playoff games.

Another important addition was made in February, when Craig MacTavish was signed as a free agent. In January 1984, while driving under the influence of alcohol, the Boston Bruins centreman was involved in a two-car collision in Peabody, Massachusetts, that resulted in the death of the other motorist. He was convicted of vehicular homicide and sentenced to a year in prison. The NHL suspended him for the entirety of the 1984–85 season, so he would not be eligible to play until the following season. He was available because the Bruins, believing he would be better able to make a fresh start somewhere other than Boston, agreed to release him from his contract. He was a crafty forward who would become known as one of the best defensive forwards in the league, and he played with passion and grit. Still, no one could have predicted how important he would prove to be to the Oilers organization.

UNDERDOGS NO MORE

When the Oilers arrived for training camp in the fall of 1984, they were still feeling pretty good about their Stanley Cup win. But when it came time to really get down to work, the impact of the win suddenly hit home. Mark Messier remembers stepping on the ice and thinking, "We have to do this again."

The reality was that teams always wanted to beat the Stanley Cup champions. The Oilers were no longer underdogs.

As the season got underway, it was clear they knew what to do—how to focus better, how to prepare. They came out with guns blazing, posting a 12–0–3 record in their first 15 games, and kept right on winning, finishing atop the Smythe Division yet again, going 49–20–11. Wayne Gretzky led the league for the fifth year running with 208 points, set a new NHL record for assists with 135, and won the Hart Trophy for the sixth time in as many years. Jari Kurri became only the third player to score 70 goals in a season, ending with 71 goals and 135 points. Paul Coffey had 121 points and won his first Norris Trophy as the NHL's best defenceman. All three made the first all-star team. Grant Fuhr played the majority of the games in goal (46), though Andy Moog spent significant time in the Oiler net, getting into 39 games.

In the division semifinals, the Los Angeles Kings twice managed to take the Oilers into overtime, but game-winning goals from Lee Fogolin and Glenn Anderson helped the Oilers sweep the series. Fuhr was named the first star in all three games. The division final against the Winnipeg Jets ended in another sweep. Fuhr was the first star of Game 1 after stopping 21 of 23 shots, while Paul Coffey came to life in Game 2, scoring two goals and adding three assists in the Oilers' 5–2 win.

Game 1 of the conference final against Chicago saw the Oilers go on a scoring rampage, with 11 goals to Chicago's two. Huddy, Kurri and Anderson scored two

apiece, while Gretzky, Coffey, Mark Napier, Willy Lindstrom and Pat Hughes contributed singles. The Oilers kept up the assault in Game 2, a 7–3 victory in which Kurri scored a hat trick. They had now won nine in a row. And adding Games 3, 4 and 5 of the previous spring's Stanley Cup final meant that they had won an NHL-record 12 consecutive playoff games.

The Oilers had also defeated Chicago in each of the teams' last seven meetings. So as they headed to the Windy City for Game 3, it was arguably with more than a little swagger. And after scoring so many goals—and winning so easily—in the first two games, the players slackened the reins and played a more freewheeling game. That night, they received a wake-up call. The Blackhawks jumped to a 2–0 lead in the first period and came out on top by a score of 5–2.

Although the Hawks didn't have the playoff experience of the Oilers, they did have some offensive power—Denis Savard had just racked up 100 points for the third time in his five NHL seasons, while sniper Steve Larmer had scored 46

The Oilers celebrate
over division rivals
The LA Kings.

goals. They made the most of their scoring ability in Game 4, winning 8–6 and evening up the series. It was after this game that Glen Sather decided to give a few players a bit of a "tongue-lashing" as Gretzky likes to call it today. He and Paul Coffey were both on Sather's hit list, among others. Their departures from the game plan, and their freewheeling on the ice had cost them. The team also held a players-only meeting where they discussed what had gone wrong and what they needed to do to win this series. Anderson said, "We talked about being too loose and how we were giving up too many goals. How we had to clean up our act defensively." These meetings gave the players a chance to speak freely. Anderson called them "sacred," saying, "Once we walked through the threshold of the [dressing room] door, we were in a safe place. Nothing was repeated outside our dressing room." Because they got along so well, they could regroup when things were going awry. Back in Edmonton, Gretzky and Coffey went to dinner on their night off with Ace Bailey, who was now scouting for the Oilers. Ace was a mentor and father figure to many of the players, especially Wayne, and he also calmly talked to the young men, almost as if it were a counselling session.

The fifth game of the series started out with back-and-forth action. Mike Krushelnyski scored first for the Oilers, but the Hawks came right back with a goal by Troy Murray. Kurri scored for the 2–1 lead, but Darryl Sutter and Steve Larmer both managed to get shots past Fuhr to take the lead. At 16:31, Kurri tied the score. The boys regrouped in the dressing room. They didn't want to lose this series. They knew how to win. But the second period didn't start well for them, as Savard scored to again put the Hawks ahead. The Oilers quickly turned on the jets, followed their game plan and scored four unanswered goals. Twenty-one seconds after Savard's goal, Messier popped one in, followed by back-to-back goals by Gretzky, the second on a power play. With momentum working in their favour, Kurri completed his hat trick and the Oilers took a 7–4 lead into the second intermission. In the third period, Coffey, Dave Hunter and Lee Fogolin added three more, and the Oilers emerged with a resounding 10–5 victory.

The fans in Edmonton had Stanley Cup fever and had been waiting for this game after watching their team lose two on television. Whatever advantages the Blackhawks had enjoyed on home ice in Games 3 and 4, the Oilers successfully neutralized them in Game 6, also played at Chicago Stadium. They didn't give the Hawks an inch, taking a 6–0 lead before bulldozing Chicago 8–2 to win the series. Kurri followed up on his Game 5 hat trick with a four-goal night—all assisted by Gretzky. Messier scored twice, and singles went to Fogolin and Anderson. The Oilers had scored 44 goals in the six

games against Chicago, and Kurri had pocketed 12 of those, giving him the NHL record for most goals in a series. He also had the most three-goal games in a year and was only the second player in NHL history to record back-to-back playoff hat tricks. (Doug Bentley of the Black Hawks was the first, in 1944.)

The Oilers were off to another Stanley Cup final, this time against the Philadelphia Flyers—the youngest team in the NHL and coached by 35-year-old Mike Keenan, who in his first season as an NHL coach had taken his team to the finals.

The series opened at the Spectrum in Philadelphia, and Keenan assigned Ron Sutter to cover Gretzky, which made it hard for the Oiler captain to make his usual plays. The Flyers outmuscled and outworked the Oilers, as well as out-shooting them 41–26. Kevin McClelland tried to get the visitors going by fighting the Flyers' Ed Hospodar, and in the second period, down by a goal, there was a line brawl after McClelland got into it with Joe Paterson. The result—a 4–1 loss—didn't sit well with the Oilers. But they weren't ready to give up the crown yet. Winning was in this team's blood, and now they had experience to go with their winning edge. In Game 2, it was the Oilers' turn to shut down the opposition. Halfway through the first period, Gretzky got his first goal of the series to take an early lead. In that period alone, there were 35 faceoffs (the average was 25), creating a game without a lot of flow. Tensions were high for both teams. Flyers Tim Kerr dropped his gloves with Dave Hunter in the second period at centre ice, and shortly after serving his penalty scored to tie the game. Just four minutes later Willy Lindstrom gave the Oilers a 2-1 lead, and then Hunter popped in the third Oilers goal on an empty net. The Oilers limited Philadelphia to just 18 shots and managed a 3–1 victory.

Games 3 through 5 were to be played in Edmonton. Buoyed by the hometown fans, Gretzky scored two goals within the first 85 seconds of the first period, working the crowd into a frenzy. By the time the buzzer sounded to end the first period, he had a hat trick. Philadelphia mounted a comeback, but the Oilers finished the game with a 4–3 win, enough to take a 2-1 lead in the series. The high didn't last long, though. Eleven minutes into Game 4, the Oilers were trailing 3-1. Later in the first period, the Oilers were on a power play when Sutter intercepted the puck and sped down the ice, hoping for a shorthanded goal. Messier chased him, caught him but also brought him down to the ice. The referee called a penalty shot—only the fifth to ever be taken in a Stanley Cup final.

From the benches, the players watched as Fuhr crouched. Sather knew that if the Flyers pushed ahead and took a three-goal lead, it could be a turning point in the series. Fuhr was ready. He read Sutter right, and when the puck came down the middle, he made the save and the fans screamed. The energy from the crowd got the adrenaline pumping—it was exactly what the team needed. Huddy popped in a goal late in the period and the Oilers were only down by one going into the second.

From then on, it was all Oilers. Anderson got the tying goal just 21

seconds into the period, while Gretzky got the go-ahead goal on a power play. Fuhr stopped a breakaway by Rick Tocchet in that second period—a huge save that, once again, reinvigorated the team. Gretzky scored his second power-play goal early in the third period to wrap up the Oilers' 5–3 win.

Two nights later, the teams met at Northlands Coliseum for what would prove to be the last game of the series. Fans had made signs that said, "The Cup Stays Here." The game featured some of the most amazing goals the Oilers had ever scored. Five minutes into the first period, Gretzky made an unbelievable blind backhand pass to set up Kurri. When Kurri slammed it home to make it 1-0, the fans went ballistic, knowing they had just witnessed magic on the ice. Lindstrom scored next for the Oilers. The Flyers came back with a Rich Sutter goal, but then Coffey put it to them, scoring two pretty goals before the end of the period, the second on the power play. That second goal featured, again, a brilliant behind-the-back pass from Gretzky. With a 4–1 lead, they hit the dressing room. The Oilers remained calm. They wanted to win on home ice and they needed to play their game, not get caught up in the dramatics of the pushing and shoving, stop and start play. In the second period, Messier and Krushelnyski put Edmonton ahead 6-1. Then Gretzky was the one to accept a blind pass, a returning of the favour from Kurri. The two linemates seemed to have a sixth sense that night, relying on feel more than sight. Including the regular season, both players scored their

Dave Semenko holds his ground to create scoring opportunities for his linemates. ▶

90th goal of the year in this game. Messier added one in the third period, during which the fans continually chanted, "The Cup stays here!" And it did. The Oilers won the game in an 8–3 victory, earning them their second Stanley Cup championship.

The crowd counted down the final seconds, and when the buzzer sounded, gloves were tossed to the ice as a mob scene developed. The players once again circled the Cup, taking turns holding it in the air, shouting hurrahs. Fans cheered for at least an hour after the game, only to spill out onto the streets and celebrate some more. Kurri's 19 goals led all playoff scorers and tied Reggie Leach of the 1975–76 Flyers for the all-time record. Wayne Gretzky won the Conn Smythe Trophy for the first time, although Kurri and Fuhr were also strong contenders.

The Oilers had proven that they weren't just a one-shot wonder. On June 5, 2017, this 1984–85 squad was named as the NHL's greatest team, as voted by fans.

Mark Messier with the Cup—and the biggest smile in the world.

1985–1986

BUCKY BREAKS THROUGH

For the Edmonton Oilers, the 1985 entry draft was nowhere near as rich as in previous years. Only one of their selections would go on to play a full NHL season, and he was taken in the ninth round, 188th overall. Still, that one player would become a cornerstone of the Oilers for years to come. Kelly Buchberger was a hard-nosed, street-fighting right winger with the Moose Jaw Warriors of the WHL. He went on to spend the 1985–86 season in junior, and most of '86–87 with the Oilers' farm team in Nova Scotia, displaying grit and determination and earning lots of penalty minutes.

COMINGS AND GOINGS

Craig MacTavish stepped on the ice in training camp knowing he'd been given a second chance. "MacT" had finished serving a one-year prison sentence, as well as a suspension from the NHL for the entire 1984–85 season. To this day, he doesn't talk much about his incarceration, but he does talk about how grateful

he is that Glen Sather signed him. MacT showed up fit and ready to play, and the Oilers were glad to have his tenacity and grit, as well as his positive attitude in the dressing room.

September 11 marked the arrival of a player who would become a well-liked member of the team and a fan favourite. Marty McSorley was acquired from the Pittsburgh Penguins, along with Tim Hrynewich and future considerations (defenceman Craig Muni), for goalie Gilles Meloche, whom the Oilers had picked up in an off-season trade. A defenceman who could move up to right wing when needed, McSorley was known as a tough-as-leather fighter, but he also liked to rush the puck and had a wicked shot from the point. With the Oilers, McSorley quickly filled the void—in terms of meanness—that had been created when Ken Linseman was traded.

Drafted by the Oilers in 1981 in the sixth round, 111th overall, defenceman Steve Smith had finally been called up to join the team in 1984–85 for two games, after serving a two-year apprenticeship in the American Hockey League. This year, he was deemed ready for the NHL.

Smith had a long reach and was a force on the blue line. He rarely got upended because of his agility on his skates—more often than not, *he* was the one doing the knocking down.

Another earlier draft pick who contributed in 1985–86 was Finnish winger Raimo Summanen. After putting up some good numbers with the Finnish club Ilves Tampere in 1983–84, he had helped out a little during the Stanley Cup playoffs and was coming off a 20-goal season in the American Hockey League. He became the latest in a long list of left wingers to get an audition on the Gretzky–Kurri line, but the hoped-for chemistry didn't materialize. After scoring 30 goals in 132 regular-season games as an Oiler, Summanen would be traded to Vancouver for Moe Lemay in March 1987.

Some old standbys took their leave of the Oilers in 1985, including Pat Hughes, who was sent to Pittsburgh on October 4. Three days later, the Penguins claimed Willy Lindstrom in the waiver draft. On December 28, Billy Carroll was traded to Detroit for Bruce Eakin, who never played a game for the Oilers.

Because Craig MacTavish played for Boston before the NHL made a headgear rule for the 1979-80 season, he never had to wear a helmet. When he joined the Oilers for the 1985-86 season, he kept the habit. He was famously the last helmetless NHL player.

Flying Economy

Being based in one of the most remote centres in the NHL—only Calgary and Vancouver were within 1,000 kilometres—meant a lot of airline travel. And in the 1980s, teams still tended to fly on commercial flights in economy class. Security wasn't as stringent in that era, either; at the gate, an attendant would hand a trusted member of the team a number of blank boarding passes—no names printed on them. Before one flight, Dave Semenko noticed that no one was covering the check-in desk. So he reached over and picked up three additional boarding passes, which he handed to the team captain, the trusted one. When Sather and assistant Bruce MacGregor showed up to board the flight, they collected the tickets and handed them out, only to be extremely puzzled when they had three left over. Their puzzlement turned to frustration and then anger within seconds. Lateness for a flight was one of Sather's cardinal sins, so he waited to discover which three players were late—and, consequently, which three would be paying fines. Everyone else boarded the plane and suddenly the door was closed, leaving Sather, MacGregor and the rest of the coaching staff still at the gate, waiting for whomever was late. The plane took off and the players soon realized that none of the coaches or management had made the flight. They cheered! Maybe there would be no practice when they landed. Maybe, just maybe, they could go out when they landed.

MORE SCORING RECORDS

The regular-season followed the established template: a 56–17–7 record for 119 points, giving Edmonton first place overall. Wayne Gretzky set a new standard for points, with 215, and shattered his year-old mark for assists, with 163. To put that achievement into perspective, he had more helpers than the runner-up in the race for the Art Ross Trophy—Mario Lemieux—had total points (141). Paul Coffey scored 48 goals, the most ever by a defenceman and two more than Bobby Orr had potted in 1974–75. With 138 points, Coffey fell just one point short of Orr's record, set in the same season.

Coffey would receive the Norris Trophy for the second time, while Gretzky won the Art Ross Trophy for the sixth year in a row, beating Lemieux by 74 points, and earned the Hart Trophy for the seventh consecutive time. But it was his linemate Jari Kurri who led the league in goals, with 68—marking the first time since 1980–81 that someone other than Gretzky was tops in this category.

In goal, Grant Fuhr and Andy Moog were still tag-teaming. Moog ended up making 47 appearances to Fuhr's 40, although Fuhr held a 29-27 edge in victories. Once the playoffs started, Fuhr was designated as the Number 1 goalie, playing in nine games while Moog made only one appearance.

SCORCHED IN THE PLAYOFFS

The 23-44-13 Vancouver Canucks were no match for the Oilers, who took the Smythe Division semifinal series in three straight, outscoring the Canucks by 17-5. In the other series, the second-place Calgary Flames made equally quick work of the Winnipeg Jets, setting up another edition of the Battle of Alberta. This time, however, the Flames were ready. Or perhaps Edmonton was not ready.

The Flames opened the series with a convincing 4-1 victory, and the game took on a Battle of Alberta energy, foretelling how this series was going to go. The first period saw each team awarded eight penalties. Semenko was in fine form, throwing his weight at whoever got in the way. He was given a game misconduct for fighting before the end of the first period. In Game 2, the Flames held a 4-2 lead after 40 minutes, before the Oilers battled back, clinging to a 5-4 lead with a minute and a half to play. Joe Mullen tied it at 18:40, but the Oilers pulled it out on Glenn Anderson's goal, assisted by Dave Lumley and Charlie Huddy, at 1:04 of OT. Calgary poured it on in Game 3, outshooting the Oilers 38-19 and scratching out a 3-2 win, taking a 2-1 lead in the series. Game 4 exploded with fights and 26 penalties, 11 of those for misconduct. Despite the many disruptions in play, the Oilers bounced back to even the series with a healthy 7-4 win.

> *"Quite frankly, every year was the same for us Flames. We always said if we could find a way to beat the Oilers, we could win the Stanley Cup . . . You knew playing the Oilers was going to be an all-out war. Even when you passed them in the hallway, it was just a quick nod. No words were ever spoken. Our team was built to beat the Oilers."* —Lanny McDonald

Gretzky scored a hat trick and added two assists. The tables turned again in Game 5, as Lanny McDonald broke a 1–1 tie at 12:35 of the second period, paving the way for a 4–1 victory and 3–2 advantage in the series. The Flames took a 2–0 lead in Game 6 before Edmonton responded with five unanswered goals to tie the series and force a seventh game.

On April 30, 1986, at Northlands Coliseum, the unthinkable happened. The Oilers had battled back from a 2–0 deficit to tie the score on Mark Messier's goal at 19:09 of the second period. The score remained knotted just past the five-minute mark of the third when rookie defenceman Steve Smith raced after a puck that was headed deep into the Oilers end. No one was around him except for Grant Fuhr. Smith picked up the puck and swung around to head back up ice, at which point he chose to make a pass across the ice. There was no risk, as the Flames were making a line change. As he

The Penticton Peach, Andy Moog, was always steady in net for the Oilers.

The Year of Bub Slug

Unlike many NHL franchises, the Oilers did not have a mascot, but for a short time in 1986, they were featured in the *Bub Slug* comic strip. Many Edmontonians will remember the full-page, weekly colour comic that began running on May 11, 1985, in *The Edmonton Journal*. The main character, Bub Slug, was Edmonton's senior waterfall maintenance man, and his wife's name was Betty. In the beginning, the comic strip, created by Gary Delainey and Gerry Rasmussen, was about the Slugs winning $6 million in Lotto 6/49. On January 4, 1986, a hockey storyline began, featuring many of the Oilers players as well as Glen Sather and Peter Pocklington, and it continued until April 5. "Of course, Bub Slug's purpose was to poke fun, which we did with the Oilers, too . . . with good intentions and respect," said Delainey. "The Oilers story was probably our most popular story sequence."

cleared the puck, it misfired off his stick and somehow hit the back of Grant Fuhr's leg, landing in the back of the Oilers net. Smith took one look at the puck and fell to his knees, burying his head in his hands. Fuhr stood frozen in front of his net, staring back at the puck. The play-by-play announcer's voice had a high-pitched note of shock as he kept repeating that the puck had gone into the Oilers net. Lanny McDonald skated around the ice, fist pumping, knowing that his team had just been given the luckiest break. The Oilers, seemingly unable to recover from the shock, lost Game 7—and their bid for a third straight Stanley Cup—by a score of 3–2. There was to be no parade on Jasper Avenue this year.

NO CELEBRATION

Peter Pocklington decided not to show up for the end-of-season team photo. Also absent, of course, was the Stanley Cup, won by the Montreal Canadiens in a five-game series against the Calgary Flames. The players, still stunned by the "Steve Smith goal," had a hard time smiling for

anything. The feeling just wasn't there.

They packed up their things and went their separate ways, bound for wherever they spent their summers. Glen Sather told the players to call him if they were in trouble—anytime, no matter where they were.

When the May 12, 1986, issue of *Sports Illustrated* hit newsstands all over North America, an article described the dethroned Edmonton Oilers as a team that was unravelling because of legal battles and drug issues. The title of the article was "The Joyless End of a Joyride," and the text referred to "rampant drug-use rumors," and reported that "at least five members have had 'substantial' cocaine problems."

Sather blasted back, denying the allegations. "That's the best example of yellow journalism I've heard in a long time," he said. "How can a magazine of that stature print something like that with no substantiation?" He added, "This article has been taken out of context with no reasonable backup. If someone on this club was convicted of using drugs, he wouldn't be here a day."

Taken earlier in the season, the Oilers were all smiles hoping for a repeat championship year.

1986–1987

FAREWELL TO FOGOLIN

Even amidst the turmoil of the drug talk and a team that had lost in a bizarre situation, Sather went about making changes. He tweaked as he always did in the off-season, but he also started to re-evaluate some of his core players.

In August, the Oilers signed a free-agent defenceman, Craig Muni. Muni had been drafted by the Toronto Maple Leafs in 1980, but over the course of six years had only been called up to play in 19 games. As luck would have it, one of the games he did get to play in was against the Oilers. Sather must have seen something in Muni that he could use on his blue line, and the 24-year-old was in uniform for the first game of the 1986–87 season. Danny Gare, a 50-goal scorer when he was with the Buffalo Sabres in 1979–80, was picked up as a free agent after being released by the Detroit Red Wings. The right winger would only get into 18 games, scoring one goal.

On December 12, Dave Semenko was called into Sather's office and told he was being traded to the Hartford Whalers.

The Oilers were getting a third-round draft choice in return.

At first, Semenko thought Sather was joking. He was an Oiler through and through. He'd been there since 1978, when the team was still in the WHA. In his first game with Hartford, he looked down at his jersey during the national anthem to see the crest—an *H* and a *W*, topped by the tail of a whale—and to him it just felt all wrong. When he arrived in Hartford, Semenko ran into the manager of the same hotel where he had slipped the fire hose under the door. The two reminisced about that time the Oilers came to town and flooded a room. Semenko's secret, of who had done the deed, was still in tact. He just nodded and laughed, not lying, but not giving away the truth either. Not only had he learned to be a better hockey player under Sather, but he'd learned a few other things as well.

On March 2, the Oilers picked up Kent Nilsson from Minnesota for a second-round pick in 1988. A former Calgary Flame, the 30-year-old Nilsson was known as a goal scorer and point producer. After the trade, he appeared in

All it takes is a stick in the wrong place. Here, Glenn Anderson fights off an Alberta boy, Ron Sutter, of the Flyers.

In March 1987, Rick Hansen visited Edmonton on his Man in Motion tour and hit the West Edmonton Mall to meet Wayne Gretzky. (He still has that gift hanging on his wall.)

17 regular-season games, scoring 5 goals and adding 12 assists for 17 points. In 21 playoff games, he scored 6 goals and earned 13 assists for a total of 19 points. A few days later, Reijo Ruotsalainen joined the Oilers. "Rexi," a puck-moving defenceman, had played five seasons for the New York Rangers but was unable to come to terms on a contract for the 1986–87 season, so he elected to play in Switzerland. Perhaps not expecting the Finnish blueliner to return to the NHL, Ranger GM Phil Esposito traded his

rights to the Oilers. He arrived in time to play 10 regular-season games, putting up 8 points, and 22 playoff games, in which he added 13 more.

As the March trading deadline drew near, Jeff Brubaker was traded to Philadelphia for Dom Campedelli, while Raimo Summanen was traded to Vancouver for 25-year-old winger Moe Lemay.

But perhaps the biggest, most heart-breaking trade of the 1986–87 season came on March 6, when Lee Fogolin was traded, along with Mark Napier and a fourth-round pick, to Buffalo for Normand Lacombe, Wayne Van Dorp and a fourth-round pick. Paul Coffey encountered the former captain just after he'd been told the news. Fogolin was sitting on a Gatorade bucket, almost in tears. Coffey and Fogolin had sat beside each other in the dressing room for seven years, and Coffey thought of him as a mentor and friend. At dinners out, Fogolin would tell Coffey he just wanted to retire as an Oiler. He looked at Coffey and said, "Take care of yourself."

This trade made Paul Coffey think long and hard about the team, and he started to think that perhaps it "wasn't about us anymore. Lee got traded for nothing."

The Sabres were scheduled to play the Oilers about a week after the trade. Gretzky ran into Fogolin before the game and saw that he was limping. He asked what was wrong, and Fogolin said his knee was sore, but he had to play because he needed to get into enough games to qualify for the pension. He told Gretzky he just wanted to retire and live back in Edmonton. Both teams went through their warm-ups and were starting to get focused. The game started and the Oilers took the lead, but Gretzky noticed that Fogolin was struggling to skate. He talked to Mark Messier and Kevin Lowe, telling them that Fogolin had a bad knee and needed his games for his pension. So collectively, they decided that they would try to keep the puck from going down the left side when Fogolin was on the ice. Every time they got the puck, if Fogolin was on the ice,

they tossed it over to the right side so he wouldn't have to skate as much. Finally, Sather noticed and asked what was going on, and when the guys told him, he shrugged and told them to continue going down the right side if that's what they wanted to do. And it *was* what they wanted to do because they respected Lee Fogolin that much.

Before the season was over, Fogolin underwent arthroscopic surgery on his knee, and he ended up retiring in September of 1987.

A FLYER REMATCH

Despite the media coverage and the roster turnover, the 1986–87 Edmonton Oilers still scored goals and won hockey games. It was another 50-win season, the club's third in four years. With 106 points, they finished first overall—also for the third time in four years—and won their sixth consecutive Smythe Division title. Jari Kurri finished with 54 goals and 108 points—his fifth straight season above 100—and Mark Messier achieved a new career high with 107 points. In just his first full NHL season, Esa Tikkanen scored 34 goals and earned 78 points. Paul Coffey led Oiler blueliners with 67 points despite missing 21 games. Andy Moog and Grant Fuhr split the time in net almost evenly (46 games to 44, Moog playing 73 more minutes), but Moog came out ahead with 28 wins to Fuhr's 22. Stealing the show once again was Wayne Gretzky, who won the league scoring race with 183 points—75 more than Kurri—to earn his seventh Art Ross

Slipping one past
Hextall—a sweet feeling.

Trophy and his eighth Hart Trophy. His 62 goals and 121 assists were also tops in the NHL.

The Oilers drew the Los Angeles Kings in the Smythe Division semifinals. Game 1 was tied 2–2 after 40 minutes, but the unheralded Tiger Williams, Bob Bourne and Bobby Carpenter provided all the offence in the third to give the visiting Kings a 5–2 victory, shocking players and fans alike. The Oilers wasted no time showing everyone who was boss as they trounced the Kings 13–3 in Game 2, Kurri scoring four goals and Gretzky registering seven points. Moog, taking over for Fuhr in the Oiler net, faced only 14 shots. Moog backstopped the Oilers to a 6–5 win in Game 3, while Fuhr returned the following night for a 6–3 victory and a 3–1 lead in the series. Gretzky led the way with five points. Fuhr also started Game 5 in Edmonton, which the Oilers won 5–4. Tikkanen's sixth goal of the series clinched the win.

Assistant equipment manager Lyle Kulchinsky (better known as "Sparky") was loved by the players.

The third-place Winnipeg Jets had upset the Calgary Flames, preventing another Battle of Alberta. But they proved to be no match for the league champions, who swept the series by scores of 3–2, 5–3, 5–2 and 4–2.

That gave the Oilers more than a week off before they had to face the Detroit Red Wings in the Campbell Conference final. The Wings were clearly the underdogs. Their regular-season record was a mediocre 34–36–10, and they had lost their last 13 games against the Oilers. Also, the Norris Division final against Toronto had gone the full seven games, leaving the club with just one day off before the series opened at Northlands. Still, Detroit managed to catch the home team off guard in Game 1, relying on physical play and Greg Stefan's goaltending to win by a score of 3–1. Again, the Oilers seemed to learn a lesson from the loss, putting together four straight victories by scores of 4–1, 2–1, 3–2 and 6–3

Mark Messier squares off against a young Steve Yzerman.

that showed they could shut down an opponent just as well as they could play a run-and-gun style.

The Stanley Cup final brought a rematch with their 1985 opponents, the Philadelphia Flyers—the only other team with more than 100 points in the regular season. Flyer coach Mike Keenan let the hockey world know that he was looking for a hard-hitting, physical, if not dirty, series. Sather countered by lining up his big bruisers: Marty McSorley, Kevin McClelland, Mark Messier and Steve Smith. With Semenko now gone, Sather also called up Kelly Buchberger, just in case. In his first pro season, with the Oilers' farm team in Nova Scotia, Buchberger had racked up more than 200 penalty minutes and was gaining a reputation as a tough player.

As he entered the dressing room, the young winger was wide-eyed and almost tongue-tied. Was he really in the same dressing room as Gretzky and Messier? This was every kid's dream in the '80s, but who could've expected that a guy drafted in the ninth round would be the one? "Bucky" didn't have flash and dash, or a skill level approaching that of Gretzky or Kurri, but he had heart, and lots of it. He played every game as if it was Game 7 of the Stanley Cup final—and that included preseason play.

In his first NHL shift, he got into a fight with Flyers tough guy Dave Brown. He didn't emerge as the winner, but it sure sparked the attention of his teammates, watching from the bench. Buchberger returned to the bench where Paul Coffey leaned in, nudged him, and said, "You just got yourself a ring."

Game 1 of the series was tied 1–1 after two periods, but then the Oilers turned up the heat, racking up goals by Glenn Anderson, Coffey and Kurri in just over nine minutes, ending up with a 4–2 win. There was no sense that Game 2 would be so easy, and it wasn't. After a scoreless first period, the Flyers held a 2–1 lead. The teams swapped scoring chances, but goaltenders Fuhr and Ron Hextall made heart-stopping saves. Anderson tied the score, 2–2, halfway through the third, setting the table for Kurri to blast home the winner in overtime.

At the Spectrum, Mark Messier opened the scoring with a shorthanded goal, and the Oilers held a commanding 3–0 lead midway through the second period. This is when the series took a turn. The Flyers shut the door on the Oilers while scoring five unanswered goals, including an empty-netter in the closing seconds, to make it 5–3 and cut Edmonton's lead in the series to 2–1.

The Oilers had little trouble winning the fourth game 4–1, but it didn't go down without drama. Hextall lost his cool as Anderson was trying to pick up a bouncing puck that the Flyer goalie claimed was already in his glove. Temperatures rose as Kent Nilsson entered Hextall's crease. The Flyer goalie wound up and whacked Nilsson across the back of the leg, and was awarded a five-minute major.

Back in Edmonton, with the home team up 3–1 in the series, the Oilers and the City of Edmonton were talking about parades and post-Cup parties and streamers and balloons and all of the celebratory stuff that goes with winning. Plans had to be put on ice, though. In Game 5, the Flyers overcame a 3–1 deficit to win 4–3. Game 6 in Philadelphia followed a similar template, the Oilers holding a 2–0 advantage until seven minutes into the second period, when the Flyers got on the board, followed by a pair in the third period to win 3–2. The series was going to a seventh game in Edmonton.

The fans showed up strong and the Stanley Cup chatter continued. The Oilers stepped on the Coliseum ice to chanting and cheering. But at 1:41 of the opening period, it was Philadelphia that scored the first goal of the game—the first time in the series this had happened. Messier showed his determination and put Edmonton on the board six minutes later. The Oilers outshot the Flyers 18–12 in the first 20 minutes, but went to the dressing room looking at a tie score. The Oilers skated the Flyers into the ground in the second period, but didn't put the puck in the net until 14:59. It was the only goal by either team in a period in which Edmonton held a 13–6 lead in shots on goal.

In the third period, Sather's scorers were skating and shooting and pinging the puck off the goalposts, but Hextall was strong in net, and wielded his stick to move players out of his way. There was a hush in the Coliseum. Oiler fans were afraid to say boo because these Flyers had pulled off so many comebacks already in this series. With 2:24 left in the third period, Glenn Anderson got an insurance goal from 35 feet out. All in all, the Oilers outshot the Flyers 12–2 in the third period and won their third Stanley Cup. Hextall was named the first star of the game and won the Conn Smythe Trophy, becoming only the fourth player to win the award despite playing on the losing team.

When Wayne Gretzky was given the Stanley Cup, instead of hoisting it over his head and skating around with it, he looked at Steve Smith, who had borne the burden of that fluke own-goal against Calgary, and handed it to him.

What a difference a year makes. Here, Steve Smith is all smiles.

1987–1988

COFFEY HOLDS OUT

To this day, many years later, Paul Coffey will say that his trade was "self-induced." He had been crushed when Lee Fogolin was traded towards the end of the 1986–87 season, and it made him second-guess the organization that he loved. He hated seeing Fogolin traded after all he'd done for the team and especially knowing that he wanted to retire as an Oiler. After the '87–88 season, Coffey wanted to discuss his contract, and the amount he was being paid, but the powers that be were resisting him. Peter Pocklington was operating a small-market team, with a pay structure that was less generous than that of many others, and the players knew they were being undercut. They had proven they were the best, but they still weren't getting paid top dollar.

Frustrated that the team wouldn't deal with him, Coffey was a no-show at training camp. Sather retaliated by taking shots at him in the media. Coffey fired back, saying his actions were less about money than they were about principle. The standoff continued until

November 24, when Coffey was traded to the Pittsburgh Penguins with Dave Hunter, a winger who had been with the Oilers since the WHA days, and Wayne Van Dorp, a minor leaguer acquired in the Fogolin trade. In return, Edmonton got centre Dave Hannan; Chris Joseph, a defence prospect the Penguins had drafted fifth overall in 1987; defence-man Moe Mantha; and Craig Simpson, a 20-year-old left winger with goal-scoring ability.

In 1985, Simpson had been playing for Michigan State University and was considered a top candidate to be drafted first overall. The Toronto Maple Leafs had the Number 1 pick that year, and Simpson made it clear he didn't want to play for them. On draft day, they bypassed Simpson and chose Wendel Clark. Simpson then went in the Number 2 slot to the Pittsburgh Penguins. In September 1985, Simpson said goodbye to the books and went to Pittsburgh's rookie camp, eventually earning a spot on the roster. As with many young players, Simpson needed time to adjust to the NHL and it took him until his third year before he felt as

Esa Tikkanen, better known as Tik, shows his emotion.

if he was making progress. Then came the shock of November 24, 1987, when he was involved in the trade of the year with Paul Coffey. Edmonton got lucky with Simpson. He thrived, finishing the season with 43 goals in just 59 games, often playing on a line with Mark Messier and Glenn Anderson.

Andy Moog was the next important player to leave. The goaltender was tired of playing roughly half the games in the regular season, but not seeing much action in the playoffs. He felt he had

done everything necessary to be a Number 1 goalie in the NHL. So, rather than return to Edmonton, he decided to join the Canadian national team and play in the 1988 Olympics, which were taking place in Calgary in February. After the Olympics, March 8, Sather sent Moog to the Boston Bruins for winger Geoff Courtnall, goalie Bill Ranford and a second-round pick in 1988.

Ranford had been drafted in the third round, 52nd overall by the Boston Bruins in 1985. His first NHL action came late in the 1985–86 season, when the Bruins called him up after his season with the New Westminster Bruins of the WHL had ended. He went 3–1 in four regular-season games, but went 0–2 in a pair of playoff games, racking up a save percentage of just .841. The following year, he appeared in 41 games, the most among Bruin goalies, but spent most of 1987–88 with Boston's farm team, the Maine Mariners.

BOSTON BLACKOUT

With the team in transition, the string of six consecutive first-place finishes ended this year. The Calgary Flames led the league with 105 points. Seven-time NHL scoring champion Wayne Gretzky, sidelined for 16 games by a knee injury, had 149 points, which left him in second place behind Mario Lemieux's 168. Lemieux would also win the Hart Trophy in 1987–88. Still, with 99 points,

the Oilers managed to finish third overall, behind Calgary and Montreal. With Andy Moog playing for the Canadian Olympic Team, Grant Fuhr appeared in a record-breaking 75 games and won 40, earning the Vezina Trophy as the NHL's top goaltender.

In the playoffs, the Oilers met the Winnipeg Jets in the first round. Edmonton took the first two games, lost the third, but came back and dominated in Games 5 and 6. Next up were the Flames, in another instalment of the Battle of Alberta. Since Coffey had been traded, Steve Smith had dominated on the blue line, leading all Edmonton defencemen, with 55 points in 1987–88. The Oilers took the Flames in four straight, although Game 2 went to overtime. Messier took a tripping penalty at 5:57 of the extra period, and the Oilers were successfully killing it. With just three seconds left of Messier's penalty, Flames goalie Mike Vernon was shocked

Jasper Avenue has changed over 40 years. Steve Smith, Charlie Huddy, Craig Simpson and Craig Muni enjoying post-Cup celebrations.

when Wayne Gretzky scored a "slapshot shortie" to win the game. This goal is one of the Oilers' most famous OT playoff winners.

After winning the first two games of the Campbell Conference final against Detroit, the Oilers dropped a 5–2 decision in Game 3. The fourth game went to overtime, and this time it was Jari Kurri who put the puck into the net. The Oilers clinched the series with a decisive 8–4 win in Game 5.

The Stanley Cup final pitted the Oilers against the Boston Bruins, and Andy Moog who was now their starter. The Oilers were feeling confident, but knew that Moog was a fighter. And from practising with them for years, Moog knew their strengths and weaknesses. They couldn't take the series lightly. Boston had finished fourth overall and eliminated the New Jersey Devils in a seven-game Wales Conference final. What followed was one of the more unusual series in Stanley Cup history. It started routinely enough. The Oilers squeezed out a 2–1 win in Game 1, as Keith Acton scored the game-winner on Andy Moog at 1:15 of the third period. Game 2 saw the Oilers take a 2–0 lead in the first period, only to surrender a pair of goals in the third. Gretzky broke the tie, beating Rejean Lemelin with 8:39 in regulation time, while Kurri scored into an empty net to give Edmonton a 4–2 win and a 2–0 lead as the series shifted to Boston. The Oilers had little trouble in Game 3, beating Lemelin and the Bruins 6–3.

Game 4, played on May 24, was a back-and-forth affair. Ten seconds in,

Glenn Anderson opened the scoring, beating Moog with a backhand shot. With a two-man advantage, Gretzky fed the puck to Esa Tikkanen at 15:33 to put Edmonton ahead 2–0. Greg Hawgood scored for the Bruins at 16:56, and it was 2–1 at the first intermission. Bruins rookie defenceman Glen Wesley scored a pair—one shorthanded, the other on the power play—early in the second period, and it was 3–2 Boston. At 16:37, on an Oiler power play, Craig Simpson tied it.

And then the lights went out.

Just as the teams lined up at centre ice for a faceoff after the Simpson goal, a power transformer outside of Boston Garden failed, leaving the arena without electricity. When it became clear that the power could not be reliably restored anytime soon, the game was cancelled and rescheduled—if necessary, it would be played at the end of the series as Game 7. This decision was in keeping with NHL bylaws, but also reflected the fact that the Garden was booked for NBA playoff games between the Boston Celtics and Detroit Pistons the next two nights. The series would resume two nights later in Edmonton. This game, originally designated as Game 5, was now Game 4. After the Bruins pulled ahead 2–1 at 9:44 of the first—on a power-play goal by former Oiler Ken Linseman—Edmonton scored five goals in a row, winning the game 6–3 and clinching (in what was still considered a sweep) their fourth Stanley Cup in five years.

This Stanley Cup win marked the beginning of a tradition that is

This on-the-ice team photo was the start of a tradition that continues today.

maintained to this day. Wayne Gretzky (who had also just won the Conn Smythe Trophy) wanted all the Oiler players to gather on the ice for a photo with the Stanley Cup. Also, he had heard the rumblings that this might be his last game as an Oiler, though he didn't want to believe it. So, before the game, he talked to the Coliseum's security staff and asked them to keep the ice clear if Edmonton won. Usually, after teams won the Stanley Cup, the ice was jammed with all kinds of people. The security guards did what Gretzky asked and limited access to the ice. The team got together, hair still sweaty, faces red, smiles huge, and in a big lump they sort-of posed. Some were lying down, some were standing—it was unprepared and uncoordinated. The moment marked the start of a tradition, and an ending for Gretzky.

1988-1989

THE TRADE

A shift in the composition of the Edmonton Oilers had begun the previous season, with Paul Coffey's holdout and trade to Pittsburgh, as well as Andy Moog joining the Olympic team and then being traded to Boston. And seemingly before the names had been engraved on the Stanley Cup for the latest championship, a truly massive, completely unexpected shockwave was due to strike.

Wayne Gretzky's contract was about to expire in 1989, and he was often in Pocklington's office talking business behind closed doors. After winning four Stanley Cups, Gretzky knew the players deserved more money than what Pocklington was paying them. He felt he had to set an example for his teammates by demanding more, because they all deserved to be paid like others in the league. Plus, Gretzky said, "I owed it to myself to at least wait until the end of the year to see what my value was on the open market." Little did he know that the new owner of the Los Angeles Kings, Bruce McNall, had already approached Pocklington during

the 1987-88 season, wanting to know if Gretzky was available and had suggested he would pay $15 million US for him. At the time, Pocklington had laughed off the offer, telling McNall that Gretzky wasn't for sale.

At the NHL awards banquet in June 1988, Pocklington arrived at Massey Hall and went looking for McNall, telling him that if he still wanted to make a deal, he was ready. McNall called him shortly after, and within a month they had it all worked out (but for signing the final papers). Of course, no one had told Gretzky that he was being traded, although his father, Walter, had been telling him to be prepared for anything. Wayne had waved his dad off, saying, "I don't think so. They wouldn't do that."

To this day, Glen Sather denies knowing anything about the trade until it was a done deal, by which time he could do nothing about it. Pocklington and Sather were both on an annual fishing trip with other NHL brass when the deal was actually being worked out. Pocklington, who usually consulted Sather on player deals, was quietly working with McNall by himself. One morning, Sather and

A new season brings big changes, with Mark Messier now wearing the C for the Oilers and Wayne Gretzky in a Kings jersey.

Harry Sinden of the Boston Bruins were sitting with their lines in the water, enjoying the peace that comes with fishing. Sinden asked Sather about the Gretzky trade rumour and Sather replied, "I don't know a thing about it." Thinking that the rumour must be just that, a rumour, Sather didn't approach Pocklington about it on that trip.

From the fishing trip, Sather went to Colorado to golf with Pocklington and a friend of the Oiler owner. At dinner, after opening a bottle of red wine, Pocklington told Sather that he was going to trade Wayne Gretzky. Sather shot back, "You're out of your #@*$ mind."

Once he had resigned himself to the fact that the trade couldn't be prevented, Sather set out to figure out how much the Oilers could get in return. With Gretzky gone, a gaping hole in the lineup would have to be filled. Sather and Pocklington both wanted Luc Robitaille, the young left winger who had won the Calder Trophy in 1986–87 and scored 53 goals and 111 points in his sophomore year, but McNall wouldn't let him go. So they settled for 20-year-old centre Jimmy Carson, who had scored 55 goals and 107 points in '87–88; 18-year-old left winger Martin Gelinas, who was playing for the Hull Olympiques of the Quebec Major Junior Hockey League; and first-round picks in 1989, 1991 and 1993, along with $15 million US in cash (roughly $18.5 million in Canadian dollars at the time). In return, the Kings got Gretzky, Marty McSorley and Mike Krushelnyski. Gretzky liked that Marty and Mike were going along with him.

The deal was announced at a press conference at Molson House on August 9. With tears in his eyes, Gretzky said, "I promised Mess I wouldn't do this." He said little else during the press conference, unable to speak and dabbing his eyes with tissues. Pocklington stood at the microphone and said, "It is with mixed emotions, a heavy heart and sincere best wishes for Wayne Gretzky that I announce, and I guess more important confirm, that the Edmonton Oilers have agreed to trade Wayne Gretzky to the Los Angeles Kings."

Next up was Glen Sather. "I don't want to try and philosophize on what's happened—because I don't think we can justify the reason why this has happened—but we're all trying to do something that's good for Wayne, for the Edmonton Oilers, for the National Hockey League. We would all like to be proud of what we do to make a living, and I think you can see here today that the reason we've won four Stanley Cups is because of the emotion we display for each other. It's genuine, and in a couple of days I know that we'll adjust to it—and I'm going to work my hardest to try and find a way to kick the hell out of the Los Angeles Kings."

He paused, then said, "But right now, I really feel a lot of empathy for Wayne and what he's going through."

The *Edmonton Journal*'s headline read, "Gretzky Gone," while the *Edmonton Sun*'s was "99 Tears."

Pocklington had shocked the Edmonton fans, because instead of working with Wayne on his contract, as everyone thought he would do, he sold him. He said that Gretzky's trade was a business deal and "a good businessman

always sells an asset at its peak." Pocklington thought that if he let Wayne test the market to find out how much he could get, he would never be able to match it anyway. Edmonton was a small market, and Gretzky would command a much higher price from a team with deeper pockets. Pocklington was already heavily indebted and was operating the Oilers off a loan from the Alberta Treasury Branch. He had come to the conclusion that he likely couldn't pay the premium for a premium player. If he traded Gretzky, perhaps he could pay off part of his loan from the ATB.

Fans felt betrayed in a huge way. Wayne Gretzky was *their* hero. Plus, after the press conference, Pocklington made a comment that upset the hockey world, and the Gretzky family. "He has an ego the size of all Manhattan," Pocklington said. "And he's a great actor. I thought he pulled it off beautifully [at the press conference] when he showed how upset he was." Then Pocklington alluded that Gretzky was crying "crocodile tears." He also said, "I think he was upset, but he wants the big dream. I call LA the Land of the Big Trip, and he wants to go where the trips are the biggest." For the fans, it wasn't just the trade that hurt, but the words.

Meanwhile, it quickly became apparent that Hollywood loved Wayne Gretzky. His arrival prompted a spike in interest in the Kings—within 36 hours of the trade, the team had fielded 2,000 requests for information about season tickets, and average attendance would grow by more than 3,000 per game in 1988–89.

"HE STUCK IT TO US"

The mood in the Oiler dressing room in the fall of 1988 was sombre, with many players—Mark Messier and Glenn Anderson among them—still shocked and

Bill Ranford played 449 games for the Oilers, the most by any goalie in the 40 years since joining the NHL.

devastated that their friend and team-mate was gone. At the beginning of the season, Mark Messier was given the C that had belonged to Number 99, while Kevin Lowe wore an A. Craig MacTavish, who by now was firmly entrenched as an Oiler, said, "Kevin Lowe could unite a lot of entities. Kevin was more diplomatic and Mark was more direct, but they worked well together."

With Gretzky gone, Edmonton's fire-power cooled off dramatically. The team scored 325 goals, its lowest total since 1979–80. Jari Kurri became the Oilers' primary offensive weapon, leading the club with 102 points—good for eighth in the NHL. Right behind him was Jimmy Carson with 100 points, including a team-high 49 goals.

Carson, drafted second overall by the Kings in 1986, had scored 37 goals in his rookie season, 1986–87, but missed out on the Calder Trophy, which was awarded to his teammate, Robitaille. A year later,

after clearing the 50-goal and 100-point barriers, his star was on the rise.

The Oilers slipped in the standings, finishing with a record of 38–34–8 and 84 points, leaving them in third place in the Smythe Division and seventh overall. Their provincial rivals, the Flames, had put up a solid record of 54–17–9 and 117 points, giving them first place in the division and in the overall standings.

In the division semifinals, Edmonton was paired with—who else—the Los Angeles Kings and Wayne Gretzky. By this time, fans had noticed that a few of the Oilers still hadn't recovered from the trade. In particular, Anderson had had a lacklustre season, managing just 64 points—the fewest since his rookie year. Young gun Craig Simpson said it was "hard because there was something missing in the dressing room."

The team also found it difficult to line up against their former captain. Usually, a team goes out on the ice with the goal of owning a traded player—tying him up, checking him, nailing him at centre ice. But this was Wayne Gretzky. The Oilers hesitated to make that bone-crushing hit or resort to playing dirty to keep him from scoring. Even so, Edmonton was able to rally late in the third period of Game 1, on goals by Tikkanen and Simpson, and win 4–3. In Game 2, the Kings got an offensive boost from Chris Kontos, an unlikely source who had joined the team in March after spending the bulk of the year in Switzerland. His hat trick powered Los Angeles to a 5–2 win. As the series moved to Northlands, the Oilers fought back, shutting out the Kings 4–0 in Game 3 and again mounting a third-period rally to win the fourth game 4–3. Ahead 3–1 in the series, they felt okay, good enough to win. But the Kings came back just as hard, winning the next two games by scores of 4–2 and 4–1.

The series was down to a seventh and final game, to be played at the Great Western Forum in Los Angeles. Gretzky opened the scoring less than a minute into the game, and although the Oilers battled to a 3–3 tie on Kevin Lowe's goal at 7:48 of the second period, the Kings found the net three more times, with Gretzky scoring a shorthanded goal—his fourth goal and 13th point of the series—into an empty net with 1:35 on the clock to make it 6–3.

After the game, the Oilers sat in the dressing room, quiet, dejected and a little angry with themselves. Sather came in as they were getting out of their equipment, sweat still glistening on their foreheads, and said, "I want you to remember what you just saw. Remember that moment. He stuck it to us. We need to move on."

Craig Simpson said it was the beginning of the end, and they all knew they had to get their heads around Gretzky's absence. What was done, was done. The Oilers needed to move forward without the Great One.

Glenn Anderson's shot is blocked by LA King Tom Laidlaw—the kind of determination that would force the Oilers to lose this series.

1989-1990

THE SHOW MUST GO ON

Does time really heal all wounds? It's an adage that the Oilers would put to the test in 1989–90.

Glen Sather, having decided to focus on his management duties, appointed John Muckler as head coach. Muckler had been Sather's assistant coach from 1982–83 through 1984–85, and was considered his co-coach during the 1988–89 season. Previously, he had coached in the minor-pro ranks since 1960, spending the 1981–82 season as head coach of the Oilers' farm team in Wichita. In 1968–69, he spent half a season behind the Minnesota North Stars bench. Former Oiler goalie Andy Moog had always cited Muckler as a huge influence, stating that he changed his attitude, making him more accountable, and "helped him mature."

In September, Grant Fuhr was sidelined by an emergency appendectomy, forcing him to miss the first 11 games of the season. Bill Ranford stepped up in his absence, backed up by Eldon "Pokey" Reddick. A shoulder injury in mid-December put Fuhr out of the

lineup for another two and a half months, cementing Ranford's status as the Number 1 goalie.

Involved in the blockbuster Gretzky trade, Martin Gelinas had escaped the pressure and the limelight by playing in only six games for the Oilers at the beginning of the 1988–89 season, after which he was sent back to Hull. Gelinas had been selected seventh overall in the 1988 entry draft after scoring 63 goals in 65 games with the Olympiques. He put on a Kings jersey on the day of the draft and never wore it again—two months later, he was traded to the Oilers. Muckler and Sather took a good look at the 19-year-old during the 1989–90 training camp and decided he was ready for the NHL.

Mark Lamb wasn't a big guy, nor was he flashy or super-skilled, but he had grit and determination and he wasn't afraid to get hurt—the Saskatchewan native had grown up around horses and bulls, and he rode both of them. Drafted 72nd overall by Calgary in 1982, he only played in one game with the Flames. He signed with the Detroit Red Wings in 1986 and got into 22 games, scoring two goals and adding an assist. The Oilers

Jari Kurri and Geoff Smith are all smiles after Kurri scores.

claimed him in the 1987 waiver draft, but he spent most of the next two seasons in the AHL. When he was called up to Edmonton, Lamb saw action on the fourth line, primarily in a checking role. Still, Muckler saw the possibility of putting him on a line with Jari Kurri and Esa Tikkanen.

Jimmy Carson, another key player in the Gretzky sale, had done well enough in his first year as an Oiler, scoring 49 goals, but he felt there was too much pressure attached to playing in "Wayne Gretzky's shadow." Four games into the season, he

quit the team and demanded a trade. Glen Sather was confused by the move, as were some of the players. Charlie Huddy said, "I know last year was rough for him. But I thought over the summer he'd gotten it together. I talked to him a bunch of times and the impression I got was he was excited." After Carson asked for the trade—and it wasn't granted—he decided to sit out, so he was suspended by the team. The Oilers then traded Carson to his hometown team, the Detroit Red Wings, on November 2, along with the popular Kevin McClelland and a

fifth-round pick, for Adam Graves, Petr Klima, Joe Murphy and Jeff Sharples.

HERE COMES THE KID LINE

A quarter of the way into the season, the Oilers were in fifth place in the Smythe Division, with a dismal 6–9–5 record. But then they caught fire, winning 9 of their next 10 games and going 10–1–2 before Fuhr hurt his shoulder. By the midpoint of the season, they were 21–12–7, with a five-point lead on Calgary, but they fell back into a funk in the new year.

During the three-day all-star break in January, the players decided to take matters into their own hands. Aside from Kevin Lowe and Mark Messier, who had been chosen to play in the all-star game in Pittsburgh, they organized a trip to Lake Louise—to go skiing, of all things. Although Sather and Muckler were well aware that skiing was a risky activity for hockey players in the middle of a season, they decided to allow the guys and their families, as well as the training staff, to make the trip. They understood the dynamics of team

Under Mark Messier's leadership, the Oilers won their fifth Stanley Cup.

bonding, especially when spouses and families were involved. To show his support for the team-building effort, Sather organized a dinner for everyone at the Post Hotel in Lake Louise.

The trip was a turning point for the team. When they returned to the ice, they won some games and seemed to be gelling again. Then, on February 25, they were thumped by the Calgary Flames, 10–4. This put them in a bad mood as they boarded the plane to Los Angeles to play the Kings. They stepped on the ice in LA with an angry edge, and the game boasted more fights than goals. Just 95 seconds into the game, Messier and McSorley started trading punches, which led to several brawls. The teams combined for 356 minutes in penalties, including 15 fighting majors. By the end of the game, seven players had been ejected, five from the Oilers. Sports commentators made

dire comments, and the NHL expressed its displeasure. Even though they had lost 4–2, this game gave the Oilers the fight they needed to get to that Stanley Cup finals. Although they were unable to mount another sustained winning streak, the team ended the season with a record of 38–28–14, good for 90 points and second place in the Smythe Division.

The Gretzky and Carson trades paid off when Muckler put Martin Gelinas, Adam Graves and Joe Murphy on a line together, a unit that came to be known as the Kid Line. Craig MacTavish said, "The Kid Line was as dominant a line as I've ever seen."

Graves, a 21-year-old left winger, had been drafted 22nd overall by the Red Wings in 1986. He appeared in nine games with Detroit in 1987–88 before being returned to his junior team, the Windsor Spitfires, and saw limited

The red hot Bill Ranford wins the Conn Smythe Trophy.

action the following season. Playing on the Kid Line helped establish his ability to tally points. Murphy had been the first-overall pick in the 1986 draft, taken just ahead of Carson. Although Detroit thought he might be ready to step right into the lineup, he spent most of his time in 1986–87 with their farm team, the Adirondack Red Wings. A year later, he scored 10 goals and added 9 assists in 50 games, but he ended up splitting '88–89 between Detroit and Adirondack.

Another new player, Petr Klima, had fled Czechoslovakia in 1985 to make North America his home. He was a brilliant skater and had a quick release and excellent puck-handling skills. Taken 86th overall in 1983, he was now

in his fifth NHL season and had already scored at least 30 goals three times.

Muckler's task over the course of the regular season was to blend these new arrivals with his core of established players—Mark Messier, Glenn Anderson, Kevin Lowe, Jari Kurri and Grant Fuhr— who had demonstrated they knew what it took to win.

In the Smythe Division semifinals, the Oilers faced the Winnipeg Jets. The series would begin without Fuhr, who had reinjured his shoulder two days before the end of the regular season. But Bill Ranford was primed, psyched and ready to play. "Billy always gave us a chance to win," said Buchberger.

But in Game 1, the Jets shocked the

The Kid Line was a force during the 1989-90 Stanley Cup run. From left to right: Joe Murphy, Adam Graves, and Martin Gelinas.

Oilers, overcoming a 4–2 deficit to win 7–5. Winnipeg held a 2–0 lead early in the third period of Game 2, but it was Edmonton's turn to mount a comeback, as Joe Murphy tied the score at 12:45 of the third period and fourth-liner Mark Lamb beat Stephane Beauregard in overtime. Ranford gave the Oilers a chance to win in Game 3, stopping 28 of 30 shots, but the Jets managed a 2–1 win on Dale Hawerchuk's goal late in the third period. The Jets were up 3–1 early in Game 4, but Edmonton tied it with less than a minute to go in the second period. Defenceman Dave Ellett beat Ranford in double overtime to give Winnipeg a 4–3 victory and a 3–1 lead in the series.

The Oilers went back to their dressing room and sat there, looking at each other. They needed to regroup. There was nothing they could do but get better. They had no choice. Remarkably, the team's offence was coming mostly from youngsters like Simpson and Murphy and unheralded players like Kelly Buchberger and Mark Lamb. Where were the leaders on the team—Messier, Lowe and MacTavish? What were they doing to help the team win?

In Game 5, the Jets took a 3–1 lead midway through the second period, and all signs pointed to an early playoff exit for the Oilers. But Ranford bore down and made save after save. Simpson and Lamb scored 13 seconds apart to tie the game. And then Messier decided to show what he was made of—why he had been named captain. At 3:53 of the third, he drilled a shot past Beauregard to win the game. The sixth game was played at the Winnipeg Arena, where the fans dressed

almost exclusively in white shirts to create the traditional playoff "whiteout" in the stands. The Oilers jumped out to a 3–0 first-period lead, but the Jets—fuelled by their white-clad fans—tied it midway through the third. This time Jari Kurri stepped up, scoring just his second goal of the series, assisted by Lamb, who now had an incredible six points. Returning to Northlands Coliseum, and their boisterous fans, the Oilers made relatively easy work of the Jets, winning 4–1, with Lamb scoring the series-clinching goal.

The division final was a rematch with Gretzky and the Los Angeles Kings. From the opening faceoff, Messier and Lowe had fire in their eyes and speed in their strides. The end result was a four-game sweep. Edmonton won the first two, at home, by scores of 7–0 and 6–1, while victories of 5–4 and 6–5—the latter in overtime—were testaments to the Oilers' determination. Tikkanen, who checked Number 99 relentlessly every time they were both on the ice, was instrumental in stopping him from doing anything spectacular.

The Chicago Blackhawks reached the Campbell Conference final having played back-to-back seven-game series. But after a 5–2 loss at Northlands, the Hawks found their second wind, winning 4–3 and 5–1 to pull ahead in the series. The fourth game was played at Chicago Stadium, and once again it was Messier who gritted his teeth. Before the game, he refused to talk to anyone and walked around with his eyes burning holes in everything in his sight line. "Mess was so focused," said

MacTavish. "You couldn't even talk to him. He played the most dominant game I've ever seen anyone play."

In front of the Chicago fans, he came out with a head of steam, running over anyone who got in his way, scoring two goals to lead his team to a 4–2 victory. The players knew that no one wanted to mess with Mess that game.

With a day off to travel between Games 4 and 5, the players remained in Chicago for the night, and suddenly they had that winning feeling again. The energy, the control, the confidence had all returned. The veterans were teaching the Kid Line that winning was something special, something that was worth every ounce of pain. This leadership showed in the next game, as they crushed the Hawks 8–4 to win the series. Anderson and Messier led the way, each with a goal and two assists.

Three nights later, the Oilers were in Boston to play the team they had swept in the 1988 final. Nobody was expecting a sweep this time, and the players were aware that the Bruins might come out with revenge on their minds. In the first period, Muckler elected to bench Petr Klima. The winger sat, for hour upon hour, the cold settling into his joints, the bench hard. Between periods, Captain Messier would tell him to "be ready." But Klima took his seat on the bench, never hearing his name called. At one point, he untied his skates and stashed his gloves behind him. The Bruins came back from a 2–0 deficit, courtesy of back-to-back goals by Ray Bourque, and the game went into overtime. The first overtime period was

John Muckler took on the role of head coach during this season. Out of the gate, he won a Stanley Cup.

intense as the puck rang off posts. Bill Ranford swiped at a puck, shot by Cam Neely, that almost trickled over the goal line. Between the first and second overtime periods, Klima headed to the dressing room. Again, Messier said, "Be ready."

The third overtime period had barely started before it was halted because the lights dimmed. Fans were quick to remember what had happened in 1988, when the game had to be cancelled. They held their breath, not wanting a repeat. Long shadows were cast on the ice as the players waited to hear the verdict. NHL president John Ziegler made his way to the ice surface at 12:32 a.m., and announced that a tripped circuit breaker was the culprit. Twenty-six minutes after the lights had gone out, they were back on and play resumed. Once again, Messier told Klima to get ready, so he tied up his skates and put on his gloves. When Muckler finally called Klima's name—with five minutes left in the third OT period—he did his duty and hopped over the boards. With everyone except Klima dog-tired, he trickled one past former Oiler Andy Moog to put away a game that had seemed destined never to end. The Oilers had been outshot 52–31, in a game that lasted 115 minutes and 13 seconds, and it was Bill Ranford who kept the Oilers in the game for so many of those minutes. But, of course, it was Petr Klima's goal that won the game.

In Game 2, Ranford was hot again. After the first period, the Oilers were up 2–1 despite being outshot 10–2. Greg Hawgood tied it early in the second, but the Oilers poured it on, scoring five unanswered goals for a decisive 7–2 win. Kurri led the scoring with three goals and two assists. Back in Edmonton for Game 3, the Bruins showed a bit of spark and won 2–1. Moog stopped 28 of 29 Edmonton shots. Glenn Anderson performed in Game 4, scoring twice and adding two assists, while Esa Tikkanen and Steve Smith worked tirelessly to shut down Boston's top forwards. The Oilers pounded through, beating the Bruins 5–1 and taking a 3–1 lead in the series.

The last game in the series started off at a frantic pace, both teams skating end to end, but no one scored. Early in the second, Anderson got the puck in the Oiler end of the rink and took off down the ice, splitting the Boston defence and drilling the puck home. He also set Simpson up for the second goal of the game, with a beautiful pass from behind the net. This goal proved to be the game-winner as the Oilers won 4–1.

For the fifth time in seven years, the Edmonton Oilers were Stanley Cup champions.

Ranford, who tied the NHL record by winning 16 playoff games (Grant Fuhr, in 1988, had set the record, followed by Mike Vernon of Calgary in 1989), was awarded the Conn Smythe Trophy. At the NHL's postseason awards banquet, Mark Messier won the Lester B. Pearson Trophy, awarded by the NHL Players' Association to the most outstanding player as chosen by the players, and the Hart Trophy as the NHL's most valuable player. Kevin Lowe, now an alternate captain, won the King Clancy Memorial Trophy for his humanitarian contributions to the community of Edmonton, something he has continued to do for years.

Messier, Anderson, Kurri, Fuhr, Lowe, Randy Gregg and Charlie Huddy had now won five Stanley Cups with the Oilers.

How many more could they win? Who would be traded next? No one could predict the Oilers' future. Fans expected more Cups, players just wanted to keep playing, and the press looked forward to more jubilation pieces. But Pocklington was struggling to keep the franchise afloat.

Road Trips

In 1984, after the Oilers won their first Stanley Cup, they looked at it in the dressing room and said, "What should we do with it?"

Glen Sather told them to be proud, show it off, wherever they saw fit. Usually, when a team won the Cup, they put it in a trophy case, behind glass. Not the Oilers. They loved the Cup and wanted to share it with friends, family and fans.

Mark Messier grew up in St. Albert, Alberta. He wanted to take the Cup there because his parents were having a barbecue for the players. Kevin Lowe had just bought himself a slick Mercedes and didn't want the Cup on his leather seats. He opened up the trunk and said, "Let's put it here." All the way to St. Albert, it clanked around in the trunk. When they arrived, the players suddenly had the idea to take it into a watering hole, the Bruin Inn. There were maybe three people in the bar at the time. Word got out (even though there were no cell phones or social media at this time), and within 30 minutes the place was packed and everyone was getting their chance to drink out of the Cup.

It even went to public schools. One time, Andy Moog took it to his daughter's school and told the administrative staff he'd pick it up at three o'clock. Panic set in because the Oilers office thought the Cup was lost. They phoned around and found out Moog had been the last one to have it. They called Andy, waking him up, and he groggily told them he'd taken it to his daughter's school. Okay, he was told, just make sure you get it back to us after three this afternoon.

In the summer months, the Cup often travelled. Players asked for it to be sent to their homes so that friends and relatives could fawn over it, drink from it, or even wash babies in it. Kevin Lowe had it sent to Montreal. Wayne Gretzky had it on his parents' property in Brantford. Andy Moog and his wife, Karla, were asked to be the grand marshals of the Peach Festival parade one year, and Andy thought it would be cool to bring the Cup to his hometown. He was told it would be shipped to Penticton and was given the flight number. Andy made his way to the airport and watched the plane arrive. When he saw the bags going around on the conveyor belt, he also saw the trunk where the Cup slept. Andy picked it up, took a peek inside, and sure enough, there was the Stanley Cup. For three days it stayed in Penticton, attended the Peach Festival luncheon and rode front and centre in a convertible down Main Street.

But it wasn't just the players who got to cart the Cup around. Assistant trainer Lyle "Sparky" Kulchinsky often put it in the back of his car to show off. On team photo day after one of the Stanley Cup wins, the players arrived, looking smart and ready for the camera. Since the team had won the Stanley Cup, it had to be in the photo; but on that morning, no one could the find the Cup. A search began, and sure enough, it was found in the back of Sparky's car.

After the 1989–90 season, when the Oilers won their fifth Stanley Cup, the NHL decided it was time for the Cup to get some supervision. The league was guided in part by a photo of Sparky in the newspaper, at West Town Ford, with the Cup being refurbished. The Stanley Cup is now handled with white gloves by representatives of the Hockey Hall of Fame, who accompany it wherever it goes.

Head medical trainer Ken Lowe catches a nap while flying with the Cup. ▶

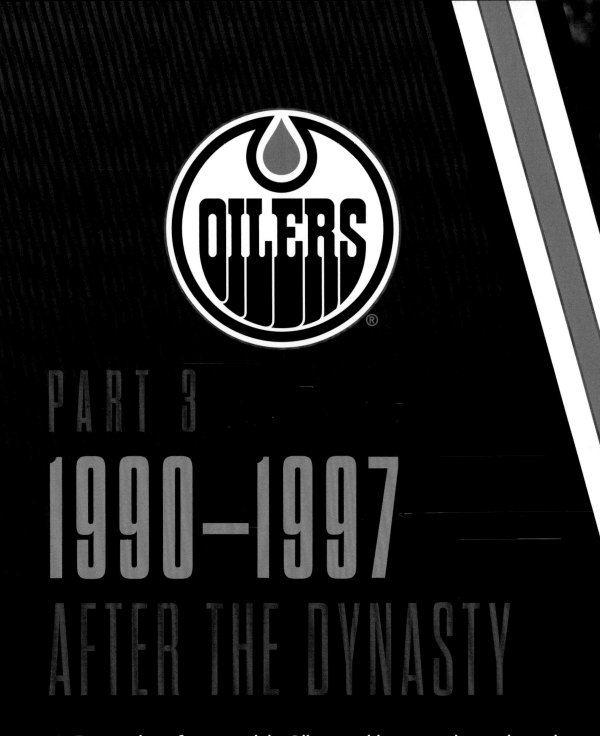

PART 3

1990–1997

AFTER THE DYNASTY

No Dynasty lasts forever and the Oilers would see many heroes leave the team in the years after the Stanley Cup championships. NHL hockey was changing too, and many new players would become fan favourites in Edmonton.

1990–1991

ADDITIONS AND SUBTRACTIONS

In the summer of 1990, the towering building that was the Edmonton Oilers continued to be disassembled, brick by brick. When a wealthy Italian approached Jari Kurri about playing for the Milan Devils, he thought long and hard about it. His contract with Edmonton was expiring, and owner Peter Pocklington wasn't putting forward the kind of deal the superstar wanted. Kurri accepted the Italian offer, signed a two-year contract and headed over to Europe. The terms included an escape clause, as well as time off to play in the World Championships, to be held in his home country of Finland in 1991. Glenn Anderson also was in dispute over his contract and sat out until October 15.

On August 31, just before the season was to begin, the *Edmonton Journal* ran a story that said Grant Fuhr had been abusing drugs for several years. It alluded that Fuhr had struggled with the issue, trying to keep it in check while performing at the high level expected of a star goaltender. There had been murmurings in the past, but three times Fuhr had been randomly selected and tested negative for drugs. As Sather told the press, "there was never any proof."

The news spread to papers all over North America. NHL president John Ziegler responded by calling for a hearing on September 26. Afterward, Ziegler issued a statement that made it clear that Fuhr, 28 at the time, had used "cocaine, an illegal drug" for about six to seven years before August 1989. Calling his conduct "dishonourable and against the welfare of the league," Ziegler suspended Fuhr for a year. He did, however, allow for a return to the team as early as February 1991, should Fuhr meet "certain conduct requirements." The league also gave the Oilers a chance to challenge the decision, but they declined.

Little-used winger Steve Graves became a free agent and signed with the Los Angeles Kings on July 16. Randy Gregg was claimed by Vancouver in the October waiver draft. Meanwhile, the Oilers brought back Ken Linseman as a free agent on August 31. Defenceman Chris Joseph, who had been part of the Paul Coffey trade and had shuttled between the AHL and NHL, earned

Petr Klima and Dave Brown celebrating a moment.

MacTavish doing some serious damage along the boards. Still not wearing a helmet.

a full-time spot with the parent club. Russian-born Anatoli Semenov, a tall, lanky forward, had been drafted by the Oilers 120th overall in 1989. He had started the 1989–90 season with Moscow Dynamo, but arrived in North America in time to play in two playoff games.

Edmonton-born Geoff Smith had been drafted 62nd overall in 1987 and, after two years at the University of North Dakota, he joined the Kamloops Blazers of the WHL. He played in 74 regular-season games in 1989–90,

earning a spot on the NHL All-Rookie Team and getting his name engraved on the Stanley Cup.

SEEING (NORTH) STARS

The season got off to a dismal start, as the Oilers were seemingly unable to find their footing—or the back of the net. A nine-game losing streak left them at 2-11-2 after 15 games. The slide coincided with team captain Mark Messier spraining his knee, sidelining him for a month. Injuries would limit him to 53 regular-season games, though he still managed to earn 64 points. It didn't take long for the team to make things right. By the halfway point in the schedule, Edmonton was at .500 with a 19–19–2 record.

A bright spot for the season was the return of Grant Fuhr. Having met all the conduct requirements tied to his suspension, he suited up for the Oilers on February 18. If there was any doubt that he was ready, he put them to rest, shutting out the New Jersey Devils. In his absence, Bill Ranford had held the fort, backed up by Pokey Reddick and Finnish goalie Kari Takko, but when Fuhr returned he was the Number 1 goalie— he played 13 of the Oilers' last 21 games. Fuhr's return provided his team with a much-needed boost. The Oilers finished the regular season third in the Smythe Division, with a record of 37–37–6. Los Angeles and Calgary battled for first place, the Kings edging the Flames by two points. Esa Tikkanen led Edmonton in scoring with 69 points and trailing him by just one point was Petr Klima, whose 40 goals paced the club.

The Smythe Division semifinals renewed the Battle of Alberta. The Oilers had to dig deep in this series, drawing on guts. The Flames had outscored them by nearly a goal a game in the regular season. If Edmonton was going to win, it wouldn't be pretty. The Oilers took the first game 3–1, but Calgary won by the same score in Game 2, Mike Vernon stopping 35 of 36 Edmonton shots. The Oilers won Game 3, at Northlands, on a buzzer-beater by

Joe Murphy with 14 seconds to go. Game 4 saw them fall behind, 2–0, before grinding out a 5–2 win, taking a 3–1 series lead. But the Flames were not about to bow down. At the Saddledome, they poured it on, firing 38 shots at Grant Fuhr en route to a 5–3 victory. The Oilers were still up a game, but the series could easily go either way.

The Coliseum crowd got a show in Game 6. In a game that went back and forth, Craig Simpson scored the only goal for Edmonton in the first period, while Paul Ranheim tied it midway through the second. It was still 1–1 as regulation time ran out. Theo Fleury broke the tie in overtime to even up the series.

Game 7 would be in Calgary at the Saddledome. The Oilers boasted a number of players with postseason experience and a burning desire to win, but so did the Flames. After 20 minutes, Calgary held a commanding 3–1 lead. The Oilers' lone goal had come from Esa Tikkanen, set up by Mark Messier and Jeff Beukeboom. In the dressing room, the Oilers regrouped. This was Calgary. They couldn't go down without a fight. They came out and steamrolled their way through the second period, tying the score on goals from Glenn Anderson and, with his second of the night, Tikkanen. The teams managed one goal each in the third period, leaving the score tied at 4–4 when the buzzer sounded. This time, the overtime hero was Tikkanen, with an unassisted goal that completed his hat trick and sent Edmonton to the division final.

For the third year in a row, the Oilers prepared to face Wayne Gretzky and the Kings. But nothing could have prepared them for what followed. This series seemed to take on a life of its own. Ranford got the start in Game 1—his first of the playoffs and his first action in nearly three weeks—and the Oilers led until 12:07 of the third, when Luc Robitaille tied it. The young superstar beat Ranford again, at 2:13 of the extra period, to give the Kings a 4–3 win. In the second game, Klima took the reins, scoring on Kelly Hrudey at 4:48 of the second OT to give the Oilers a 4–3 win. Back on home ice, for the third game in a row, the score was tied 3–3 at the end of regulation time. The first overtime went by with no scoring, and Tikkanen—who was having an unbelievable series—ended it 48 seconds into the second extra frame. Proving that they were more than just their superstars, the Oilers beat the Kings 4–2 in Game 4 on goals by Charlie Huddy, Joe Murphy, Martin Gelinas and Petr Klima. But the Kings, powered by a Robitaille hat trick, rallied with a 5–2 win in Game 5.

Leading the series 3–2, the Oilers returned to Northlands Coliseum, where their fans were ready for them to end it. Tikkanen, Klima, Simpson, MacTavish and the Kid Line had all been playing gutsy hockey. Simpson opened the scoring at 7:49 of the first period, and Tikkanen gave the Oilers a 2–0 lead two minutes into the second.

The Kings responded with three consecutive goals. At 12:38 of the third, Tikkanen tied the score, and for the fourth time in the series, the game went into OT with the score tied at three. At 16:57 of the overtime period, MacTavish skated toward the net, and when the puck was passed out front, he slapped at it. The puck sank to the back of the net and MacTavish, wearing a huge grin, fell into the net, too. Players landed on top of him, celebrating. The Oilers had won the Smythe Division title.

Whether the Oilers ran out of steam, or were exhausted from playing so much hockey in the division final, they just weren't the same team when they met the Minnesota North Stars. Despite finishing the regular season with a 27–39–14 record and fourth place in the Norris Division, the North Stars had upset the top two teams in the league, Chicago and St. Louis, on their way to the Campbell Conference final. The energy-depleted Oilers just couldn't generate the kind of explosive offence that had served them so well in the past, and they lost the series, four games to one. They dropped Game 1 by a score of 3–1, and lost 7–3, 5–1 and 3–2 in Games 3 through 5. They did show a glimpse of their old selves in Game 2, outscoring Minnesota 7–2, including a hat trick by Klima and a pair by Glenn Anderson. The whole team contributed, with singles coming from Huddy and Semenov, but this game alone wasn't enough to keep the Cup dream alive.

Grant Fuhr returned early with a clean slate from his one-year NHL suspension. He was subdued in style, but still flashy in ability.

1991-1992

RECESSION AND REGRESSION

Alberta's economy took a hit during the 1980s, as interest rates skyrocketed and oil prices crashed. Rumours surfaced that Peter Pocklington was running out of money. Indeed, many of the player moves the Oilers made, beginning with the Paul Coffey trade, were motivated at least in part by money. The team's success on the ice didn't seem to result in a surplus of cash. In fact, it was just the opposite. Surprisingly, during the Oilers' dynasty years, empty seats at Northlands Coliseum weren't uncommon in the first few playoff rounds. Fans just assumed the team would go deep into the playoffs, so they chose not to attend until the conference finals and Stanley Cup finals. The forgone revenue hurt Pocklington. And with each winning season, players were also seeking more money and salaries were rising to levels that Pocklington couldn't afford. Pocklington claimed that he lost between three and four million dollars a year after 1988, and upwards of $10 million a year in the early '90s.

A ROSTER MAKEOVER

In recent years, attendance at Minnesota North Stars games had been sliding, and owners George and Gordon Gund sought permission to move the club to the San Francisco Bay area. The NHL denied the request, but agreed to sell the brothers an expansion franchise, to be based in San Jose, that would begin play in the fall of 1991. The Gunds sold the North Stars in the spring of 1990, and in an unusual arrangement, they were allowed to claim 14 skaters and two goaltenders from Minnesota after the 1990–91 season. On May 30, an expansion draft was held, involving not only San Jose but Minnesota as well. Huddy, a dressing-room favourite who had played 694 regular-season games for the Oilers over 11 seasons, and won five Stanley Cup rings, was one of the players the North Stars selected. Less than a month after the expansion draft, he was dealt to Los Angeles, where he was reunited with former teammate Wayvne Gretzky.

Another longtime Oiler was already ticketed for the West Coast. On the day of the expansion draft, Edmonton

Scott Mellanby arrived in Edmonton as a much needed, hard hitting forward.

traded Jari Kurri's rights to Philadelphia, along with big, tough winger Dave Brown and defence prospect Corey Foster, for enforcer Craig Berube, right winger Scott Mellanby and Flyer farmhand Craig Fisher. The Flyers immediately dealt Kurri to the Kings.

On September 19, Berube, Glenn Anderson and Grant Fuhr were sent to the Toronto Maple Leafs in exchange for centreman Vincent Damphousse, goaltender Peter Ing, defenceman Luke Richardson, left winger Scott Thornton, future considerations and cash. And on October 2, Steve Smith was traded to Chicago for defenceman Dave Manson and a third-round pick in 1992.

But perhaps the biggest bombshell was yet to be dropped. Two days later, the Oilers dealt Mark Messier to the New York Rangers, along with future considerations, for centre Bernie Nicholls, tough guy Louie DeBrusk and Steven Rice, a right winger who had been the Rangers' first-round pick in 1989. Part 2 of this deal took place on November 12, when Jeff Beukeboom was sent to New York for defenceman David Shaw. (On January 21, 1992, Shaw was traded to Minnesota for defenceman Brian Glynn.) Pocklington also received cash as part of the trade.

Messier would be joined in New York by Adam Graves, who signed with the Rangers as a free agent on September 3.

Finally, on October 7, two-time Oiler Ken Linseman was traded to Toronto for cash. Compared with the team that had reached the conference final against Minnesota just five months earlier, the Oilers team that took the ice for the 1991–92 season was nearly unrecognizable.

With few of his friends left, steady defenceman Kevin Lowe accepted the role of captain. Craig MacTavish was named as an alternate captain. Getting this team to gel would be a tall order, made all the more challenging because head coach John Muckler had moved on, having been successfully wooed by the Buffalo Sabres. In his place was Ted Green, who was no stranger to the Edmonton Oilers. An old friend of general manager Glen Sather—the two were teammates on the Boston Bruins in the late 1960s—Green had been an Oiler assistant coach since the 1982–83 season. He knew about winning championships, having been with Edmonton for all five Stanley Cup wins and having played on a Cup-winning team with Boston in 1972. He would have been part of the Bruins' memorable 1970 championship run, but for a violent on-ice incident during the preseason. In an exhibition game against the St. Louis Blues in September 1969, Green collided with left winger Wayne Maki in the Boston zone. Green turned and swung his stick at Maki, just missing him, and Maki retaliated by swinging back, cracking Green on his helmetless head. Green dropped to the ice. Ace Bailey, who would go on to play and scout for the Oilers, was on the Bruins bench, and he jumped over the boards to protect his teammate. Green suffered a fractured skull that required the insertion of a metal plate and was out for the year. He returned for two more seasons with the Bruins, after which he jumped to the World Hockey Association, winning the Avco Cup with New England in 1973 and with Winnipeg in 1976 and '78.

A mix of new players and vets made up the Oilers roster. From top left to bottom right: Vincent Damphousse, Luke Richardson, Dave Manson, and Kevin Lowe, who was now sporting the C.

Despite the loss of so many high-profile players, the 1991–92 Oilers boasted their fair share of talent. Damphousse had been a sixth-overall pick in 1986, and in 1989–90 he racked up 94 points.

Known for his ability to play a hard-hitting game as well as score goals, Scott Mellanby came to the Oilers after playing five years with the Flyers. He had sat out a good chunk of the 1989–90 season because of nerve and tendon damage to his forearm. During the off-season, Mellanby was trying to protect a friend in a bar and his arm was cut with a broken

beer bottle. After managing just 23 points in 57 games, he rebounded in 1990–91, scoring 20 goals and 41 points and spending 155 minutes in the penalty box.

Bernie Nicholls was 30 years old when he showed up in the Edmonton Oilers dressing room. A former Los Angeles King, Nicholls had three 100-point seasons on his resumé, including a career-high 70 goals and 150 points in 1988–89, the year Gretzky was traded to LA. Injuries limited him to 50 games in 1991–92, but he still managed 20 goals and 29 assists.

After John Muckler took a job with the Buffalo Sabres, the Oilers hired Ted Green as head coach.

The Oilers lost a defenceman and a tough guy when they traded Steve Smith, but Dave Manson was ready to step into the role. He pushed and shoved in front of the net, clearing opponents out of the crease. He was a solid scrapper, and had a searing shot on the power play. During this season, Manson was punched in the throat by Sergio Momesso, which permanently damaged his vocal cords. The damage caused him to speak softly, in a raspy voice, but that somehow made him even more menacing. His nickname was, simply, "Charlie."

A stay-at-home defenceman who didn't put up big numbers, Luke Richardson was solid in the Oilers zone, blocking shots and doing the dirty work if needed. He wasn't flashy, but he lent a touch of class to the Oiler blue line.

Norm Maciver had turned pro in 1986 and was traded to the Oilers in 1989, but he had spent most of his time in the minors. His break came in 1991–92, when the 27-year-old defenceman won a full-time job on an Oilers team that was rebuilding. He'd never been drafted as he was considered too small for the NHL. Despite that, he played a tough game and could stare down the best players. Plus, he could move the puck.

HERE COME THE HAWKS

With so many new faces, Ted Green had his work cut out for him. Not unexpectedly, the season started off slowly. After 20 games, the Oilers had a 6–11–3 record. While they no longer had a roster loaded with superstars, they had good players who were willing to work. After a strong second half, they had improved to 36–34–10, good enough for third place in the Smythe Division. Vincent Damphousse led the club with 38 goals and 51 assists for 89 points. Joe Murphy followed him with 35 goals and 82 points, and although Bernie Nicholls was injured for 30 games, he still notched 49 points. "Charlie" Manson led the defencemen in scoring with 15 goals and 47 points. He also accumulated the most penalty minutes, with 220. His blueline partner, Maciver, had an impressive 40 points in 59 games. Bill Ranford played in 67 games, rested occasionally by Peter Ing (12 games), Norm Foster (10) and Ron Tugnutt (3).

The team had qualified for the playoffs for the 13th year in a row, and would meet the Los Angeles Kings in the first round. For an Oilers fan, the Kings' lineup had many familiar faces: Wayne Gretzky, Jari Kurri, Marty McSorley, Charlie Huddy, and most recently, Paul Coffey, picked up in a late-February trade with Pittsburgh. They also boasted goal scorers like Luc Robitaille and Tony Granato. Coach Green wanted to shut down the LA offence, so he made sure that Kelly Buchberger was on the ice with Gretzky. Green said to the press, "I'm telling you, Wayne will be dreaming about Kelly Buchberger the next two games."

The Oilers succeeded in Game 1, keeping the Kings off the scoreboard until late in the third period and winning 3–1, but they took an 8–5 beating in the second game. McSorley took a run at Buchberger late in the second period, punching him hard.

Bucky responded, initiating a brawl. Later, Los Angeles general manager Rogie Vachon claimed Buchberger "bit McSorley on the neck." Bucky was one of eight players to draw a misconduct penalty in the closing seconds. Gretzky and Coffey each tallied four points, while Kurri had three and Huddy scored a goal. Both teams kept a lid on their tempers in Games 3 and 4 in Edmonton, swapping 4–3 victories. Buchberger kept Gretzky in check and managed a lone assist in the fourth game. Edmonton rebounded from a 2–0 deficit in Game 5, winning 5–2 despite being outshot 44–25. Game 6 was all Oilers, as they clinched the series with a 3–0 win.

The Smythe final pitted the Oilers against the Vancouver Canucks. Game 1 was a back-and-forth affair that ended in a 4–3 overtime victory. Goals in regulation time came from Maciver, Nicholls and Damphousse, while Murphy scored the game-winner. Coach Pat Quinn's team put on a show in Game 2, winning 4–0 and holding the Oilers to just 14 shots on goal. The Oilers came back hard in Game 3. Chris Joseph opened the scoring at 15:33 of the first period, assisted by Nicholls and Murphy. In the second period, Murphy scored on the power play, and at 4:35 of the third, he netted the game-winner. Late in the period, again with the man advantage, he completed the hat trick. Brian Glynn scored into an empty net to close out a 5–2 win. Game 4 in Edmonton was another seesaw. Edmonton opened the

scoring with a goal by Petr Klima at 14:11 of the first period, but Vancouver quickly responded. Esa Tikkanen gave the Oilers the lead with seven seconds to go, but again Vancouver tied it, nine minutes into the second period. The game-winner came in the final minute of the second period, thanks to Scott Mellanby.

Edmonton held a 3–1 lead in the series, but Vancouver took it to the Oilers in Game 5, building a commanding 4–0 lead. The Oilers rallied in the third period on power-play goals by Murphy and Manson, and with 33 seconds to play they were still hustling, as Mark Lamb put the puck past Canucks goalie Kirk McLean to make it 4–3. But as hard as they battled, they just couldn't tie the game up. Back on home ice for Game 6, the Oilers got goals from MacTavish, Damphousse and Tikkanen, while Ranford made 26 saves to preserve a 3–0, series-clinching victory. It had been an intense series, and the fans took to the streets after the game, chanting, "Let's go, Oilers!"

Edmonton was off to the Campbell Conference final.

Led by Steve Larmer and Jeremy Roenick, the Chicago Blackhawks quickly brought the Oilers back down to earth, delivering an 8–2 thumping in Game 1. Losses of 4–2, 4–3 and 5–1 followed, and on March 22 the Oilers' season, along with any hopes of a sixth championship, came to an end.

It would be 14 years before they came as close to hoisting the Cup again.

Louis DeBrusk wasn't afraid to take a punch of two. ▶

1992–1993

THE LAST OF THE DYNASTY

As the 75th anniversary of the NHL neared, the league expanded into a new market, which was also a historic one. The Ottawa Senators shared a name with one of the NHL's original teams, a franchise that played in the league from 1917–18 until 1933–34. The Senators joined Boston, Buffalo, Hartford, Montreal and Quebec in the Adams Division. The Tampa Bay Lightning was the league's first franchise in Florida, and it would play in the Norris Division, a distant rival to Chicago, Detroit, Minnesota, St. Louis and Toronto. NHL membership now stood at 24 clubs.

In the expansion draft, the Oilers lost Anatoli Semenov to Tampa Bay and Mark Lamb to Ottawa. Meanwhile, for a combination of financial and competitive reasons, the Oilers' roster remained in flux. Vincent Damphousse, the team's leading scorer in 1991–92, was dealt to Montreal on August 27, along with a fourth-round pick in '93, for Shayne Corson, Brent Gilchrist and Vladimir Vujtek.

Corson was a 26-year-old power forward who had had a banner season in 1989-90, with 31 goals and 75 points. He also came with the gritty qualities that suited the Oilers. He had a reputation for having a bit of a mean streak, and leadership skills. He had worn the C for Canada at the World Junior Championship. At 25, Brent Gilchrist was coming off a career year, with 23 goals and 50 points. Like Corson, Gilchrist had been with the Canadiens when they went to the Stanley Cup final against Calgary in 1989. Unlike Corson, Gilchrist would be gone before the season was over. A 20-year-old left winger, Vladimir Vujtek served as a utility player, moving up and down between Edmonton and the farm team in Cape Breton.

Two key players were absent on opening night because they were holding out for new contracts. Joe Murphy was starting to realize his potential and made a stand for himself. Even more conspicuous by his absence was team captain Kevin Lowe—who had appeared in a franchise-record 966 games and was the last remaining Oiler

With Kevin Lowe gone to the New York Rangers, Craig MacTavish took over the Oilers leadership role.

to have played on all five Stanley Cup championship teams. Both sat on the sidelines while they awaited trades. As the season began, Craig MacTavish was wearing the C.

As trade talks dragged on, the Oilers stumbled out of the gate, going 1–8–1 in their first 10 games, including a 6–1 wash by the expansion Tampa Bay Lightning. Finally, on December 11, Lowe was traded to the New York Rangers for Roman Oksiuta and a third-round pick in 1993. A little over a month later, on January 13, Bernie Nicholls was traded to New Jersey for left winger Zdeno Ciger and centre Kevin Todd. In February, Murphy was sent to the Chicago Blackhawks for defenceman Igor Kravchuk and centre Dean McAmmond.

As the trade deadline drew near, it was clear that the Oilers would not be making the postseason. On March 3, Edmonton lost a fan favourite and a quintessential Oiler when Esa Tikkanen was traded to the Rangers for Doug Weight. In an awkward twist, the Oilers were scheduled to play at Madison Square Garden on the day of the trade. On game day, MacTavish saw Tikkanen in the hotel elevator with his bag and asked, "Tik, where are you going? It's not time to leave yet." Tikkanen explained that he had just learned he would be playing for New York that night. Buchberger was in the dressing room when a young Doug Weight walked in, sat down beside him and

Igor Kravchuk played 17 games with the Oilers in the 1992-93 season, but an impressive 80 games in the next season.

Although he had some moves, Brent Gilchrist only lasted one season with the Oilers as the revolving door kept things moving.

started getting into his hockey gear. When the game started, there was Tik, wearing a white Ranger jersey, while Weight stood on the opposite side of the rink, wearing a blue Oilers jersey.

The 1992–93 season turned out to be one of the worst in Oilers history. They recorded several franchise lows: 242 goals, 26 wins and 60 points. Twenty-five years later, their 50 losses are still a club record. They finished fifth in the Smythe Division, missing the playoffs for the first time since joining the NHL—by 27 points. Petr Klima led the team in scoring with 32 goals and just 48 points, while Shayne Corson managed 16 goals and 47 points and spent 209 minutes in the penalty box. Dave Manson still protected the blue line, leading the team with 210 penalty minutes and also led Oiler D-men with 15 goals and 45 points. Bill Ranford played 67 games in goal, winning 17 while posting a career-high 38 losses. Ron Tugnutt, picked up in a trade with Quebec in March 1992, was in net for 26 games, going 9–12–2.

The poor performance was reflected at the box office, as attendance dropped, averaging only 14,855 compared to the 17,009 of the 1990–91 season. Peter Pocklington's losses continued to rise. The franchise seemed to be losing steam, despite all efforts. Pocklington repeatedly threatened that he would move the team to a new home—Hamilton, Ontario, came up as one such option.

1993–1994

SHUFFLING DIVISIONS AND THE ROSTER

In 1993, for the third year in a row, the National Hockey League expanded, adding the Miami-based Florida Panthers and the Mighty Ducks of Anaheim. The 26 teams were then reorganized into a new divisional alignment, the NHL's first major overhaul since 1981–82. The names of the divisions (Adams, Norris, Patrick and Smythe) and conferences (Clarence Campbell and Prince of Wales), which had been in place since 1974, were scrapped. In their place were geographic terms the league considered to be more user-friendly. The Campbell Conference was renamed the Western Conference, while the Wales became the Eastern. The Smythe and Norris Divisions were now called Pacific and Central, while Adams and Patrick gave way to Northeast and Atlantic.

Three teams switched divisions. Pittsburgh moved from the Atlantic to the Northeast, Tampa Bay from the Central to the Atlantic, and Winnipeg from the Pacific to the Central. The Oilers remained in the Pacific Division with Calgary, Los Angeles, San Jose,

Vancouver and the new expansion team in Anaheim. A new, basketball-style playoff format was also introduced where the first-place team in each conference would play the eighth-place team, second against seventh, third against sixth, and fourth against fifth. Playoff teams would not necessarily face division rivals as they had been doing since 1982.

The Oilers started this new season knowing they would have to win games without Scott Mellanby, claimed by Florida in the expansion draft, and Ron Tugnutt, taken by Anaheim. In late June, Martin Gelinas was traded to Quebec, along with a sixth-round pick, for winger Scott Pearson. Petr Klima was sent to Tampa Bay for a third-round pick, in the 1994 draft.

The NHL Entry Draft took place on June 26 at the Colisee in Quebec City, and their dismal showing in 1992–93 earned the Oilers the seventh-overall pick. Their choice was Jason Arnott of the Oshawa Generals, a big power forward who had scored 41 goals in 56 games in the OHL the year before. When Arnott reported for training camp that fall, Coach Ted Green felt the soon-to-be-19-year-old was ready

Big Jason Arnott played his first season with the Oilers at the age of 19.

to step right into the NHL. In Arnott's first NHL game, on October 6, 1993, he popped the puck in the net, and kept up a productive pace throughout his rookie season, tallying 68 points, including 33 goals. He also racked up 104 penalty minutes. He made the NHL All-Rookie Team and placed second behind New Jersey Devils goalie Martin Brodeur in the voting for the Calder Memorial Trophy.

Just before the season was to start the Oilers traded veteran Craig Simpson, who had won two Stanley Cups with the Oilers, in 1988 and 1990. His playoff experience left the team and headed to Buffalo for Jozef Cierny and a fourth-round pick in 1994.

SLATS MAKES A HARD CALL

Despite opening the season with back-to-back victories, the Oilers were winless in 21 of their next 22 games. By the time of the American Thanksgiving holiday, their record was 3–18–3, the worst in the NHL. In the Pacific Division, they trailed the expansion Mighty Ducks by nine points. Someone needed to be held accountable, so head coach Ted Green was fired. General manager Glen Sather, who last coached the team in 1988–89, returned to a familiar position behind the bench. He was assisted by former Oilers goalie Ron Low, who had been on the coaching staff since 1990, and Kevin Primeau, now in his third year with Edmonton. Team captain Craig MacTavish said, "It was hard on us players because Green was so emotional and passionate and such a terrific person." But Green was taking the losses personally, and was getting gallstones from the stress. On road trips, he would lie down on the plane because he was in such pain. Players were feeling the strain of losing, too. Losing wasn't fun.

IN THE BASEMENT

Under Sather's guidance, the team improved, and they ended the season with a record of 25–45–14 for 64 points—four more than in 1992–93. Even so, it wasn't nearly enough to get them into the playoffs, nor even to keep them out of last place in their division. They finished 33 points behind the division-leading Calgary Flames.

There was some cause for optimism, however. Doug Weight led the Oilers in scoring with 74 points and a team-high 50 assists. Jason Arnott had 68, including a club-leading 33 goals. Zdeno Ciger had 57 points, and Shayne Corson racked up 54, including 25 goals. Igor Kravchuk was the high-scoring defenceman, with 50 points. Scott Pearson registered 19 goals, 37 points and 165 penalty minutes. Rounding out the top 10 were

At the age of 22, Steven Rice was another youngster to crack the Oilers roster.

defenceman Bob Beers (37), winger Steven Rice (32), and blueliners Fredrik Olausson and Ilja Byakin (28 each).

Doug Weight had wasted no time putting on the Oilers jersey. Right from the start, he showed energy, enthusiasm and offensive talent. In the dressing room, he could motivate and boost his teammates to new heights. On the ice, he gave it his all and it didn't take long

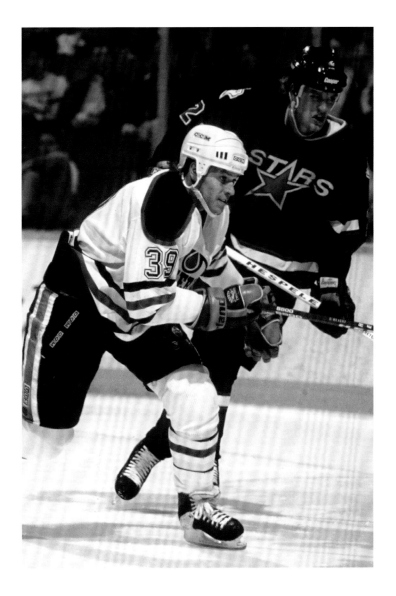

Late in the 1992-93 season, Doug Weight arrived to the Oilers bench. In 1993-94, he showed his worth and then some, playing in 80 games.

Nicholls trade in January 1993. He had good hands and an ability to find openings. Kravchuk was a Russian defenceman with good mobility and stickhandling skills, and he proved to be an asset on the power play.

Pearson was a role player with a bit of an aggressive streak. Bob Beers arrived on November 11, when Chris Joseph was traded to Tampa Bay, and this was his only year with the Oilers. Rice, acquired in the Messier trade, had been in the Oilers system since 1991, and he finally landed a full-time spot in the lineup in 1993-94. Swedish born Fredrik Olausson had been acquired from Winnipeg on December 6 and brought a calm, collected presence to the team.

In March, the Oilers traded Dave "Charlie" Manson to Winnipeg for forward Mats Lindgren and defenceman Boris Mironov, plus a couple of draft picks. A few days later, on March 19, they said goodbye to another captain when Craig MacTavish was sent to the New York Rangers for rookie centre Todd Marchant. For the remainder of the season, Corson wore the C.

Sather had approached MacTavish and asked him what he wanted. The reply was, "I want to play on a team that has a chance to win a championship." MacT suggested the Detroit Red Wings. Sather traded him to the Rangers. Maybe Slats knew what he was doing, because MacTavish arrived just in time to win another Stanley Cup with the Rangers—alongside six other former Oilers: Jeff Beukeboom, Esa Tikkanen, Mark Messier, Adam Graves, Glenn Anderson and Kevin Lowe.

for him to become a fan favourite. Before the New York Rangers drafted Weight 34th overall in the 1990 Entry Draft he had been on a scholarship at Lake Superior State University, where he earned second-team All-America honours and was one of the top-20 scorers in the school's history. Born in Slovakia, Ciger had arrived in Edmonton as part of the Bernie

1994–1995

POCKLINGTON GETS THE COLISEUM

If anyone doubted that Oiler fans were frustrated with a team that had missed the playoffs two years in a row, the evidence could be found at the box office. In 1993–94, the average attendance at Northlands Coliseum was just 13,437—well below the 17,000 needed to make ends meet. Many nights, the team played to a half-empty arena and gate receipts were an important revenue source. Peter Pocklington was struggling to keep his franchise afloat, and now he started to complain that Edmonton was a weak hockey market, one that lacked the support of large corporations. He felt it was dominated by "mom and pop operations." Through radio and print media outlets, he began threatening to move the team to the US. Several other Canadian franchises were indicating that they, too, were finding it hard, if not impossible, to put together teams good enough to challenge for the Stanley Cup.

In the spring of 1994, following the regular season, Pocklington made a move to cut Northlands out of the operation of the Coliseum, taking control of the arena himself. Prime Minister Jean Chretien's government was giving out grants to cities for infrastructure projects, and the City of Edmonton got one for $10 million to upgrade the arena. Pocklington made a deal with the city and Northlands, under which he would pay Northlands to rent the building if he could have control of the operations, including staffing and concert bookings. He would receive the money from ticket sales, as well as food and beverage sales, but he would also carry out the major renovations that the arena needed—including 39 new luxury boxes on the mezzanine that would complement the existing 16 skyboxes, and a new scoreboard, an upgraded sound system and new seats. The city, wanting the improvements to go ahead, sided with Pocklington. He was granted the lease and control, but in return he was required to sign an agreement stating that, before he sold the team to outside interests, local Edmonton buyers had to be offered the chance to purchase the Oilers for $100 million Canadian ($80 million US at the time). The local buyer (or buyers) would have 45 days to come

With MacT gone, the C was sewn onto Shayne Corson's sweater.

up with the funds. This agreement was put in place partly to restrict the Alberta Treasury Board from selling the team to pay off outstanding loans Pocklington had with the ATB at the time. The goal was to provide a bit of assurance that the Oilers would remain in Edmonton.

With the deal in place, renovations began in July 1994 on the newly named Edmonton Coliseum.

LOCAL CONTENT

With two picks in the top-six slots, the Oilers were poised to add a couple of impact players in the first round of the 1994 entry draft. With the fourth pick, obtained from Winnipeg in the Dave Manson trade, they chose Jason Bonsignore, a six-foot-four centreman out of Rochester, New York, who was rated as the sixth-best prospect in the draft pool by the NHL's Central Scouting Bureau. He didn't quite pan out, appearing in just 21 games for Edmonton before he was traded to Tampa Bay. But with the sixth pick, the Oilers found their winner. As a 17-year-old in 1993–94, Banff-born Ryan Smyth had been a scoring machine with the Moose Jaw Warriors of the WHL, tallying 105 points. The Oilers were quick to call his name, and it was a proud moment for the gritty power forward and his family, because it meant he would be playing in Alberta. He played another year in Moose Jaw, recording 41 goals and 86 points in regular-season play, adding 15 points in 10 playoff games. During that year, he also appeared in three games with the Oilers.

THE LEAGUE'S FIRST LOCKOUT

On October 1, 1994, with players and management unable to agree to a new collective agreement, Commissioner Gary Bettman announced that the NHL was locking out its players. The puck would not drop on the 1994–95 season. Bettman was an aggressive young executive who, acting on behalf of the owners of the NHL's 26 teams, aimed to curtail rising player salaries. Owners of small-market franchises like the Oilers claimed that the gap between what they could afford and the budgets of wealthier teams was growing, and they were getting left behind. The league called its proposal a "tax plan," while the NHL Players' Association countered that it was a salary cap in disguise. The players said they were actually agreeable to a small tax on their

salaries, if the proceeds went into a fund to help smaller-market teams, but the owners insisted that curtailing payrolls, and not revenue-sharing, was the solution they were seeking.

Even with the looming threat of a shortened season, players showed up at the rink, laced their skates, and went ahead with training camps and pre-season games. But then everything came to a halt with the announcement of the lockout. The owners indicated that they were willing to cancel games, and forgo revenue, until they got the settlement they wanted.

In the media, owners talked about how sorry they were about the potential loss of a season of hockey, while the players continued to hold firm on their demands. As the weeks—and months—passed, the owners started to realize that the entire season was actually at risk. In early January, after 103 days, a settlement was reached. Ownership got a cap on rookie salaries and changes to the arbitration system, but no salary cap or "tax plan." That issue was put aside for now.

A SHORTENED SEASON

In the wake of the lockout, a 48-game schedule was drawn up, with teams playing only within their conference. The Oilers had only a week and a half to get ready for their first game, against the Mighty Ducks of Anaheim at the Edmonton Coliseum. Not all players had been idle during the lockout—some had gone to Europe, while others played in exhibition games. And many rookies

Todd Marchant would become a regular fixture on the Oilers roster, scoring key goals when called on.

would come to be known as a durable two-way centre.

Another rookie was David Oliver, a winger Edmonton drafted in the seventh round, 144th overall, in 1991. He played another three years for the University of Michigan before joining the Oilers in 1994. Excited at making the roster in training camp, he then had to accept an assignment to Cape Breton for the duration of the lockout. He made the best of it, registering 29 points in 32 games, and when the NHL season finally got underway, he had 16 goals and 30 points in 44 games.

After he was acquired from Toronto in the blockbuster trade that sent Glenn Anderson, Craig Berube and Grant Fuhr east, Scott Thornton shuttled between Cape Breton and Edmonton. When the Cape Breton Oilers won the Calder Cup (the championship of the AHL) in 1993, Thornton's grinding and checking skills were important contributions. He never shied away from the corners, and whenever he was called up, he played an important checking role with the Oilers. He finally got to play in the NHL on a consistent basis in the 1993–94 season, when he appeared in 61 games. And in 1994–95, he played in 47 of 48 games, pocketing 10 goals and 12 assists for 22 points, putting him seventh in team scoring.

After riding out the better part of '93–94 behind the Oiler bench, Glen Sather focused on his GM role, promoting George Burnett to head coach. He'd coached the Cape Breton Oilers to their 1993 Calder Cup win. Ron Low and Kevin Primeau were back as assistant coaches. The Oilers came out of the gate relatively strong, posting a record of 12–13–2

were sent to the minors, including Todd Marchant, who had come to the Oilers in the Craig MacTavish trade. The 21-year-old centre had 22 goals and 47 points in 38 games with the Cape Breton Oilers. He was fast, had good hands and worked hard, and he made his mark after the lockout with 27 points in 45 games for the Oilers. He

through 27 games, putting them in second place in the Pacific Division. Then the wheels fell off. A tie in Dallas was followed by a nine-game losing streak that put them in last place in the Western Conference. After the seventh consecutive loss, Burnett was let go and replaced with Low. The club went 5–7–1 after the coaching change, but in such a short season, they simply ran out of time. They finished with a 17–27–4 record for 38 points, four points shy of a playoff berth.

1995–1996

A HOMETOWN DRAFT

For the first time ever, the NHL Entry Draft was held in Edmonton, on July 8, 1995, and the Oilers' staff worked tirelessly to make it a day to remember. Over 10,000 fans showed up to watch the event at Northlands Coliseum. They were eager to see what the home team would do with the sixth-overall pick. Two standouts from Alberta were highly rated: Shane Doan from Halkirk, who had just been named most valuable player in the Memorial Cup tournament, won by his Kamloops Blazers; and Jarome Iginla, who was born in Edmonton and had played minor hockey in St. Albert. He was Doan's teammate on the Blazers and had been named the most sportsmanlike player at the Memorial Cup.

When it was time for the Oilers to pick, the fans started chanting, "Doan, Doan, Doan." Yet Glen Sather, Barry Fraser and the rest of the Oilers brass walked to the stage and called out the name Steve Kelly. He was a centre with the Prince Albert Raiders of the WHL and had far fewer points than Doan,

but he had speed. Kelly would play just 27 games with Edmonton.

The Oilers had better luck with their second pick, 31st overall. Montreal native Georges Laraque was a left winger with the St. Jean Lynx of the Quebec Major Junior Hockey League who had scored 19 goals and racked up 259 minutes in penalties. The Oilers knew he might need another year of junior, but they liked his toughness and ability to stir things up on the ice, and even throw a punch or two.

NICHOLS RAISES DOLLARS

In the summer of 1995, the Quebec Nordiques moved to Denver, becoming the Colorado Avalanche. And the Winnipeg Jets made a formal announcement on August 15 that they would be moving at the end of the 1995-96 season. The remaining Canadian franchises, including Edmonton, continued to struggle financially, particularly when the Canadian dollar was trading between 70 and 75 cents US. The NHL addressed the problem by instituting a Canadian Currency Assistance Plan

(CCAP) that provided $2.5 million to Canadian teams in need, provided that they met targets for sales of season tickets, luxury boxes and rink-board advertising. To qualify, the Oilers would need to reach 13,000 season tickets, while selling 90 percent of their corporate suites and 100 percent of the ad space on the boards.

To aid with the season-ticket drive, a meeting was organized at the Mayfair Golf and Country Club, and a group called Friends of the Oilers (FOTO), made up of local businesspeople interested in helping keep the team in Edmonton, was formed. Cal Nichols, who had been in the oil and natural gas business before founding Gasland Properties, an Alberta holding company with diverse investments, heard about the meeting from his friend James Cumming, who was the past president of the Edmonton Chamber of Commerce. Nichols agreed to go, as he had a connection with Glenn Anderson—in his playing days, Anderson had a Gasland endorsement agreement. Besides which, he was a true-blue Oilers fan.

"Not much happened at the first meeting," said Nichols. Over the summer, there were more rumblings about the team moving, and more meetings at the Mayfair. Finally, in late fall, both Pocklington and Sather told the businessmen who regularly showed up at the meetings, including Nichols, that the only hope of keeping the team in Edmonton was the CCAP. Pocklington told the businesspeople to hit up their colleagues to spur ticket sales. Doctors should approach other doctors, owners

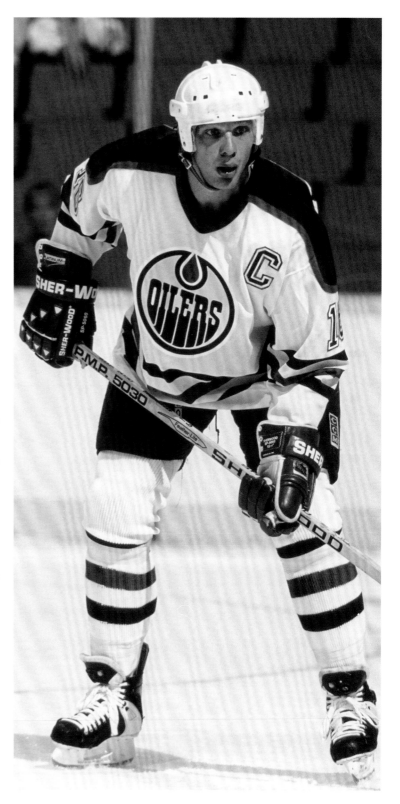

Young Georges Laraque originally wore #24 before donning Dave Semenko's old #27, which suited him well.

Kelly Buchberger stood the test of time with the Oilers and it paid off when he was given the C after Corson's early exit.

of gas stations should talk to other gas station owners.

As Christmas came and went, and then New Year's Day and Valentine's Day, little progress was made and the plan stalled. Nichols decided to change the strategy. He spoke to his contacts in the business community, convincing them to spread the word by approaching their supply networks. By April 1996, FOTO still didn't have the tickets sold and the deadline was drawing near. Finally, Nichols lashed out at larger corporations, almost shaming them into supporting FOTO and the Oilers. He told the media that corporations should be "contributors, not

bystanders." A branch of FOTO was formed, called SEATS—Shrewd Eleven Aggressive Ticket Salesmen. Local radio stations got on board and started talking it up to promote SEATS to their listeners.

Then SEATS came up with the brilliant idea to create a directory of all the businesses and corporations that helped the team. They could showcase their businesses and get some advertising in return for their contribution. They worked the word *community* into all slogans and they *were* aggressive when they approached businesses, even with those who didn't live in Alberta but always came in for games. Nichols let everyone know he

Doug Weight played a full eight seasons for the Oilers and was a fan favourite.

wasn't doing it for Pocklington but for the community. FOTO and SEATS even went so far as to produce a commercial that aired on local television. They obtained footage of fans of the Winnipeg Jets—who played their last game on April 28, 1996, before moving to Arizona— waving goodbye on the team's last day in Winnipeg. The ad showed the tearful fans waving for 27 seconds, and at the end it said, "FOTO. Have you done your part?"

The campaign worked. After the ad aired, the phones started ringing. The public shaming of businesses also had an effect. By the deadline, FOTO had managed to get the season-ticket numbers up to 13,000, and all the luxury boxes were sold. There was a big celebration at City Hall, and the members of FOTO were recognized for giving back to the community. This group of loyal Edmonton fans had saved the Oilers from moving. However, the financial problems were not solved permanently.

A NEW GOALIE AND AN OLD WINGER

The Oilers had now gone three straight years without a playoff berth, and Sather had some hard calls to make. He had already decided that it was time for head coach George Burnett to move on, and reliable Ron Low was given the position. Captain Shayne Corson was also on Sather's list. They'd had a few battles, not seeing eye-to-eye on some things. When Corson became a free agent at the end of the 1994-95 season, he was signed by St. Louis. The Oilers had the right to match the offer, but opted instead to accept two first-round picks from the

Blues as compensation. They then swapped the picks back to St. Louis for goalie Curtis Joseph and the rights to winger Mike Grier, who was playing for Boston University. This turned out to be a stellar move for the Oilers.

Joseph, known as "Cujo," followed a different route to the NHL than many players. Instead of playing in the Ontario Hockey League, he decided to get an education, accepting a scholarship at the University of Wisconsin. He excelled in college hockey and was named to the Western Collegiate Hockey Association's First All-Star Team in 1988-89. After just one year, he signed with St. Louis as a free agent—he was never drafted. Now, after spending six years in St. Louis, including four as the Number 1 goalie, Joseph was coming to Edmonton.

September arrived, and Joseph and Sather hadn't come to terms on his contract. So Joseph played for the Las Vegas Thunder of the International Hockey League, getting sunshine instead of snow. Finally, in January, a deal was made. This allowed Sather to trade long-time Oiler Bill Ranford to the Boston Bruins for right winger Mariusz Czerkawski (an up-and-coming youngster with potential), defenceman Sean Brown and a first-round draft pick. Czerkawski had been drafted by Boston in the fifth round, 106th overall, in 1991, and made his NHL debut late in the 1993-94 season. In 37 games after the trade, he scored 12 goals and had 17 assists for 29 points, enough for ninth on the Oilers at the end of the season.

January also saw the (brief) return of

Glenn Anderson. Now 35, the right winger had started the season in Germany. The Vancouver Canucks signed him as a free agent, but he had to clear waivers to re-enter the NHL, and Glen Sather snapped him up. He wanted Anderson's leadership in the dressing room. He played in 17 games, scoring four goals and earning six assists, before the St. Louis Blues claimed him off the waiver wire on March 12.

CUJO PROVIDES HOPE

With Shayne Corson's bags packed, the captaincy fell to Kelly Buchberger, who wore the C with pride, feeling honoured to be chosen as the team leader. He was living a dream, not only playing in the NHL, but being the captain of a team as well.

The Oilers lost their first four regular-season games, which essentially set the pace for the season. By the time Curtis Joseph started playing in net, more than 40 games were gone and the Oilers' record was a dismal 14–23–6. Joseph's arrival turned the tide. The fans, who were back at games because of FOTO, began cheering again. In 33 games, Joseph had a 15–16–2 record. The Oilers ended the season with 68 points and a 30–44–8 record, putting them fifth in the Pacific Division. They missed the playoffs again, but with Cujo in net, they seemed to be on the right track.

Leading the way in points was Doug Weight, the first Edmonton player since Mark Messier in 1989–90 to break the 100-point barrier, with 104. Zdeno Ciger led the team in goals, with 31, and his 70 points were second only to Weight. Jason Arnott had 59 points, including a healthy 28 goals, while David Oliver put up 20 goals and 39 points. Todd Marchant had 38 points, with 19 goals. Miroslav Satan, a Slovakian drafted by the Oilers in the fifth round in 1993, had 35 points with 18 goals.

Dean McAmmond, who became an Oiler in the Joe Murphy trade back in 1993, had split his time between Edmonton and Cape Breton in 1993–94, and a severed Achilles tendon kept him on the sidelines for most of the shortened 1994–95 season. This season, he was able to get into 53 games, scoring 15 goals and 30 points. Leading the defencemen was Boris Mironov, with 32 points, including eight goals. Fellow blueliner Jeff Norton, picked up in a January trade that sent Igor Kravchuk to St. Louis, helped the Oilers with 20 points in 30 games. The 30-year-old Norton was in his ninth NHL season, having spent time with the New York Islanders, San Jose Sharks and St. Louis Blues. Known best for his crisp passes and effectiveness on the power play, Norton joined the Oilers at a much-needed time.

Youngster Ryan Smyth showed his worth, playing 48 games and scoring his first NHL goal against Calgary on November 24—a power-play marker early in the second period against Trevor Kidd.

 Alberta born Ryan Smyth was drafted by Edmonton and became a household name with Oilers fans. His emotional play spoke volumes.

1996–1997

"VICIOUS" REJOINS THE TEAM

After a successful ticket drive by FOTO, it appeared the team's troubles might be over. And the Oilers added some veteran leadership on September 9 when Kevin Lowe became an unrestricted free agent. Sather knew the 37-year-old defenceman would be able to work with the young rookies, and with an eye towards the future, his contract included a two-year coaching deal that would kick in whenever he retired. Buchberger was still wearing the C, but he welcomed Lowe's input and advice, knowing it was coming from a player with a winning edge.

On June 4, goalie Bob Essensa had come to the Oilers in a trade with the Detroit Red Wings, and he proved to be not only popular in the dressing room but a tremendous backup to Curtis Joseph. He immediately fit right in, becoming good friends with Buchberger, who liked his attitude and willingness to work. Essensa had started his career with Winnipeg, making the NHL All-Rookie Team in 1989–90 and winning the Molson Cup as the Jets' most valuable player. In 1991–92 the Jets allowed the third-fewest goals in the NHL, and Essensa ranked third in the voting for the Vezina Trophy, behind Patrick Roy of Montreal and Kirk McLean of Vancouver. A trade from the struggling Jets to first-place Detroit at the March 1994 deadline looked like it might benefit Essensa, but after giving up nine goals in the first two games of the playoffs against San Jose, he was replaced with Chris Osgood. The Wings acquired Mike Vernon from Calgary during the off-season, and Essensa was relegated to the minors for two years. The move to Edmonton offered him a fresh start.

Just ahead of training camp, on September 6, the Oilers sent Scott Thornton to Montreal for right winger Andrei Kovalenko. His 32 goals in 1996–97 would rank second behind Ryan Smyth's 39, while his 59 points were third on the team.

RETURN TO THE POSTSEASON

With a healthy amount of scoring ability and a solid goaltending tandem, the '96–97 Oilers made progress. Doug Weight again led the club in scoring, with 82 points.

Wins were more frequent this season and making the playoffs again was a reason for celebrating.

His 61 assists were fifth-best in the league. In his first full season, young Ryan Smyth set the goal-scoring pace and had 61 points. Curtis Joseph was making unbelievable saves in net, and Lowe was a respected presence in the dressing room, although he missed some games because of an inner-ear infection. On November 26, the Oilers walloped the Calgary Flames 10–1, with goals from 10 different players: Buchberger,

Mariusz Czerkawski, Kovalenko, Mats Lindgren, Todd Marchant, Bryan Marchment, Dean McAmmond, Dan McGillis, Miroslav Satan and Weight.

The regular season ended with a record of 36–37–9 and 81 points, enough for third place in the Pacific Division and a ticket to the playoffs. In the conference quarter-finals, they were paired up with the Dallas Stars. With 104 points, the Stars were second overall in the NHL and were seen as strong contenders for the Stanley Cup. They had solid offensive players in Mike Modano, Joe Nieuwendyk and Pat Verbeek, while ex-Oiler Andy Moog was their Number 1 goalie. The Oilers were definitely the underdogs.

Before Game 1 at Reunion Arena in Dallas, Lowe stood up in the dressing room. When he re-signed with the Oilers, his contract included a $50,000 bonus if Edmonton won its first-round series. He told his teammates that if they upset Dallas, he would take them all to dinner on his tab.

Dallas took the first game 5–3, but the Oilers came back strong in Game 2, blanking the Stars 4–0. Cujo blocked 25 shots.

Fans still talk about Game 3, one of the most exciting games in Oilers history. Dallas was holding a 3–0 lead with four minutes left in the third period, and disgruntled fans started leaving the Coliseum. But then, from the stairwells and hallways, those who had drifted away from the game could suddenly hear cheering. Doug Weight had scored, making it 3–1. Even so, a Stars win seemed inevitable. At 17:44, with Dallas killing an interference penalty to defenceman Sergei Zubov, Kovalenko scored. The Oilers trailed by a single goal. Twelve seconds later, the unthinkable happened and the Oilers scored a third time, this time courtesy of Mike Grier. Those still in the building went crazy, standing up, clapping and cheering, and the fans who had left started to rush back in, trying to figure out what was going on. Those who had already driven off and were listening to the

final minutes on the radio must have wondered why they had bailed out on the game, and some even starting turning back.

In overtime, the play was frenzied and marked by back-and-forth action. Cujo, who hadn't been beaten since 8:07 of the second period, kept his team in the game, ultimately making 39 saves. Finally, at 9:15 of the extra period, the Oilers took possession of the puck

This was Mike Grier's debut season with the Oilers, and the NHL. He was a hard worker and put in a full six seasons in Edmonton.

Russian born Andrei Kovalenko scored some important goals for the Oilers during the 1996-97 playoff run.

and rushed down the ice. In dramatic fashion, Kelly Buchberger scored.

Suddenly the team had confidence. Their forwards were scoring and their goalie was standing on his head, showing his quick reflexes and tremendous agility.

Dallas wasn't ready to give up so easily, and they beat the Oilers in a hard-fought fourth game by a score of 4–3 to tie the series at two games each. In Game 5, Edmonton dished up another shock,

winning again in overtime. This time, the game was scoreless after 60 minutes, and remained so after 20 minutes of overtime. Finally, 22 seconds into the fifth period, young Ryan Smyth broke the stalemate, giving the Oilers a 3–2 series lead.

Again, Dallas fought back and took the sixth game, 3–2. The deciding game was to be played in Dallas. Late in the third, the score was 3–3. With precious little time left, Joseph made an incredible save,

but gave up a rebound. He was down, out of position, as Nieuwendyk slapped at the puck to put it into the wide-open net. Dallas fans thought for sure their team was headed to the next round. But somehow, Joseph reached across with his stick. The puck banged off it and flew away from the goal. The Oilers quickly picked it up and rushed the other way.

Drawing on every last reserve of energy and adrenaline, the Oilers fought hard. Buchberger literally fought—he won himself a trip to the penalty box for mixing it up with Richard Matvichuk. With the teams playing four on four, Bucky watched from the penalty box. And as Todd Marchant started wheeling down the ice, he rose to his feet. "When the defenceman [Grant Ledyard] blew a wheel," said Buchberger, "Toddy just went by him and shot left side low."

Moog didn't make the save, and the Oilers won the series in seven games. Lowe, true to his word, took all the

players out in Dallas on his bonus money. The bill came to $16,000. Where they went is a secret long kept by the players. Some things stay in the dressing room.

For the Western Conference semifinals, the Oilers had to play the defending Stanley Cup champions, the Colorado Avalanche. The Avs had taken the Presidents' Trophy by finishing first overall with 107 points in the regular season. The Oilers seemed to have run out of gas in this series, losing the first two games in Denver, 5–1 and 4–1. They put up a valiant effort for the home fans in Game 3, coming from behind to win 4–3, but Colorado outlasted them in the next two games, taking the series 4–1 on a couple of one-goal decisions.

It wasn't a fairy-tale ending, but the fans weren't upset. After a four-year absence, their beloved Oilers had made the playoffs and played dramatic, exciting hockey. There was once again optimism in the City of Champions.

Curtis Joseph, or "Cujo," brought his incredible reflexes to the Oilers, helping them get past their playoff drought.

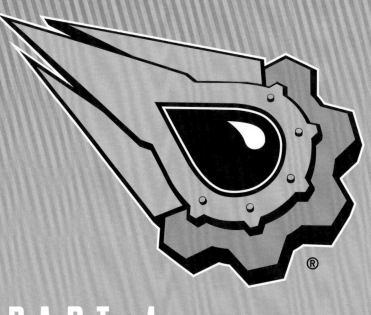

PART 4
1997–2003
EDMONTON'S TEAM

This was a turbulent period for the Oilers, on and off the ice. While the team was up and down in the standings, there were big changes on the horizon for the ownership. Peter Pocklington was out, and a determined group of investors came together to keep the Oilers in Edmonton.

1997–1998

GOLFING PUT ON HOLD

At the NHL Entry Draft, held in Pittsburgh on June 21, the Oilers were scheduled to pick 14th, a fair bit later than they had been accustomed to in recent years. General manager Glen Sather listened intently while such future stars as Joe Thornton, Patrick Marleau, Roberto Luongo and Marian Hossa were taken off the board. When Edmonton's turn came, he made an unusual call: right winger Michel Riesen, the first-ever player to be drafted out of Switzerland. Riesen was a fast skater and crafty forward who spent the 1997–98 season with HC Davos in his home country. He would spend three seasons with the Oilers' farm team in Hamilton, but his NHL career consisted of just 12 games in 2000–01, in which he notched a lone assist and drew two minor penalties.

Of the 10 players the Oilers selected that day, only one went on to a lengthy NHL career. Edmonton-born Jason Chimera was a big winger with the Medicine Hat Tigers of the WHL.

After a couple more years in junior and an apprenticeship in Hamilton, he cracked the Oiler lineup in 2002, and as of 2017–18 was still playing, with the New York Islanders, having appeared in over 1,000 NHL games.

A few weeks after the draft, the Oilers welcomed a familiar face back to the coaching staff. Ted Green, who had been a head coach and assistant coach with the club in the past, joined head coach Ron Low behind the bench. Rounding out the staff was Bob McCammon, who had won a Stanley Cup with the Oilers in 1987 as director of player development. He also had experience as a head coach with Philadelphia and Vancouver, and he rejoined the Oilers in 1995–96.

Over the summer, Luke Richardson became a free agent, and on July 23 he signed with Philadelphia. On the 28th, Scott Fraser, a 25-year-old centreman who had spent the previous season with three minor-league teams, was signed. And on August 25, Mariusz Czerkawski was sent to the New York Islanders for the rights to winger Dan LaCouture, a member of the Boston University Terriers in 1996–97.

A Michigan State Spartan, Rem Murray played a full six seasons with the Oilers.

The season got off to a slow start, almost as if the Oilers were still thinking about the summer sun. After 20 games, they had a dismal 5–10–5 record. Although they were in a three-way tie for eighth place in the conference, and therefore were still in the playoff hunt, this kind of performance fires up general managers and fans alike—not to mention the media, who start talking about who needs to be traded. As the new year approached, the funk continued, and on December 30, with the team's record at 11–19–9, Sather sent Jason Bonsignore, Steve Kelly and Bryan Marchment to Tampa Bay for Paul Comrie and Roman Hamrlik.

Bonsignore and Kelly had been first-round picks—fourth and fifth overall, respectively—for the Oilers. Neither had established a foothold in the big league, but they were still considered prospects. The Oilers would miss Marchment, an edgy defenceman who, the year before, had logged 20 minutes a game on the blue line. A first-round pick of the Winnipeg Jets in 1987, he'd come to Edmonton in August 1994. The media consistently praised his play and had voted him the Oilers' top defenceman in 1996 and 1997. But Sather wanted to make changes, mix things up.

For Edmonton, the key to the trade was Czech-born Hamrlik. Back in 1992, the Lightning had selected him first overall in their first-ever NHL draft, and he had stepped right into their lineup. He was a quiet kind of defenceman, steady and reliable, but he could play it rough if needed. Edmonton-born Comrie was a centre, playing in his second year at the University of Denver.

Czech-born Roman Hamrlik added some punch to the Oilers blue line.

The dressing-room staff had barely had a chance to rearrange the name-plates on the players' stalls when, on January 4, Sather pulled the trigger on what was perhaps the biggest trade of the season. After four and a half seasons, Jason Arnott was on his way to New Jersey with minor-league defenceman Bryan Muir for wingers Bill Guerin and Valeri Zelepukin.

Bill Guerin came to the Oilers and sparked some energy into the team. He was popular in the dressing room.

Coming to Edmonton with Stanley Cup experience, Guerin was a strong two-way forward. In addition to his size, which he wasn't afraid to use, he was a very fast skater. In 40 games after the trade, Guerin scored 13 goals and put up 29 points.

Guerin's arrival touched off a six-game winning streak, and Curtis Joseph was a driving force in net over the last

half of the schedule. However, the month of March found Sather still tweaking the roster. On March 9, minor-league blueliner Scott Ferguson was sent to Ottawa for Czech-born defenceman Frantisek Musil. The 33-year-old Musil, known as "Frank," had defected to North America as a teen and broken into the NHL with the Minnesota North Stars in 1986. At six foot three and over 200 pounds, he played a steady blueline game, making up for a lack of flash with good balance and strength. He also had an edge that at times could turn nasty.

At the trade deadline, defenceman Janne Niinimaa was brought in from the Philadelphia Flyers, though it meant the departure of Dan McGillis, a big young defenceman who had a promising rookie season in 1996–97. The Oilers were looking for more flash and dash, and felt Niinimaa's more offensively oriented style would help them. Like McGillis, the swift-skating Niinimaa had made his debut the year before, collecting 44 points and earning a spot on the NHL's All-Rookie Team. The Flyers had gone to the Stanley Cup final in '97, so the 22-year-old Finn was playoff-tested as well. Niinimaa quickly became the Oilers' top defence-man in terms of ice time, and he quarterbacked the power play. A character in the dressing room—who always insisted on playing heavy metal music—Niinimaa also became a media favourite because he told it like it was. If things were going well, he said so, and if they were bad, he didn't hesitate to comment, often using choice words, much to the media's delight.

The rejuvenated Oilers finished the season at 35–37–10, once again placing

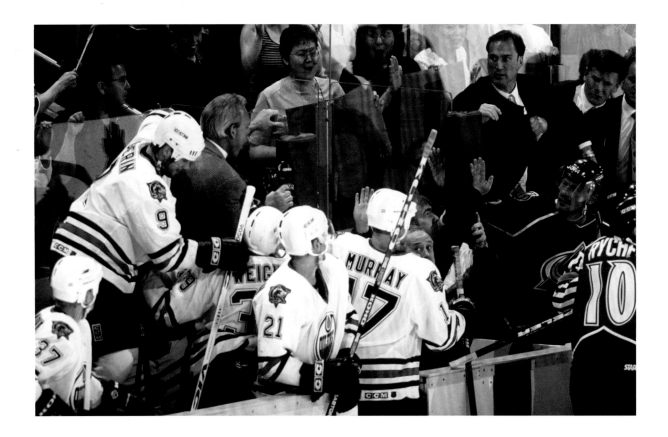

them third in their division and seventh in the conference.

For the fifth consecutive time, Doug Weight led the club in scoring with 70 points, including 26 goals. The only other 20-goal scorer on the Oilers was Ryan Smyth, who added 13 assists for 33 points in 65 games.

Trailing Weight was the kid from Grande Cache, Dean McAmmond, who had a bit of a breakout season with 50 points and 19 goals. Defenceman and alternate captain Boris Mironov led the Oiler defence lineup with 46 points, including 16 goals.

Joseph appeared in 71 games, while Essensa got into 16. In a 17-game stretch between February 2 and March 21, Cujo recorded four shutouts, taking his already-impressive season total to eight (fourth in the league in that category).

In the first postseason round, the Oilers were rematched with Colorado, who with 95 points had won the Pacific Division. The Oilers were used to playing the role of underdog, and they headed into the series, which opened on enemy ice, knowing they would have to elevate their game. They caught a break prior to Game 1, when the news broke that Avalanche captain Joe Sakic wouldn't be in the lineup. There was no score in the game until 15:31 of the second period, when Peter Forsberg put one past Curtis Joseph. Cujo waved his stick in the air, complaining about a crease violation,

Head Coach Ron Low protects his players, ready to pounce over to the visitor's bench in a game against Colorado.

but the goal stood and the period ended with the Avalanche leading 1–0. Then, just 17 seconds into the third period, Forsberg scored again, this time on a wraparound. The Oilers, who had gone 0-for-6 on the power play, finally beat Roy with the man advantage at 11:02 of the third, as Bill Guerin brought them within a goal. The floodgates had opened. Only a minute and 20 seconds later, Todd Marchant saw a loose puck and sped down the ice, beating an Avalanche defenceman. Dean McAmmond rushed the net, going to the left side, and Marchant sent him a perfect pass that he tapped in. The Oilers had tied the game on a tic-tac-toe play.

Less than two and half minutes later, Ryan Smyth and Tony Hrkac crashed the net in an aggressive forecheck and the puck got loose, allowing Boris Mironov to smack it past Roy for the go-ahead goal. Although the Avalanche jammed away at the front of the net in the dying seconds of the third period, they couldn't get another puck past Joseph. At the end of the game, Cujo talked about the hacking and whacking and the fact that there were probably six or seven broken sticks during the game.

Bolstered by the return of Sakic, the Avalanche came back in Game 2. Before the game was three minutes in, Valeri Kamensky and Peter Forsberg had made it 2–0. The commentators wondered if the series would now turn. Had the Oilers scored their one and only upset? Halfway through the game, with Colorado leading 4–1, Ron Low pulled Joseph in favour of Essensa. It looked to be a mercy pull, but the intention was to give Cujo time to

rest up for Game 3. The final score was 5–2 Avalanche.

An eager crowd greeted the Oilers for Game 3 at the Coliseum. The Avs again leapt to a 2–0 lead after the first period, but Edmonton pulled it together and mounted a comeback on goals from Mironov and Weight. Claude Lemieux made it 4–2 at 2:14 of the third frame, but Guerin brought the home side within one. Then came a break. With just under eight minutes to go, the Oilers were cycling the puck around the Avalanche zone. When it came to Buchberger, he sent a beautiful backhand shot past Roy, tying the game. The fans went crazy, banging on the glass. The game went to overtime, but it was Sakic who sent a bullet past Cujo to end it.

Still in Edmonton for Game 4, Smyth opened the scoring at 17:52 of the first period. But that was the only goal the Oilers could muster. They lost 3–1 and were heading back to Colorado trailing 3–1 in the series.

But this team had a habit of fighting back. After Stephane Yelle popped the puck into the Edmonton net to give Colorado a 1–0 lead at 16:20 of the first period, the Oilers bore down and played their gritty hockey. Even so, they were unable to solve Roy and the Colorado defence. During the second intermission, they looked at each other in the dressing room and Buchberger said, "It's too damn early to golf." Just over four minutes into the third, with the Oilers on a power play, there was a scramble in front of the net. When the puck landed on Guerin's stick, he wound up and blasted it from the hash marks to tie the game. Shortly after, Mike Grier found himself with the puck, bearing down on Roy. When he couldn't find anyone open to pass to, he made a long wraparound move, sneaking the puck past the goal line. Now the score was 2–1 Edmonton.

The Avalanche jammed at Joseph for the rest of the period, trying to tie the game, but he held strong. At the end of the third, Colorado pulled Roy for the extra attacker. Grier saw the puck leaving the Oilers zone and raced after it, winning the battle with the Avalanche defenceman behind the net. He snuck the puck into the empty net, sealing the win with a final score of 3–1.

The series evened up in Edmonton, when Joseph earned a 2–0 shutout win in Game 6. The first goal was scored by Drake Berehowsky, who hadn't scored for the Oilers since the first game of the season, back in October. His goal injected some much-needed energy into the crowd. With that, the Oilers held strong and kept the lead, adding one more goal by Mironov. But it was Joseph who stole the show. At the end of the game, the fans were chanting, "Cujo! Cujo! Cujo!"

That wasn't the only yelling during this game. Oilers coach Ron Low was furious at his Colorado counterpart, Marc Crawford, for putting two known fighters—Jeff Odgers and Warren Rychel—on the ice with four seconds left. Low tried to get at Crawford, who screamed at Low until his face turned purple.

The war of words continued after the game, via the media. Low jabbed at Crawford, saying, "Great move. I guess

he was figuring on both of them scoring."

"Ronnie's memory can't be that bad," Crawford retaliated. "Doesn't he remember who he had on at the 19:50 mark in Game 2?"

Still, the Oilers were excited by the 2–0 win and looked forward to Game 7 in Colorado. They got the outcome they were hoping for. Another shutout, this time with a goal each from Niinimaa,

Cujo's mask, a picture of a rabid dog from the 1983 horror movie *Cujo*, was a hit with Oilers fans.

Guerin, Marchant and Lindgren. But it was Joseph who was again the hero of the game, stopping 31 pucks. At the other end of the rink, Patrick Roy let in those four goals on just 17 shots.

Next up were the Dallas Stars—once again, the Oilers were meeting the Presidents' Trophy winners in the second round. This was a hard-fought, low-scoring series, and try as they might, the Oilers just couldn't get the puck past Ed Belfour, whose 1.88 goals against average had led the league. The Oilers lost the first game 3–1, but evened the series with a 2–0 win. Game 3 was scoreless until 13:07 of overtime, when Benoit Hogue gave Dallas a 1–0 victory. The fourth and fifth games were lost by scores of 3–1 and 2–1.

Now it was time to golf.

POCKLINGTON PACKS IT IN

The 1996–97 season had ended on a high note on the ice, but behind the scenes, things seemed to be going downhill. The ticket drive, though successful, was only a Band-Aid solution to the Oilers' financial problems. It was no secret that Pocklington was indebted to the Alberta Treasury Branch. When the bank called in the loan, Pocklington had no choice but to put the team up for sale.

There were roadblocks to selling the team, with the City of Edmonton and Northlands. Pocklington was leasing from Northlands at the time under the location agreement that he had signed in 1994. The deal bound the Oilers to the Coliseum until 2004, as well as stipulating that, should Pocklington reach an agreement with an outside buyer, Northlands and the City of Edmonton each had 45 days in which to seek local interests willing to buy the team for $100 million Canadian and keep it in Edmonton.

In the fall of 1997, talk started to circulate that Leslie Alexander, owner of the Houston Rockets of the National Basketball Association as well as an arena football franchise and the Houston Comets of the WNBA, was interested in buying the team and moving it south. Nothing was substantiated, and there was no official offer, but the rumours

Sather Enters the Hall of Fame

Glen Sather was inducted into the Hockey Hall of Fame on November 17, 1997, in the Builder category. The high point of his nearly two decades as head coach and general manager of the Oilers would have to be the five Stanley Cup championships—the first just five years after the Oilers had been admitted to the NHL.

were flying. Two other Houston business-men, Chuck Watson (owner of the Houston Aeros of the International Hockey League) and Robert McNair, also expressed interest. However, their offer fizzled because they didn't want to own a team that was required to play in Edmonton for three years, which would have been the case under the existing agreement with Northlands. If the team were to move, the remaining years on the Northlands agreement would have to be bought out—a too expensive prospect for a buyer already investing millions.

As this went on, so did the Oilers' 1997-98 season. The players did their best to stay focused on hockey and shut out any uncertainty about the future of the franchise. Meanwhile, Cal Nichols, who had been instrumental in the FOTO ticket drive, thought he might be able to assemble a group of investors from Edmonton to buy the team. The first person he called was Bruce Saville, who developed and marketed billing solutions for the telecommunications industry. One of his major clients had been the City of Edmonton. Saville, having sold his company for millions and with "cash to blow," was in immedi-ately. He had never met Nichols, but felt he owed something to the city. He put forward $5 million, and later said, "I didn't do it as an investment."

Nichols continued to work the phones, bringing other businessmen on board, including Jim F. Hole, who became chairman of the board; and Gary Gregg, brother of former Oiler Randy Gregg.

As the partnership grew, it adopted

the name Edmonton Investors Group, or EIG, and set a goal of raising $60 million operating capital. (They only needed $50 million, but they wanted the extra for assurance.) A bank loan for another $50 million would give EIG the stake it needed. Contributions ranged between $1 million (officially the minimum, although in some cases inves-tors pooled their contributions, so some bought in for as little as $200,000) and $5 million.

The struggle to reach the $60-million goal continued throughout 1997. By December, only nine soft letters of intent to invest had been received and the finish line was nowhere in sight. In January 1998, Nichols met with Larry Makelki in Edmonton. Makelki lived in Lloydminster and was in the oilfield supply business. He and his accountant, Bruce Pennock, listened to the pitch and were persuaded to put $5 million into the pot. Makelki also worked his oil field contacts to raise another $7 million. As Nichols later said, "It was really the blue-collar millionaires that pulled all this together. It all seemed to start happening when the industrial communities were approached."

Nichols and the EIG were determined to make this work, but then the situa-tion intensified when Leslie Alexander of Houston re-emerged in February with a firm offer to buy the Oilers. The ATB accepted the offer, starting the clock on the 45-day time frame for either the city or Northlands to come up with a local bid.

Less than 24 hours before the dead-line, the EIG group met in a boardroom, prior to a press conference where they were to announce that they had the money. They had recruited 37 investors, but eleventh hour changes had left them a million dollars short.

Time was ticking. They went around the table. Who would invest a bit more? Everyone passed. They tried a second time, with no luck. Finally, on the third go-round, Saville said, "I will put in $500,000." With this, two more investors decided that they would contribute another $250,000 each. The group, led by Nichols, headed down to the press conference to announce that EIG would become the new owners of the Oilers.

The EIG investors were a diverse group of Edmonton business people. Each contributed what they could, and then a little more, to save their team.

Dave Addie—Lloydminster; Neal Allen—Nisku; Jakab Ambrosius—Edmonton; Ted Barrett—Los Angeles; Manuel Balsa—Edmonton; Edward E. Bean—Edmonton; Gordon Buchanan—Edmonton; Bill Butler—Edmonton; Michael Dalton—Kelowna; *The Edmonton Journal*; Ernie Elko—Edmonton; Gary Gregg—Edmonton; Don Hamilton—Edmonton;

Ron Hodgson—Edmonton; Tom Mayson—Edmonton; Jim Hole—Edmonton; Gerald Knoll—Nisku; Wally Kuchar—Edmonton/Nisku; Lloydminster Consortium of Five: Marcel and Roger Roberge; Keith Weaver; Rusty Stalwick (Vermillion); Brian Nilsson; Larry Makelki—Lloydminster; Todd McFarlane—Phoenix; Tim Melton—Edmonton;

Art Mihalcheon—Edmonton; Cal Nichols—Edmonton; Al Owens—Edmonton; Dick Paine—Edmonton; Harold and Cathy Roozen—Edmonton; Bruce Saville—Edmonton; Dale Sheard—Edmonton; Simon Sochatsky—Edmonton; Barry Weaver—Edmonton; Jim Woods—Edmonton; Jim Zanello—Edmonton; Dick Colf—Portland.

1998–1999

"I'M OUT OF HERE"

The headline in the July 23, 1998, edition of the *Edmonton Sun* consisted of a simple declaration, in bold, black capital letters, that marked the end of years of frustration and speculation. "I'M OUT OF HERE" was Peter Pocklington's final message to the people of Edmonton. The *Journal* marked the occasion by proclaiming, "Puck Packs It In." The sale of the Oilers prompted an outpouring of articles on the good and the bad of Pocklington's legacy, what he had done for the city and what he had failed to do in the end.

After selling the Oilers to the EIG, Pocklington remained for a time in Edmonton. But when the ATB seized his personal collections, including the contents of his wine cellar, Pocklington decided it was time to leave Edmonton. The mood in the city was mixed.

But while some irate fans were glad to see him go, there was one person who maintained that he would miss Pocklington: Glen Sather. They'd had a good working relationship, and Peter rarely got in the way of Glen's decisions. After so many years together, they were friends.

The Oilers were staying in Edmonton, and with Sather as GM, Ron Low as head coach and Kelly Buchberger as captain, there was an element of stability. On July 31, Kevin Lowe retired. At the press conference announcing his decision, he held his emotions in check until the very end, but then he could no longer hold back the tears. But he wasn't leaving altogether. Although he was retiring from the game he loved, he had a new position behind the bench as assistant coach.

Trades were abundant this year, as Sather—minus his friend Pocklington, but now with 38 owners to answer to (the group started with 37, but had attracted another investor after the deadline)—continued to swap out more expensive players for more affordable options. This was no easy feat in Edmonton, where fans still remembered watching superstars on the ice at the Coliseum. But without a salary cap, the small-market Oilers still couldn't attract or retain them. The team had new owners, but old problems. And some of the shareholders were testing Sather, although he worked well with the board chairman Jim F. Hole.

Ethan Moreau started his journey with the Oilers in the 1998-99 season and played ten more years with the club.

Two Lowes, and a Low behind the bench. Brothers Kevin (assistant coach) and Ken (head medical trainer) hug the wall, while Ron Low stands on the bench.

The arena, which had been called the Edmonton Coliseum for the past few years, was to take on yet another name in 1998–99. Barry Weaver, part of the EIG consortium, had founded Skyreach, a company that specialized in heavy construction equipment, in 1977. This year, in a deal that would add to the Oilers' revenue streams, he bought the naming rights to the arena for five years and renamed it Skyreach Centre.

HELLOS AND GOODBYES

At the draft in June, the Oilers placed bets on a number of prospects who didn't pan out. One who did go on to make an impact was Shawn Horcoff, a centre from Trail, British Columbia, who had just finished his second season of collegiate hockey at Michigan State University. Taken in the fourth round, 99th overall, Horcoff had a strong work ethic and perseverance, among the many positive attributes that appealed to the Oilers. He elected to complete his education before cracking the Edmonton lineup in 2000–01.

Not long after the draft, it was time for fans to say goodbye to their treasured goalie, as Curtis Joseph became a free agent. Joseph's stock was high, given that he had been a driving force behind the Oilers reaching the second playoff round in each of the past two years, and a number of teams were interested in signing him. Once again, the fans were upset, and they expressed it on radio talk shows. Cujo had been a bright spot, giving them hope, but it all came down to money. He ended up signing with the Toronto Maple Leafs. With this, Bob Essensa inherited the Number 1 spot.

The return of a natural enforcer. Marty McSorley was involved in the Gretzky trade, the biggest trade in the history of hockey, but eventually made his way back to Edmonton.

On October 1, Drake Berehowsky, Greg de Vries and Eric Fichaud were sent to the expansion Nashville Predators for centre Jim Dowd and Russian-born goaltender Mikhail Shtalenkov, who would back up Essensa for part of the year, playing in 34 games before being traded to Phoenix.

The Predators also claimed Zdeno Ciger in the waiver draft. And Petr Klima was signed as a free agent by Detroit.

Sather filled one of the voids in the lineup by signing a veteran Oiler and old fan favourite. Marty McSorley added that so-needed tough guy piece to the team. Sather also signed Pat Falloon, who the San Jose Sharks had drafted second overall in 1991. The right winger, who'd had a few 20-goal seasons, had split 1997–98 between the Philadelphia Flyers and Ottawa Senators.

OVERTURNED GOALS

Despite an injury that kept top scorer Doug Weight out of action for nearly three months, the Oilers got off to a decent start, and as January gave way to February they were a game under .500. Then the team went into a nosedive, dropping to 25–33–10 as of March 17— leaving them on the bubble as far as the playoffs were concerned. As the trading deadline approached, Glen Sather initiated a quartet of deals in an effort to get his team back on track.

On March 20, Mats Lindgren was traded to the New York Islanders, along with an eighth-round pick, for starting goaltender Tommy Salo. Wearing the bright yellow-and-blue Tre Kronor jersey, Salo had helped his country win the gold medal in the 1994 Winter Olympics, and since then had been a fixture in the Swedish net in international play. He may not have had the catlike reflexes of Curtis Joseph, but he had a skill set that coach Ron Low thought would work. Low, a goalie himself, said, "Salo was consistent in the net. Perhaps not as flashy as Curtis, but he didn't let in a lot of bad goals. If you don't have any bad goals with a team, you don't have to deal with deflation. Plus he had a tremendous work ethic."

The very same day, Sather packaged Boris Mironov, Dean McAmmond and defenceman Jonas Elofsson—who was playing in Sweden—to the Chicago Blackhawks for left wingers Ethan Moreau and Chad Kilger, defenceman Christian Laflamme and right winger Daniel Cleary. Moreau had been drafted 14th overall by Chicago in 1994, and had been a full-time NHLer since 1996–97. He was a grinder and a checker, able to kill penalties, block shots and even fight tough guys bigger than him. Laflamme had been drafted in the second round by Chicago in 1995 after a successful year in the QMJHL, and was in his second full year with the Hawks. Kilger had been drafted fourth overall in 1995 by Anaheim, who hoped he might turn out to be a good linemate for Paul Kariya. He also had the size and mean streak associated with a power forward. He had shown flashes of the ability that had made him such a high pick, but not enough to prevent him from being traded, first to Winnipeg and then to Chicago. One of the few Newfoundlanders to reach the

NHL, Daniel Cleary had been drafted 13th overall by the Blackhawks in 1997, after starring with the Belleville Bulls of the Ontario Hockey League. He had split the 1998–99 season between the Hawks and their farm team in Portland, Maine.

Having added some youth up front, the Oilers then looked for some experienced help on the blue line. On March 23, in exchange for a fourth-round pick in 1999 and a second-rounder in 2000, Edmonton acquired 25-year-old Jason Smith from the Toronto Maple Leafs.

Tommy Salo was a key ingredient in the Oilers making the playoffs in 1999. This image, from 2003, shows the design for a third Oilers jersey. It depicted a metallic meteor-like oil drop, and was created by artist Todd McFarlane. The gear rivets on the crest represented the five Stanley Cups the Oilers had won. It was the alternate jersey from 2001–2007.

He was a big, solid player, strong on his stick, and a leader.

With Salo in the crease, the Oilers won eight of their 14 remaining games. Making the playoffs came down to the third-to-last game of the season, on April 12, when they travelled to San Jose to play the Sharks. After 40 minutes, they were down by a goal. As they regrouped in the dressing room, the word came through that the Calgary Flames had lost to the Vancouver Canucks. This was welcome news for the Oilers, because it meant that if they could win this game, they would clinch eighth place and a playoff berth. They were buzzing as they headed down the tunnel to the ice surface. Rem Murray tied the game at 13:47 of the third period, while Todd Marchant made it 3–2 for the Oilers at 14:32. The Sharks bit back with a goal by Alexander Korolyuk at 17:02, and pulled ahead on Mike Ricci's goal at the 19-minute mark. Marchant came to the rescue once again. With 18 seconds to play, he rifled a shot past Steve Shields to tie the score at 4–4. The buzzer went seconds later, and at 3:55 of overtime, the leggy rookie Tom Poti caught a pass from Doug Weight, headed to the slot and sniped in a wrist shot. The Oilers swarmed the ice. They were heading to the playoffs.

The players were thrilled that their season would be extended, but the bad news was that they would have to play the Dallas Stars in the conference quarter-finals. The Stars had finished the season with a league-leading 114 points, 36 points more than eighth-seeded

Edmonton. The Oilers were simply outmatched. They battled admirably in the first two games, losing a pair of intense matches by scores of 2–1 and 3–2. Despite being outshot 65–32 these were close games for the Oilers.

The series shifted to the Skyreach Centre for Game 3. Fans were psyched and there was a two-hour tailgate party before face-off. The noise level in the arena was incredible, especially when Ryan Smyth started the scoring in the first period. Edmonton kept battling and was ahead 2–0 after Ryan Smyth scored again, 24 seconds into the third. The fans thought their team had the game won. Then the unthinkable happened. The Stars came back and scored three unanswered goals, leaving with a 3–2 victory and a 3–0 lead in the series. Even more frustrating, for fans and players, was that three Edmonton goals weren't counted because of crease violations. One fan's quote in the Edmonton Journal said it all: "First Star: video goal judge. Second Star: the ref. Third Star: the other ref. The Oilers should have won 5-2." It didn't seem right to the disgruntled fans who left the arena shaking their heads. Salo had stood on his head. The fans were convinced that the Oilers had done everything they had to do to win. To them, the refs interfered.

Emotions were on full display for Game 4, played on April 27, for multiple reasons. Eight nights previous, in front of an emotional crowd at Madison Square Garden in New York, the Great One had hung up his skates for good. Edmonton fans felt the sting and sadness in his retirement, because all these years later, they still considered him an Oiler. So when he surprised the crowd of 17,100 by stepping out to centre ice to drop the puck, waving to the crowd, they went crazy. He talked briefly to Oilers captain Kelly Buchberger and Stars captain Joe Nieuwendyk before the ceremony, then, in true Wayne Gretzky fashion, he headed off the ice and disappeared to let the Oilers play their game. And what a game! After a scoreless first period, Ryan Smyth managed to get one past Ed Belfour at 4:47 of the second. The lead held until, with 34 seconds in the period, Nieuwendyk scored on a Dallas power play. Todd Marchant gave Edmonton a 2–1 lead six and a half minutes into the third, but with the Stars again enjoying the man advantage at 11:05, Jamie Langenbrunner made it 2–2.

There was no further scoring in the third period. Or in 20 minutes of over-time. Or *40* minutes. When games go on this long, anything can happen, including a lucky bounce. Sadly for the Skyreach crowd, that kind of luck was with the Dallas Stars this time. At 17:34 of the third overtime period, with the clocks reading 1:03 a.m., the puck came to Stars defenceman Sergei Zubov at the point. He drilled a shot toward the Edmonton goal—the 56th shot Salo faced in the marathon—and it went in off the leg of Nieuwendyk, capping the longest game either team had played to that date. The Stars won the game 3–2, and swept the series, advancing to the conference semifinals. They would go on to win the Stanley Cup.

The two games played in Edmonton had been wild and unusual. Even the

presence of the Great One wasn't enough to turn Edmonton's fortunes. The Dallas Stars would go on to win the Stanley Cup on, ironically, a controversial goal where Brett Hull scored with his foot in the crease. The refs allowed the goal saying Hull had possession. Apparently, the league had sent out a private memo to the teams earlier that season that said that a skate could be in the crease if the player was in control of the puck, so Hull's goal was a good goal.

Anthem singer Paul Lorieau had a 30-year stint with the Oilers, from 1981–2011. His last game was April 8, 2011. He passed away on July 2, 2013.

1999–2000

IT RUNS IN THE FAMILY

The Oilers found some local talent in the entry draft in Boston. Mike Comrie of the University of Michigan Wolverines, taken in the third round, 91st overall, had attended Jasper Place High School in Edmonton and played provincial Junior A for the St. Albert Saints. His roots in Alberta were deep. His father, Bill, had played for Wild Bill Hunter's Edmonton Oil Kings in 1968–69. In 1969, Bill's father, Herb Comrie, passed away, so he gave up hockey to look after the family furniture business, which eventually turned into the national chain The Brick. "I was supposed to go to Chicago's camp that fall," said Bill. "We had no money. And my mom had never worked. My dad had $10,000 worth of life insurance. So I had to stay home and help out." Luckily for Mike Comrie, he inherited his father's hockey genes. He didn't come to the Oilers right away, returning to college for one more season, but his brother Paul did get called up for 15 games in 1999–2000.

FROM LOW TO LOWE

With the addition of the Atlanta Thrashers to the NHL fold, an expansion draft was held on June 25. Longtime Oiler—and, until now, the team captain—Kelly Buchberger, was left unprotected, and the Thrashers claimed him. The Oilers were losing a player who treated every game, even in preseason, like the seventh game of the Stanley Cup final. Doug Weight was named to succeed Buchberger as captain.

In early June, Ron Low revealed that he was leaving the Oilers after serving as head coach for four full years plus part of a fifth. At 341 regular-season games, plus 29 in the playoffs, only Glen Sather had had a longer tenure behind the Edmonton bench. Low's departure came after he and Glen Sather failed to come to terms on a new contract.

Former Oiler defenceman Kevin Lowe, who had debuted as an assistant coach in the fall of 1998, was named the club's seventh head coach in the NHL era. Lowe, with six Stanley Cup championships to his name, was called the "heir apparent" in the media. "You have to be

Cowboy Bill Flett

On July 12, 1999, at the age of 56, Cowboy Bill Flett, a fan favourite who played for the WHA Edmonton Oilers and also played in the NHL Oilers' inaugural season, passed away. Cowboy played 13 years in the NHL and WHA, breaking in with the expansion Los Angeles Kings in 1967–68. He scored the first hat trick in Kings history. In the middle of his fifth season, he was traded to the Philadelphia Flyers, winning a Stanley Cup with the "Broad Street Bullies" in 1973–74. He went on to play with the Toronto Maple Leafs and Atlanta Flames before moving to the Oilers. In all this time, in every new city, he still wore his cowboy boots.

a leader and Kevin Lowe is one heck of a leader. I think he's going to do one hell of a job," said Sather. From the day he drafted the young blueliner in 1979, Sather had had faith in Lowe and knew he was "heads and tails" above all the other draft picks. His leadership qualities would now be put to the test like never before.

FRICTION IN THE MANAGEMENT SUITE

Glen Sather dug in hard and tried his best to work under the supervision of 38 owners, but in 1999 tensions came to a head. The budget he had to work with was tight, and he wasn't sure how he could put together a competitive team with so little money. Plus, it was no secret that he was butting heads with the EIG. The group wanted more transparency around how Sather spent the team's money, while Slats had been accustomed to a great deal of autonomy

under a single owner, Peter Pocklington. The sheer size of the ownership group made decision-making hard. From the EIG point of view, they had a right to accountability. Sather now had to constantly consult and he was bothered not only because he felt he was losing control, but because he thought what happened in the boardroom wasn't staying in the boardroom. "My biggest complaint was that everything that happened in that boardroom became public," said Sather at the time. "It has to stay there and it just hasn't stayed there. I don't like that way of operating."

Talk swirled about the strained relationship between Sather and the EIG for the entire season. Sports pundits were constantly speculating. Many articles were devoted to the topic, and the uncertainty played out on the airwaves as well—call-in shows allowed fans to put in their two cents' worth. His contract was up at the end of the year. Would he go? Would EIG let him walk? Who would take over?

ANOTHER MEETING WITH DALLAS

As the season approached, Lowe liked the look of his team. "They are a gritty bunch," he said. He hired a trusted friend and former Oiler captain, Craig MacTavish, to be his assistant coach.

Ethan Moreau and Jason Smith gave the team some fresh legs. Moreau was only 24 as the season began, and he quickly earned a reputation as a hard-working, two-way forward with an impressive fitness level (he was known as a gym rat). He liked to crank guys along the boards or at centre ice if they got in his way. Fans loved the grit and determination Smith showed in his play. Even when injured, he kept playing, as if pain didn't matter. If he got cut during a game, he'd get stitched up in the hall, instead of the dressing room, so he could get back to the bench as quickly as possible.

Another player who had an impact on the team this season was Alex Selivanov, who arrived from Tampa Bay in January

With Kelly Buchberger gone, Doug Weight became the tenth captain of the Edmonton Oilers.

WAYNE, WELCOME HOME

Celebrating the Great One

On October 1, 1999, the Oilers retired Wayne Gretzky's number and raised a banner dedicated to him to the Skyreach Centre rafters. That night, Edmonton was hosting the New York Rangers, the last team Gretzky had suited up for. He stepped on the ice, now in his suit and tie instead of his gear and Oilers jersey. The red carpet was rolled out and his family was invited to walk with him to centre ice. Both his mother Phyllis and his father Walter were there, as well as his wife, Janet, and three children, Paulina, Ty and Trevor. As a surprise, Dave Semenko, Mark Messier and Jari Kurri also stepped onto the ice. In an emotional moment for everyone, but especially for Gretzky, his banner was brought out by his good friend, Joey Moss, a man with Down syndrome whom he had helped get a job with the Oilers equipment staff years before—a job Joey still held. After he hugged Joey, the banner was raised and fireworks went off.

Weeks later, on November 23, Wayne Gretzky was inducted into the Hockey Hall of Fame. He was the second Edmonton Oiler to be inducted, following Glen Sather, and the first to go in as a player.

After playing 12 games in the 1998–99 season, Jason Smith became a steady blue liner in the 1999–00 season, and a leader in the dressing room.

of 1999, part of a three-cornered deal that sent Andrei Kovalenko to Philadelphia. The winger scored 27 goals and contributed 20 assists, placing him third on the team. Doug Weight rebounded after missing most of 1998–99 with injuries, and led the way with 72 points, including 21 goals. Ryan

Smyth again proved his worth as a first-round draft pick by leading in goal scoring with 28. His 54 points were second to Weight. The blue line was balanced by Roman Hamrlik, Janne Niinimaa and Jason Smith.

In his first full season in the NHL, Georges Laraque—wearing Dave

Semenko's old Number 27 jersey—used his body to push opponents away from the crease. Though he knew how to fight, he was no bully. If an opponent didn't want to drop the gloves, he backed off. But he also proved he could be more than a tough guy and imposing presence. On February 21, he scored a hat trick against Los Angeles. His three-goal night helped put the Oilers in first place in the Northwest Division. No one expected such a performance from a role player, and perhaps no one was more shocked than Laraque. After the game, he said, "I would never have thought I would see a hat on the ice for me. It's unbelievable." Captain Doug Weight also commented: "We got the big guy putting it in the back of the net. Georges is a kid at heart. We created a monster now!"

Coach Lowe was known to get emotional at times—during one game, he threw a pack of Juicy Fruit gum on the ice. Another time, it was a tube of ointment. But perhaps emotional involvement was exactly what the team needed. They ended the season with 88 points, the highest total they'd had since 1990, when they won the Stanley Cup. They finished second in their division, eight points behind Colorado, and seventh in the Western Conference.

Not only had Edmonton qualified for the playoffs for the fourth straight season, but they were about to face the Dallas Stars for the fourth year in a row.

With much the same lineup as the year before, the Stars again took the first two games, 2–1 and 3–0. Ed Belfour was keeping his cool, even when Ryan Smyth crashed the net again and again. But Game 3 was a different story. Doug Weight showed Oilers fans why he wore the C. With 8:40 gone in the first period, he controlled a bouncing puck that had hit his leg and put it in the net. The play was reviewed and the goal stood. Jim Dowd scored a minute and 16 seconds later, and then Weight's second goal came at the 17-minute mark, putting the Oilers up 3–0. In the first period alone, the Oilers had 22 shots, a franchise record. A little over six minutes into the second period, on the power play, Weight completed his hat trick. Edmonton went on to win the game 5–2. Unfortunately, the Oilers lost the next two games, closely fought battles of 4–3 and 3–2.

Even though they couldn't get past Dallas, there were some bright points in the series. Boyd Devereaux had worked hard in these games. The Oilers had drafted Devereaux sixth overall in 1996. This was his first season as a full-timer, and in this series he showed that he could be a good utility player for the team.

At the end of the season, Lowe said, "In the stretch run and playoffs, there's no doubt we needed a few more players, particularly up front, with an edge to them. We'd like one or two more disturbers out there."

As head coach, Kevin Lowe was known to be emotional. He could kick trashcans, or join in the celebrations.

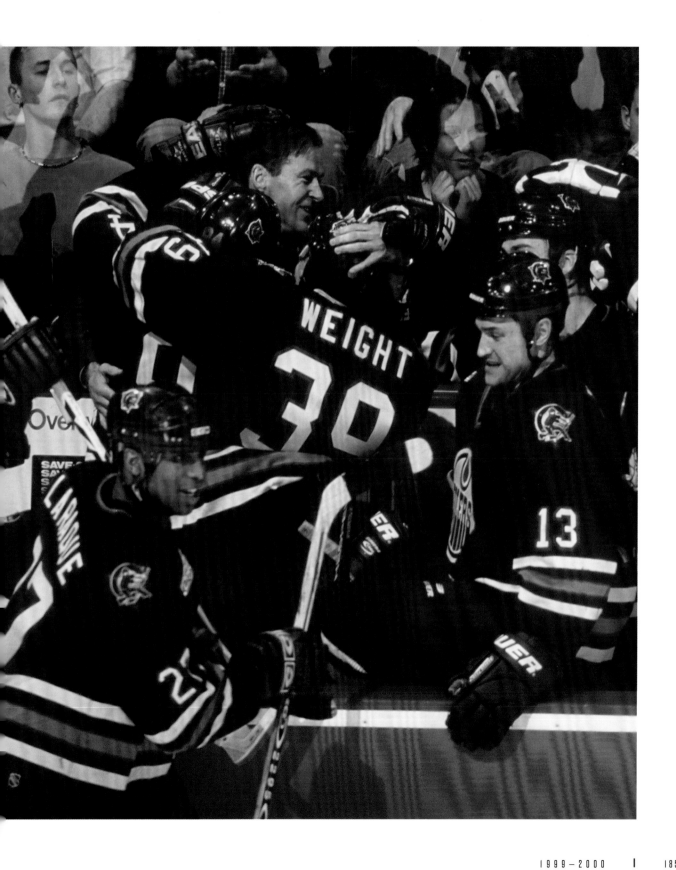

2000–2001

CHANGING OF THE GUARD

On May 19, sixteen years to the date of the Oilers winning their first Stanley Cup, Glen Sather stood behind a podium at the Skyreach Centre and announced his resignation. He had been devoted to and loved the Oilers organization. He was a legend in Edmonton, having started as a player with the WHA Oilers before taking over the coaching reins and remaining behind the bench as they joined the NHL. For years, as general manager, he had worked tirelessly to put competitive teams on the ice and had lately, amidst the ever-changing lineups, become the face of the franchise, the one constant. He had taken the Oilers to five Stanley Cup championships, nurtured boys into men, and was loved by the fans.

In the days leading up to the announcement, Bruce Saville and Jim F. Hole had taken on the task of negotiating a contract with Sather. Their fellow directors wouldn't approve the amount they proposed to offer. But that wasn't what got to Sather. He had wanted to give outgoing head scout Barry Fraser a watch to commemorate his service to the Oilers,

and that request, too, had been denied by the board. Today, Sather says, "It was a watch, for someone who had put in years of service. To me, it was time to go."

At the news conference, Glen Sather, always the prankster, mentioned that he'd read his horoscope on the plane, which said, "A clash of wills is almost inevitable, whether it's at work or home . . . just back off." It was a joke, but one that had meaning. He had done exactly that—backed off.

He stood in front of the media and gave his farewell speech. It didn't take Glen Sather long to get another job. A couple of weeks later, he ended up with the New York Rangers, the landing spot of so many famous Oilers before him.

BEGINNINGS

News of Sather's departure caused season-ticket sales to cool. This gave cause for concern, because the club needed to meet a quota of 13,000 subscribers to qualify for the NHL's $3 million subsidy—something it had been able to do every year since the FOTO drive back in 1996.

On New Year's Eve, Albertan Mike Comrie was signed to one of the highest rookie contracts.

Fans were saddened and disgruntled at Sather's sudden resignation, but the board had to deal with the question of who would take over as general manager.

The answer wasn't long in coming. They went to Kevin Lowe. But Lowe was also being pursued by Glen Sather to help on the bench with the New York Rangers. Today Lowe remembers his decision. On June 9, after several weeks of deliberation on his part, Kevin Lowe accepted the position with the Oilers. At 41, Lowe was just two years into his retirement as a player, followed by a year each as assistant coach and head coach, making him perhaps the most fast-tracked GM in NHL history.

Once Lowe signed on as GM, his first order of business was to hire a head coach. On June 22, he handed the reins to his teammate and friend Craig MacTavish.

With his work cut out for him, Lowe spent the summer getting up to speed on the financial realities of running a small-market team, making decisions about which players should stay and who should go.

Lowe made his first trade on June 24, acquiring Eric Brewer, Josh Green and the 35th-overall pick from the New York Islanders in exchange for Roman Hamrlik. Brewer, the fifth-overall pick in 1997, had had a good junior career with the Prince George Cougars of the WHL, playing the Canadian Hockey League Top Prospects Game. He was also an alternate captain for Canada's silver medal–winning team at the World Junior Championships in 1998. In his rookie season, 1998–99, he played 63 games for the Islanders, but split 1999–2000 between New York and their farm club, the Lowell Lock Monsters. An all-around defenceman with good hockey sense, the 21-year-old would play 315 games over the next four seasons for Edmonton.

On November 15, Lowe made a deal that was motivated at least in part by money. Bill Guerin was due to become a restricted free agent at the season's end, and with 22 points in Edmonton's first 21 games, his value and potential asking price were both on the rise. Rather than let him walk away in the off-season, the Oilers wanted to get a player in return, and Lowe felt that now was the time. So he sent Guerin to the Boston Bruins for Anson Carter, along with a first-round pick and a second-rounder in 2001.

Carter's path to Edmonton had taken many twists and turns. Back in 1992, he had waited a long time to hear his name called during the entry draft. Finally, with the 220th pick overall, the Quebec Nordiques selected him from the Wexford Raiders, a Junior A team in his hometown of Scarborough, Ontario. He attended Michigan State University for the next four years, after which the Nordiques—who had moved to Colorado—traded him to the Washington Capitals. Then, during his rookie season of 1996–97, the Caps traded him to Boston. His contract expired after the 1999–2000 season and, unable to come to terms with Bruins GM Harry Sinden, he waited for a trade and a new deal.

While he wasn't expected to match Guerin's offensive output, he had a couple of 20-goal seasons to his credit and he was four years younger. He fit

A welcome addition to the Oilers blue line, Eric Brewer had been a fifth overall pick in the 1997 NHL Entry draft.

Anson Carter filled some big shoes when he arrived in Edmonton after the Oilers traded Bill Guerin.

right in with the Oilers, coming fourth in scoring with 16 goals and 42 points in just 61 games.

In regular-season play, captain Doug Weight led the team on and off the ice. Playing in all 82 games, he put up 25 goals and 65 assists for 90 points—placing him eighth in the NHL. Ryan Smyth spent the summer wrangling with Lowe over a new contract, and was almost a no-show at training camp. But he signed a new deal on September 25, settling for less than he wanted. He rewarded the team, scoring 31 goals and recording a career-high 70 points, the second-highest total on the Oilers. Mike Comrie had left college and signed with the Kootenay Ice of the WHL, exploding for 39 goals and 70 points in 37 games. On New Year's eve, he signed a three-year, $10-million deal—well above the going rate for rookies. He racked up eight goals and 22 points in 41 games with Edmonton.

Todd Marchant garnered 39 points, Mike Grier and Rem Murray chipped in 36 each, and young Dan Cleary had 35. Georges Laraque may not have been the top scorer, but he made his mark, roughing up the opposition and sitting in the box for a total of 148 minutes. Playing fourth-line minutes, he contributed 13 goals and 29 points.

Tommy Salo was a workhorse in net, playing in 73 of 82 games, chalking up eight shutouts and winning a career-high 36 games. Backup goalies Joaquin Gage and Dominic Roussel got a lot of rest, appearing in just five and eight games, respectively.

The defence roster was a physical net bunch. Niinimaa and Poti led them with 46 and 32 points, while Brewer, Smith and Igor Ulanov provided an intimidating presence. Frank Musil was back after missing the entire 1999-2000 season with a spinal-cord injury suffered when he slid into the boards in practice. He returned in October 2000 and played the steady blueline game he was renowned for, but after appearing in just 13 games, the injury resurfaced, leaving him with weakness in his right arm. Unfortunately for the Oilers, his season was over as was his career.

STARS IN THE SKY

In mid-February, the Oilers had a nine-game winning streak, providing a much-needed boost to their playoff chances. They finished the season with a record of 39 wins, 31 losses (three in overtime) and 12 ties—their first winning record since 1991-92—and 93 points, a total they hadn't reached since the Cup-winning 1987-88 season. They again placed second in the Northwest Division, and were seeded sixth in the Western Conference.

And, perhaps unsurprisingly, for the fifth straight year, the Oilers were up against the Dallas Stars. In the 1980s, the Oilers had been known for their creative thinking and high-scoring game. After the lockout, the Stars became the team that led the way with their "trap" style. Their wins often came by stifling the opposition, holding a one goal advantage. With Ken Hitchcock, in his sixth year behind the bench as head coach of the Stars, this series would be a grind.

According to Hitchcock, "No matter where you went in Edmonton during playoffs, you were a villain. Even if you were born and raised in Edmonton, like me. You knew when you were playing Edmonton in playoffs. You were playing the entire city and you better realize that."

One day, he went to the Hotel McDonald to get a coffee and saw a homeless man asking for money. "I gave [him] a twenty-dollar bill," said Hitchcock. "And when I left him, he said

Posing for that casual team photo.

'I hope the Oilers beat the crap out of you tonight.' Everyone in Edmonton was a fan."

Game 1 started off on the right foot, with Ryan Smyth getting the first goal of the series. Dallas replied with a power-play marker by Mike Modano with just under two minutes to play in the second period, and won it on Jamie Langenbrunner's goal at 2:08 of overtime. The Oilers were ready for Game 2, but Dallas scored first this time, just 26 seconds into the game. Then the period got interesting. Dan Cleary popped one in for Edmonton to tie the score. Dallas replied not even two minutes later to regain the lead, and just 22 seconds after *that*, Georges Laraque responded with Edmonton's second goal. This rare bit of back-and-forth action was giving Dallas fans reason to cheer, but it was also firing up the Oilers bench. Before the period was over, Rem Murray scored to make it 3–2 for Edmonton. After the intermission, the Oilers returned to the ice convinced they could win the game. On a power play, Anson Carter blasted the puck past Ed Belfour to take a 4–2 lead. Dallas worked hard to come back, and managed to beat Salo once, early in the third period. But the score remained 4–3 and the Oilers won.

With a 1–1 series split, the Oilers returned home. Dallas took the lead early in the first period, and made it 2–0 six minutes into the third. With the last minute of play in regulation about to be announced, the Oilers, playing physical hockey, raced down the ice. Belfour left his net to try to clear the puck, but Laraque forechecked him, went deep, picked up the puck and snapped off a short pass to Smyth, who was beside the wide-open net. The time was 18:57 and the Oilers were on the scoreboard. With the fans back in the game, waving white towels and cheering, the Oilers desperately tried to get possession of the puck. When the Stars iced it, Edmonton coach MacTavish called a timeout.

The next faceoff was crucial. When play resumed, Smyth lined up to take it, but was waved out of the circle by the linesman. Murray stepped in and won the draw. The Oilers moved the puck around, jockeying for position in hopes of creating an opening in the Stars defence. When Brewer blasted a shot from the blue line, Murray was in the right position to tip it past Belfour. With 6.4 seconds left on the clock, the Oilers had tied the game. Tension reigned throughout the extra period, and with

just 12 seconds left on the clock, Dallas managed to put one past Salo.

Down two games to one, but with at least one more home game, the Oilers felt they could finally break the curse and eliminate the Stars. A confident team took the ice. No goals were scored in the first period, and it was Anson Carter who put the Oilers up 1–0 midway through the second. In the third, Dallas scored to tie the game, but by the time the buzzer sounded there had been no more scoring action. Another OT period was on the agenda. Posts, crossbars, diving goalies—these extra minutes had it all. In the end, it was young Mike Comrie who scored the winning goal, his first of the playoffs, at 17:19.

In Game 5, the Oilers found themselves trailing 2–0 after 40 minutes. But in the span of less than three minutes at the top of the period, they scored a trio of goals: Carter at 2:32, Weight (back from his game misconduct for checking from behind in Game 4) at 3:04 and Brewer on the power play at 5:29. Ahead for the first time in the game, the lead lasted for 10 minutes before John MacLean scored to tie it up. For the third game in five, the Oilers were facing overtime. And this time, it was Kirk Muller of Dallas who scored the winner.

Down but not out, the Oilers headed home for Game 6. Smyth scored first, and the Oilers held their 1–0 lead until the third period, when the Stars pounced and popped three goals past Salo. This time, there was no recovery.

Even with the loss, Craig MacTavish's debut as head coach was successful, as was Kevin Lowe's first season as GM.

Garnet "Ace" Bailey

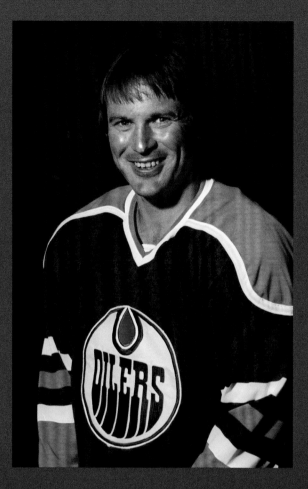

On September 11, 2001, former Oilers and Oil Kings winger Garnet "Ace" Bailey boarded United Airlines Flight 175 at Boston's Logan Airport, heading to Los Angeles for the opening of the Kings' training camp (he was the team's director of pro scouting). He never made it to LA. The plane he was on was hijacked during the terror attacks and crashed into the south tower of the World Trade Center in New York City.

Bailey, a former Boston Bruin, Detroit Red Wing, St. Louis Blue and Washington Capital, played only 38 games with the Oilers, in 1978–79. The following season, he coached Edmonton's farm team, the Houston Apollos of the Central Hockey League, and moved with them to Wichita a year later before joining the Oilers' scouting staff in 1982. He was with the club for 13 seasons before moving to the Kings.

On that fateful September day, Wayne Gretzky was devastated at the loss of his friend. "He had a huge influence because, listen, every human—everyone—has his bad days. You know, Ace had that influence on me because he knew the position that I was going to be in, that people didn't want to hear me having a bad day or a bad time. He taught me a lot about dealing with fans and people, but also about dealing with the media and things like that."

Ace Bailey had an infectious personality and was loved in the dressing room. Later, when he was scouting, players often went to him for guidance. "He had a presence about him," said Gretzky, who fought back tears after he heard the news. "I don't think he had any enemies because he was so well-liked by anyone, and he would do anything for anybody. He was very generous and very outgoing—he was just a tremendous man."

2001–2002

WEIGHT LOSS

The season had ended and the lake was beckoning, but Kevin Lowe was holed up, making trades, with a particular eye towards trying to save money to keep within the constraints of his budget. With each passing year, the economics of operating as a small-market team were cursing the Oilers. Players wanted more money, and many deservedly so, but the Oilers just didn't have the resources to offer raises.

Captain Doug Weight was one of those players. He was due to become a free agent in the summer of 2002, and as the team's leading scorer in seven of the last eight seasons, his asking price was bound to be high. So on June 30, Lowe sent him to the St. Louis Blues, along with Michel Riesen, for Jochen Hecht, Marty Reasoner and Jan Horacek.

Weight's departure left a leadership void, as well as an offensive one—in 588 regular-season games, he had recorded 577 points. The captaincy passed to defenceman Jason Smith, who was considered a veteran on this young team.

Riesen had never lived up to the expectations that came with being a first-round pick, and he wasn't able to play the Oilers' physical game

German-born Hecht came to the Oilers after two full seasons with St. Louis. The left winger had established himself as a two-way forward. A centre-man from Western New York, Reasoner had been a scorer when he played for Boston College. After parts of three seasons with the Blues, he was being called upon to be more of a role player. From the beginning, he was popular in the Oiler dressing room. Horacek, a Czech-born defenceman, never made the roster with Edmonton.

The Oilers had already taken a step that they hoped would add some scoring to their lineup, using the 13th-overall pick in the draft to select winger Ales Hemsky of the Hull Olympiques. In his first season of major junior hockey, Hemsky had logged 100 points in 68 games. On July 12, Edmonton signed free agent Steve Staios, a reliable defenceman who management hoped would also provide some offence. Staios had been drafted by the St. Louis Blues

in 1991, but after spending a few years in their farm system he had been traded to Boston in 1996. Stops in Vancouver and Atlanta followed.

Finally, head coach Craig MacTavish recruited a former teammate, Charlie Huddy, to join him behind the bench as assistant coach.

TWO POINTS SHY

The season started off on the upswing. By mid-December the Oilers had 44 points in 35 games and led the Northwest Division. What happened next is a bit of a mystery, but the Oilers fell into a slump that they just couldn't seem to get out of, going 9–16–7–1 in their next 33 games, falling 14 points behind Colorado. On March 19, Lowe traded forward Rem Murray and defenceman Tom Poti, who had just won a silver medal in the Olympics with Team USA, to the New York Rangers for left winger Mike York and a fourth-round pick in the 2002 draft. On the same day, they traded defenceman Sean Brown to the Boston Bruins for blueline prospect Bobby Allen.

York had been on a top scoring line with Eric Lindros and Theo Fleury. The hope was he would give the Oilers an offensive spark and help them earn a playoff spot. But in the last 12 regular-season games for the Oilers, he produced only two goals and two assists.

Despite going undefeated in nine games between March 14 and April 2, the Oilers fell just short of making the playoffs. The Vancouver Canucks ramped it up and came out just two points ahead of Edmonton. The race came down to the wire, but the Oilers' hopes were dashed when they lost their next-to-last game of the season to Calgary.

The Oilers came within one game of making the playoffs. If only they hadn't lost that last Battle of Alberta game.

Mike Comrie was MacTavish's go-to forward. He topped the team in scoring with 33 goals and 60 points. Anson Carter also racked up 60 points, on 28 goals and 32 assists. Ryan Smyth suffered a broken ankle in November and missed 21 games, but was able to contribute 50 points in 61 games. D-man Janne Niinimaa had 39 assists and 44 points to lead the defence corps.

Tommy Salo played 69 games in net, winning 30 and earning six shutouts. He had two new backups this year, Jussi Markkanen (14 games) and Ty Conklin (four games). Niinimaa, Smith, Eric Brewer and Steve Staios held the line against opposing scorers. All told, this year's edition of the Oilers allowed just 182 goals—only Colorado, with 169 goals against, was stingier.

Disappointing as it was to miss the playoffs, it seemed the club was doing a solid job of rebuilding for the future.

With Doug Weight heading off, Jason Smith's steadiness on ice and positive presence in the dressing room earned him the captaincy.

Jari Kurri's Banner Is Raised

The arena was dark, except for a spotlight shone in the direction of the players' gate. In that spotlight stood Jari Kurri in full gear. He skated onto the ice and waved his stick in the air, and the fans in the arena went crazy, cheering him. It was October 6, 2001, and the Oilers were playing their home opener against the Phoenix Coyotes, a team that Wayne Gretzky was now a part-owner of, but before the puck was dropped, Jari Kurri's Number 17 jersey was retired.

With his family by his side, having travelled from Finland, Jari watched in awe as his banner was raised to the rafters of the Skyreach Centre, next to Wayne Gretzky's Number 99 and Al Hamilton's Number 3. Lit up in the arena were the words "JARI, WELCOME HOME."

When he stepped up to the microphone, Jari talked about how the city of Edmonton and Oiler fans had always made him feel at home, and how the team had given him a chance to play in the National Hockey League. General manager Kevin Lowe, a former teammate of Jari's, described best how Numbers 99 and 17 had always been a magic combination: "I know Oilers fans have many terrific memories of the phrase 'Gretzky to Kurri . . . scores!'" He went on to say that Kurri was one of the best European players to play the game and an integral part of the Oilers during their Stanley Cup championship years.

Kurri was also inducted into the NHL Hockey Hall of Fame on November 12, 2001—the first Finnish player to be so honoured and the third Oiler.

2002-2003

SECOND TIME AROUND

The Oilers had 15 picks scattered across the nine rounds of the 2002 draft in Toronto, but the one who clicked was their third selection, taken 36th overall. Centreman Jarret Stoll had actually been drafted before, by the Calgary Flames, 46th overall, in 2000. But the Flames were unable to sign him, and with his rights due to expire on June 1, 2002, they traded him to the Toronto Maple Leafs. Toronto tried to notify the NHL office by fax, but it didn't go through, and that odd failure meant Stoll was able to re-enter the draft in 2002. Stoll was now 20 years old and had the benefit of two more years' worth of seasoning with the Kootenay Ice of the WHL. He played primarily for the Oilers' Hamilton farm team in 2002–03, appearing in four games with Edmonton.

OVERCOMING A SLOW START

The 2002–03 edition of the team could rely on a solid core of forwards. Todd Marchant, Ryan Smyth, Mike Comrie, Anson Carter and Mike York all ended up with 20 or more goals for the season. Plus, 19-year-old Ales Hemsky and 24-year-old Shawn Horcoff were showing their worth, and were being groomed by Coach MacTavish to play bigger roles in the future.

Still, the season started off slowly, the Oilers winning only one game in their first seven. But then the team picked up steam, and by the March 11 trade deadline they were sitting in a playoff position. On that final day of trading, the team dealt some fan favourites who had been with the Oilers for a while. Janne Niinimaa was traded, along with a second round pick in 2003, to the New York Islanders for wingers Brad Isbister and Raffi Torres. Anson Carter and rookie defenceman Ales Pisa were sent to the New York Rangers for right winger Radek Dvorak and defenceman Cory Cross.

Edmonton-born Isbister had had some good years with the Islanders, though he had spent some time on injured reserve in 2002–03. He played in the Oilers' last 13 regular-season games, recording five points, and appeared in all six playoff games. A young, offensively minded hard-hitter,

Farewell to Wild Bill

The Oilers lost a founder and a true hockey man on December 16, 2002, when Wild Bill Hunter died after battling cancer for four years. Hunter was instrumental in starting the World Hockey Association and the Alberta (and then Edmonton) Oilers. He also helped get Northlands Coliseum built, and although he had sold the Oilers by the time they joined the NHL, he was recognized for playing a huge part in the team existing. Hunter had been inducted into Canada's Sports Hall of Fame and was appointed to the Order of Canada. He was a man with a vision, and that was to bring professional hockey to Edmonton. General Manager Kevin Lowe said, "Wild Bill had stayed involved with the team until his last days."

Torres was only 21 and was sent to Hamilton for the rest of the season. He would slot into a full-time role in 2003–04. Czech-born Dvorak had scored 30 goals for the Rangers in 2000–01 and helped out on offence down the stretch with Edmonton. Cross came from Lloydminster, Alberta, and prior to turning pro he'd played with the University of Alberta Golden Bears, winning a national collegiate champion-ship in 1992. Now 32 and with a decade's worth of NHL experience, he added depth and expertise to the Oilers blue line.

Edmonton finished the season with a 36–26–11–9 record and 92 points, good enough for fourth place in the Northwest Division and the final playoff spot in the Western Conference.

IF IT'S APRIL, WE MUST BE IN DALLAS

For the sixth time in seven years, the Oilers were matched with the Dallas Stars in the first round of the playoffs. When Edmonton prevailed 2–1 in Game 1 at the American Airlines Center in Dallas, fans back home got excited.

Oozing confidence, the Oilers got a wake-up call in Game 2. Marty Reasoner opened the scoring, but the Stars potted six unanswered goals to even the series.

Former Oiler Jason Arnott led the charge with a goal and two assists.

Even so, the crowd at the Skyreach Centre was hooting and hollering, as only Edmonton fans can do, as the puck dropped for Game 3. It was as if the 6–1 shellacking had made their passion even louder. The arena shook and fans waved colourful signs, painted their faces, wore crazy wigs and stood on their feet for every rush and hard hit. They taunted Stars goalie Marty Turco, waving noodles at him. On the bench, Craig MacTavish sometimes had to communicate with his players using hand gestures because they couldn't hear him. Defenceman Steve Staios had a hard time talking to his blueline partner, Jason Smith.

Arnott continued his assault, scoring the first goal of the game midway through the first period, and the 1–0 lead held up throughout the second. Early in the third, Tommy Salo cleared the puck to Mike York, but it was Georges Laraque who ended up in scoring position. He slapped it in the net for the Oilers, giving Salo an assist on the goal. Jere Lehtinen responded to make it 2–1 Dallas, but with the fans behind them, the Oilers pounded back. Fernando Pisani, a 26-year-old rookie who was drafted by the Oilers in 1996, made the most of his opportunity, tying the game. Not a minute later, Dvorak scored to give the Oilers a 3–2 lead and the win. "They were almost like a sixth man," Laraque said of the fans after the game. Dvorak added, "The game is much easier for us because of them."

But not even 17,000 rabid fans could help the Oilers in Game 4, a 3–1 loss. With the series tied, the teams headed back to Texas. In the first period, Dallas scored on a power play after Ethan Moreau drew a double minor. Less than a minute later—this time with D-man Scott Ferguson in the box for obstruction—they made it 2–0. The Stars had little trouble skating to a 5–2 victory.

Once again, the Oiler faithful put glitter in their hair and paint on their faces for Game 6, and one even wore a tinfoil Stanley Cup. Down 2–0 after the first period, Smyth and Horcoff each scored to tie it up in the second. Things were looking good. But Mike Modano's goal at 13:08 of the third was all the Stars needed to put the game away. Despite outplaying Dallas on this night, the Oilers were going home for the summer.

The loss didn't sit well with the Oilers' coaching and management team. Lowe visited the dressing room after the game and let the team know what he thought. In his opinion, they hadn't played hard enough to win.

Consequently, some of the players became upset, some feathers were ruffled, and the summer became blackened by holdouts and contract issues.

Veteran centre Todd Marchant, an Oiler since 1994, wasn't sure about his future. He was soon to become an unrestricted free agent, and with 20 goals and 60 assists he was coming off a career year. It was the same old story for the Edmonton Oilers. There was little doubt that another team would pay Marchant more than the Oilers could afford.

PART 5

2003—2018

EDMONTON FIRST

A new era begins for the Oilers, bringing the first ever Heritage Classic game, a tremendous run to the Stanley Cup finals, a new owner, and a beautiful new arena. And years of rebuilding delivers exciting potential for the future.

2003-2004

FREE-AGENT DEPARTURES

On July 1, fast-skating Todd Marchant became an unrestricted free agent, and it wouldn't be long before a team offered him a contract he couldn't refuse. More than one club expressed interest, but he signed a multiyear deal with the Columbus Blue Jackets after just two days on the market.

Mike Comrie was also without a contract as of Canada Day, but as a restricted free agent he lacked leverage. Negotiations were unproductive. As autumn came to Edmonton and the leaves began to turn golden, Comrie remained unsigned, so he didn't report for training camp or take part in preseason action. At one point, general manager Kevin Lowe approached the Mighty Ducks of Anaheim, offering Comrie's rights in exchange for a prospect, Corey Perry, and a first-round draft pick. The deal-breaker was a question over fair value. Lowe wanted Comrie to "compensate the Oilers for all the money they'd paid him [signing bonus] because Corey Perry was unsigned and the Oilers knew they

would have to pay him a couple of million in a signing bonus, of which our ownership didn't want to pay." Lowe held firm. "In our minds, it's not fair market value, so we asked Mike Comrie to top up the deal." Today, Lowe adds, "The interesting thing is, the Comries apparently thought it was fair and were considering paying the money themselves, but the Players Association heard about it and nixed it. Could you imagine the precedent that would have set!"

And so, without the compensation deal in place, the standoff began. Lowe was willing to wait for a more suitable trade, which came on December 16. Comrie was sent to the Philadelphia Flyers for defenceman Jeff Woywitka, a first-round pick in 2004 and a third-rounder in 2005. Woywitka had been drafted 27th overall by the Flyers in 2001, and the Flyers still considered him a top prospect, but his name never graced the Edmonton Oilers score sheet.

On November 17, the Oilers signed 41-year-old Adam Oates as a free agent. Oates had played with Anaheim the year before, helping them get to the Stanley Cup finals. Oates came to the Oilers not having trained—no one had signed him after the previous season—and he struggled in his swan song. But he had great things to say about the 60 games he played for Edmonton in his one season there. "I was playing with Hemsky and I was older than both of his parents," said Oates to the Edmonton Journal. "But they treated me great. It's a first-class organization."

RENAMING THE RINK FOR REXALL

Edmonton billionaire Daryl Katz put his mark on the Oilers for the first time in November 2003, when he paid to change the name of the arena from Skyreach Centre to Rexall Place for 10 years. Skyreach Equipment, owned by Barry Weaver, was going through some financial difficulties, so Weaver was more than willing to give up the name to another local businessman. Born in 1961 in Edmonton, Katz had attended Ross Sheppard High School, going on to the University of Alberta for his undergrad degree and law school.

His father, Barry, ran two drugstores when he was growing up, and Katz eventually took over the business, building it into a billion-dollar venture. Katz had been at U of A in the '80s, when the Oilers dynasty was picking up steam, and he loved the team. In that era, Edmonton still had the feeling of a small town, and Oilers like Kevin Lowe, Mark Messier and Wayne Gretzky made friends with some of the locals their age, including Katz. To him, nothing could have been better or more exciting than those Stanley Cup championships and the

friendships he developed over those wonderful years. "We were a young city with a young team and the best hockey player the world had ever seen," he said.

The electric atmosphere that overtook the city during those years still burned in Daryl's mind a couple of decades later, so putting the name of his family's drugstore chain on the arena was a thrill. And if it helped advertise the business, it was a win-win.

THE HERITAGE CLASSIC

Two days after the renaming of the arena, the NHL played its first regular-season outdoor game in Edmonton. Fifteen years later, fans are familiar with the many Heritage Classics and Winter Classics and Stadium Series games that have been played, but in 2003 it was truly a novelty. The game was the brainchild of three men, who cooked up the idea on a plane trip home from Los Angeles after the NHL All-Star Game in 2002: Oilers governor and chairman of the board of the Edmonton Investors Group, Cal Nichols; Oilers president and CEO Pat LaForge; and Oilers VP of Marketing Allan Watt. They had been pondering the type of hockey on display at the all-star game, feeeling it didn't show the game's skill, speed and competitiveness. Typically, that event was more about the owners and sponsors schmoozing and having fun while NHL players happened to be on the ice.

The Oilers desperately needed more revenue, and LaForge was always thinking of new strategies. Towards that end, the club had already put in a bid to host

the 2004 NHL All-Star Game. The three
men sat side by side, LaForge in the
middle seat with his tray down, jotting
down ideas on napkins.

As they brainstormed, LaForge suddenly remembered a research study that
Molson had done, asking what fans
would like to see in regards to professional hockey. One of the insights that
the study had produced was that fans
wanted to see NHL players playing on
an outdoor pond. What about Lake
Louise? Pat wrote that down. The ideas
kept flowing, and by the time the plane
landed, there was a renewed focus on
the outdoor concept.

Lake Louise proved unworkable, but

LaForge went to the management of
Commonwealth Stadium and found out
that, yes, a quality sheet of outdoor ice
could be installed there. Then came the
matter of persuading the NHL to sign
on to the idea. LaForge devised a plan.
The Oilers talked to Wayne Gretzky,
who was instantly convinced, and out
of their conversation came an idea:
What if they held an alumni game as
well as the regular-season game?

Next, the Oilers pitched the package to
NHL commissioner Gary Bettman, who
was not keen on the idea. Undeterred,
the Oilers staff met to brainstorm and
keep the idea alive. When Glen Sather
was called, he joked that he had left

Steve Staios joined the
roster in 2001–02 and
stayed for seven seasons.
Here, he celebrates a
moment in the first
Heritage Classic game.

Edmonton to get out of the cold—why would he want to come back and play in an outdoor game? In reality, he was too committed to the New York Rangers to get away. So they turned to the president of the Montreal Canadiens, Pierre Boivin. Boivin didn't immediately agree, but neither did he reject it. Since Gretzky had shown interest, they went back to him for further conversations.

The work was challenging. The executive director of the players' association, Bob Goodenow, was concerned for the safety of the players, while Bettman just didn't think it was a sound idea. But, with persistence from the Oilers, they finally both agreed it was worth investigation. On the alumni side, LaForge engaged in a bit of scheming, approaching Gretzky and telling him, "Guy Lafleur and Larry Robinson challenge you to put a team together."

Gretzky simply responded, "Let them know I'm up to the challenge."

Next, the Oilers got in touch with the Montreal Canadiens, and Guy Lafleur: "Wayne Gretzky challenges you. He'll pick a team from Oilers history and you'll pick a team from Montreal history. He challenges you to play outdoors in Edmonton." The Canadiens were quick to respond: "Wayne! Wayne challenges us?"

The alumni game was played on the afternoon of November 22, 2003. Ticket sales were phenomenal, even though they were priced higher than Oilers tickets usually went for. Commonwealth Stadium seats 57,000 and there was a full house that afternoon, despite temperatures of –22 degrees Celsius. Edmonton is known for cold weather, but the average temperature at that time of year is around 3 degrees. The mass of

Even the frigid Edmonton cold couldn't stop these players from having fun at the Heritage Classic alumni game.

cold air arrived just a few days before the game and it was too late to consider a change of plans.

Gretzky and Lafleur's teams put on a show, even though you could see their breath. The dressing rooms were heated, as were the benches, and none of the players complained. Edmonton fans didn't complain, either. They were thrilled to be a part of such a fantastic spectacle.

Then came the main event that evening. Just before the present-day Oilers and Canadiens faced off, a meeting took place in a stadium hallway between Bettman, Goodenow, and production crew members. Should they go ahead? Was it safe for the players to play in such cold weather? This wasn't an exhibition game, and no one wanted to see injuries or unfair playing conditions. Finally, Bettman decided that he was going to stop the game. Fortunately, the Oilers' team doctor, David Reid, spoke up: "My father flew a bomber from France to England over the English Channel with a broken windshield in colder weather than this and he survived." It was enough.

The game went on as scheduled, and the event showed Edmontonians that hockey was alive and well in their city. It was so successful that the media began to speculate on what it meant for the future. An *Edmonton Journal* article appeared shortly afterward, under the headline "Will Heritage games spring up around NHL?" The subtitle that followed was more direct: "Successful precedent set in Edmonton that could and should be copied elsewhere."

Both alumni and current players loved the event. Messier said, "It's not only the 57,000 who came to see the game, it's the 57,000 who came with enthusiasm. That's what's incredible about it—I guess that's what makes Edmonton special."

Georges Laraque added to that: "I thought that after the first game when they saw Wayne, everybody was going to go home because it was so cold out there. At the bench we had warmers, but the fans didn't. But they stayed for both games. You looked around and the stands were packed."

AN UP-AND-DOWN SEASON

The Heritage Classic may have boosted both morale and the bottom line, but there was no escaping the fact that the Oilers were a small-market team without a large budget for player salaries in a league where payrolls were strongly tied to on-ice success. With the collective bargaining agreement between the players' association and the league due to expire in September 2004, the two sides had already begun negotiations. The owners were again looking for a deal that included a salary cap, which they viewed as the solution to escalating player salaries.

Meanwhile, there was a season to be played. In the run-up to the Heritage Classic, the Oilers had a record of 10–7–2–0, but then they went into a midseason slump, going 10–17–6–1 in their next 34 games. As January ended, they were in last place in the Northwest Division and 12th in the Western

Mark Messier looks for a pass from a fellow Oiler alumnus.

A Night for Number 31

On October 9, 2003, prior to the Oilers' game against the San Jose Sharks, the spotlight was trained on the net. In the crease stood a goalie, in full gear, a mask covering his face. He lifted his mask, and the fans, who loved these ceremonies, raised their voices to the rafters. Grant Fuhr waved and skated around the ice, making sure he did a complete lap. With his family by his side, Fuhr's Number 31 jersey was retired and a commemorative banner was raised.

In a press conference prior to the event, Fuhr had said, "This is beyond my wildest dreams, especially growing up here. I used to watch the Oilers when they were in the WHA, playing at the old Edmonton Gardens. They were the Alberta Oilers back then, and I hate to admit how long ago that was. I'd go to the games with my dad, watching Jack Norris in goal and Ken Brown, and then they brought in Jacques Plante. He was in his mid–40s then, but he was a legend."

Fuhr had always wanted to be a goalie. The years he spent defending the Oiler net were spectacular, and he had been a big part of the Cup-winning teams. He may not have recorded the most shutouts of any goaltender, but his team was young and fast and played a run-and-gun style of hockey. Fuhr was often left alone to save the day.

Fuhr was also inducted into the Hockey Hall of Fame on November 3, becoming the fourth Oiler to receive the honour. During his induction ceremony, it was said that "Fuhr often never received his due because he played for a team capable of scoring on every shift and allowing a breakaway on every other." He was finally getting his due.

Conference. They rallied in the final third of the season, going 16–5–4–4, and the hot streak continued even after the trading deadline, when starting goalie Tommy Salo was dealt to the Colorado Avalanche for defenceman Tom Gilbert, a prospect currently playing for the University of Wisconsin, and a sixth-round pick in 2005. Picking up the slack in net was Ty Conklin, who had signed with the Oilers in 2001. The Oilers also acquired Petr Nedved from the Rangers in March. He contributed 15 points in 16 games as Edmonton tried to make that push into the postseason.

Although no Oiler reached 60 points this year, Edmonton was ninth in the league in scoring. Ryan Smyth led the way with 23 goals and 36 assists, while Raffi Torres and Ethan Moreau each had 20. They scored more goals than they gave up, and Conklin's .912 save percentage was a tick above the NHL average.

But despite the end-of-season effort, the Oilers finished ninth in the West, two points out of the playoffs. For the Oilers, not only was their summer vacation beginning early, but this time it would last a lot longer than anyone might've expected.

Raffi Torres scores the game-winning goal in his Oilers debut, the same night that Fuhr's banner was raised.

2004-2005

THE SEASON NOT PLAYED

On September 15, 2004, the NHL Board of Governors voted unanimously to lock out the players for the second time in the league's history, effective the following day. Players and management, who hadn't met for negotiations in nearly a week, were unable to see eye to eye on a host of items, including a hard salary cap.

In 1994–95, the two sides had been able to come together on a deal that salvaged the year, with a shortened season and the Stanley Cup playoffs. The owners' resolve was much stronger this time, and by February 16, 2005, still with no deal in place, NHL commissioner Gary Bettman announced that the entire season, including the playoffs, would be cancelled. "We profoundly regret the suffering this has caused our fans, our business partners and the thousands of people who depend on our industry for their livelihoods," Bettman said. "If you want to know how I feel, I'll summarize it in one word—terrible."

The executive director of the NHL Players' Association, Bob Goodenow, commented too: "Every day that this thing continues, we don't think it's good for the game." He felt the players had been prepared to make enough concessions and shouldn't have to give any more. "Every offer by the players moved in the owners' direction," he said. "Keep one thing perfectly clear. The players never asked for more money— they just asked for a marketplace."

It took until July 13 for an agreement to be reached, and nine days later, on July 22, the lockout officially ended. It had lasted 10 months and six days. Under the new collective bargaining agreement there would be new free-agency rules, a new drug-testing policy, and changes in the rules of play, including the introduction of a shootout to break the tie in any game that remained deadlocked after five minutes of four-on-four overtime. Of the greatest interest to the Oilers were a salary cap and a one-time 24 percent cut in player salaries. Finally, they might be able to afford some better players to bolster their roster.

Paul Coffey celebrates winning the Cup, 1984 (left). Coffey poses (right) with Hockey Hall of Fame Chairman Bill Hay.

Number 7 Enters the Hall

While the NHL didn't play hockey this season, the Hall of Fame still had its annual induction ceremony. On November 8, 2004, fast-skating, high-scoring defenceman Paul Coffey was inducted. He was the fifth Oiler to stand up in such a way and speak about the sport he loved so much. In his speech, he commented on his time in Edmonton and how much he had learned. He told the story of how after practice one day, as a rookie, he took his practice jersey off and attempted to throw it on the ping-pong table that was in the middle of the room. It fell to the floor. Before he could get over to pick it up, Lee Fogolin walked over, picked up the jersey, folded it, and placed it on the table. He walked away, giving Coffey a look, and quietly said, "Never, ever throw your jersey on the floor." Coffey also noted that the Oilers were filled with superstars, but it was the character guys, like Semenko, Hunter, McSorley, McClelland, Jackson and Sparky (assistant equipment manager Lyle Kulchisky) that made going to the rink fun.

2005-2006

ADDING SOME STAR POWER

General manager Kevin Lowe wasted no time in using the new CBA to his club's advantage. The NHL had instilled a salary cap of $39 million for the 2005–06 season, which meant teams with bigger pre-lockout budgets had to make extreme cuts to their payrolls, in part by unloading players. This is how the Oilers were able to land Hart and Norris Trophy-winning defenceman Chris Pronger from the St. Louis Blues on August 2. In return, the Blues got defencemen Eric Brewer, Jeff Woywitka and Doug Lynch. Pronger stood six foot six and was tough and mean. Best of all, he was able to quarterback the power play with his booming shot from the point. As a junior, he had been named the Canadian Hockey League's Defenceman of the Year, and his Peterborough Petes had reached the Memorial Cup final. He'd also won gold medals in the World Junior Championship (1993), the World Championship (1997) and the Olympics (2002). In the NHL, in addition to MVP and top-defenceman honours in 2000, he'd been a first-team all-star. He was a

winner. According to Lowe, "Acquiring Chris Pronger and signing him to a new six year contract (the largest by far in Oilers history at the time) in the summer of 2005 represented the dawn of a new era for Edmonton. A ton of credit goes to Craig MacTavish for his influencing Pronger to come to Edmonton. After the 2004–05 work stoppage, the new Collective Bargaining Agreement was predicted to provide a fairer landscape for small market teams like the Oilers and Chris coming to Edmonton was a direct result of that."

The next day, the Oilers added another award-winning player: two-way centre Michael Peca of the New York Islanders. To get him, Lowe sent Mike York and a fourth-round draft pick to Long Island. Peca had received the Frank J. Selke Trophy as the NHL's best defensive forward in both the 1996–97 and 2001–02 seasons. He had also been the captain of the Buffalo Sabres when they went to the Stanley Cup finals in 1999. His nickname, "Captain Crunch," reflected his style of play.

Because of the lockout, the 2005 NHL Entry Draft was unusual in many ways.

Chris Pronger quarterbacked the Oilers blue line for the 2005–06 season, and cleared tough players (such as Brendan Shanahan) from the slot.

First of all, it was held on July 30 and 31, about a month later than usual, and it wasn't open to the public. Because no games had been played in 2004–05, there were no standings on which to base the draft order—which raised the question of how to determine which team would get the right to select highly touted centreman Sidney Crosby. The solution the NHL arrived at was to hold a lottery, awarding each team between one and three ping pong balls based on their performance in recent years. The Pittsburgh Penguins, one of the teams that got three balls, won the lottery and the Number 1 pick. The Oilers, among the group that received two balls, got the 25th slot, and they selected left winger Andrew Cogliano from St. Michael's College School in Toronto. He chose to attend the University of Michigan in 2005–06.

A CINDERELLA STORY

This first season after the lockout was a Cinderella story for the Oilers. As Kevin Lowe said, "We were the poster child for the lockout."

Craig MacTavish was back as head coach, assisted by former Oiler players Charlie Huddy and Craig Simpson, as well as Billy Moore, who had been with the team since June 2000. Moore's career with Edmonton started back when he played on the 1966–67 Memorial Cup Edmonton Oil Kings. Opening night found Oilers fans in a complete frenzy. After being denied NHL hockey for the last 16 months, they showed up two hours early and cheered relentlessly as their beloved team stepped on the ice. Shawn Horcoff scored twice to lead the Oilers to a 4–3 victory over the Colorado Avalanche.

Wins in the first three games generated an early buzz, but after a seven-game losing streak, followed by a five-game winning string, fans were left wondering what to expect from this year's team. Mid-November found them with a record of nine wins, nine losses in regulation and a loss in overtime. It certainly wasn't the worst start the franchise had ever had, but it wasn't great, either. The Oilers needed to regroup and push ahead, and that's exactly what happened. They went on a tear, winning 21 of their next 36 games. They were not only in the playoff picture, but were in a four-way battle for first place in the Northwest Division.

By this point, Lowe had added some veteran help on the blue line, trading Jani Rita and Cory Cross to Pittsburgh for Dick Tarnstrom, and minor-leaguer Tony Salmelainen to Chicago for Jaroslav Spacek. On March 8, looking for an upgrade in goal, he traded Edmonton's first-round pick in 2006 and a third-rounder in 2007 to the Minnesota Wild

for Dwayne Roloson. In 2003–04, Roloson had played in the NHL All-Star Game and led the league in save percentage. When he dropped his first three games, allowing 13 goals, fans and media alike questioned whether the team had overpaid, but in time he grew more comfortable in an Oilers jersey.

The next day, at the trade deadline, Marty Reasoner, Yan Stastny and a second-round pick were dealt to Boston (the Bruins ended up drafting Milan Lucic) for offensively minded Russian winger Sergei Samsonov, who put up 16 points in 19 games down the stretch.

As the team continued their up and down season, chatter continued over the roster moves. Fans kept their hopes up as Edmonton remained in the playoff hunt.

On the morning of April 13, after 80 games, the Oilers sat in eighth place in the Western Conference, a single point ahead of the Vancouver Canucks. Both teams were scheduled to play that night, and an Oiler victory over Anaheim,

Ready to jump when the buzzer goes, on the bench and in the seats. Edmonton was glad to be back in the playoffs, winning games and series.

A Fitting Goodbye

"The only word that describes it for me is overwhelming," said Paul Coffey when his Number 7 jersey was retired on October 18, 2005. The fastest, smoothest skater to ever play in the NHL laced up his skates and did a lap around the ice before the Oilers took on the Phoenix Coyotes. Even at 44, he made it look easy. The sight of Coffey skating on the Rexall Place ice was a definite crowd-pleaser. Because of his contract dispute, the defenceman had never had the chance to have a fitting goodbye when he left the Oilers, so this was an extra-special night for him as well as the fans. His immediate family was beside him, as well as former teammates Wayne Gretzky—who was coaching the visiting Coyotes—and Kevin Lowe. "I remember going into Boston Garden and seeing Bobby Orr's jersey [in the rafters]," said Coffey, "thinking, 'Wouldn't that be great, but it will probably never happen.'" Looking back now, it's hard to imagine a defenceman more deserving than Paul Coffey.

Bettman watching a playoff game with owner Cal Nichols. Perhaps sizing up how smaller market teams were fairing after the lockout?

combined with a Vancouver loss to San Jose in regulation time, would clinch a postseason berth for Edmonton.

Ales Hemsky's goal at 19:26 of the third period gave the Oilers a 2–1 decision over the Mighty Ducks, and the players and coaches hurried to the players' lounge to catch the end of the Canucks–Sharks game, which had started 90 minutes after their own. Vancouver led 3–2 after the second period, but San Jose came back to take a 4–3 lead midway through the third. There was a silence in the room and all eyes were glued to the television screen. Everyone held their breath until Jonathan Cheechoo's empty-netter in the final seconds put the game out of Vancouver's reach. The room erupted in cheering.

Edmonton went on to win at home against Colorado, finishing with a 41–28–13 record, giving them 95 points. Several Oilers had breakout seasons. Hemsky led the club with 58 assists and 77 points. Horcoff had 73 points, including 22 goals, while Jarret Stoll notched 22 goals and 68 points. Ryan Smyth led

the team in goals, with 36, and was fourth in points, with 66. To no one's surprise, Chris Pronger led Oiler defence-men—with 56 points, including 12 goals.

Fernando Pisani, the crafty Edmonton-born forward drafted in the eighth round in 1996, contributed 18 goals and 37 points. Signed as a free agent by Edmonton in 2001, Marc-Andre Bergeron was a fast-skating defenceman who liked to carry the puck from one end of the rink to the other.

The Oilers' opponents in the Western Conference quarter-final were the Detroit Red Wings, who had finished atop the NHL with 58 wins and 124 points—21 more than the Oilers. Detroit was considered the overwhelming favou-rite. But Oiler captain Jason Smith didn't see it that way. "We liked each other. We were a close group and we hung out at the rink and away from the rink. There was no drama with this team, and we even had fun with our families. We all had one goal in mind."

The first game, played at Joe Louis

Arena, was everything playoff action was supposed to be. Detroit took a 1-0 lead on Robert Lang's first-period power-play goal, but by the midpoint of the game it was 2-1 Oilers on the strength of power-play markers by Samsonov and Pronger. Former Oiler Kirk Maltby tied the game with six minutes left in regulation time, and scored the winner at 2:39 of the second overtime period on the Red Wings' 57th shot of the game.

Before the Oilers lined up for the faceoff in Game 2, Coach MacTavish called rookie Brad Winchester over. He explained the playoff tradition in Detroit, one that dates back to 1952 where fans throw an octopus on the ice, and an arena worker retrieves it and twirls it around to get the fans going. MacTavish told Winchester that when the octopus was thrown onto the ice surface, he should go and get it. Winchester nodded his head. As a rookie, he was in no position to turn down a request from the coach. Sure enough, in warm-up, an octopus landed on the ice, Winchester quickly skated over, picked it up with his bare hand and carried it to the Oilers bench.

Did this bold gesture turn the tables? Hockey players are superstitious guys. Or maybe it relieved the pressure on the visiting Oilers. Either way, they came back from a 2-1 deficit to win 4-2 and tie the series, with Winchester scoring the go-ahead goal. Back in Edmonton for Game 3, the crowd noise blasted off the walls of Rexall Place. The Oilers took an early 1-0 lead on a goal by Jaroslav Spacek, and the goal stood up for eight minutes before Henrik Zetterberg tied it up on a Detroit power play. Crashing the net, Smyth landed the puck in the back of the net to take the team to the dressing room with a 2-1 lead. All looked good for the Oilers in the second, when Raffi Torres scored. Then the wheels fell off and Detroit scored two goals in just 18 seconds in the third, forcing overtime. Finally, at 8:44 of the second extra period, Jarret Stoll saved the day, making the fans in Rexall scream as he scored the

Fernando Pisani was a force during the Oilers Stanley Cup run. He had 14 goals and 4 assists in 24 playoff games.

game-winner to give the Oilers a 2–1 lead in the series.

The team's power-play units showed their strength in Game 4, also played in Edmonton. The Oilers kicked things off at 7:22 of the first, as Pisani scored while Detroit's Jason Williams sat out with a penalty for hooking. But at 13:25, with Steve Staios in the box, Detroit's Tomas Holmstrom scored with the man advantage. In the last minute of the first period, Detroit pulled ahead on Robert Lang's goal—the only one of the game to be scored at even strength. Not to be outdone, Spacek tied it in the second, but Nicklas Lidstrom and Henrik Zetterberg gave Detroit the win in the third period.

Prior to Game 5, MacTavish again instructed Winchester to grab the octopus, but this time, he wore a rubber glove under his hockey glove. In Game 2, he had learned his lesson—the Octopus stunk. He proudly brought the trophy back to the Oilers bench and all the guys laughed. They were fired up, but no goals were scored in that first period. The second period was a different story. Goals by Pisani, Smyth and Horcoff gave the Oilers a 3–0 lead. The Oilers defence, especially Pronger, played a solid game, and Roloson stopped 30 of 32 shots. After 40 minutes, it was 3–1 Edmonton. The Red Wings pressed, but came up just short, able to muster only one more goal with 22 seconds left in the game. The Oilers had a 3–2 victory *and* a 3–2 series lead.

As the teams returned to Edmonton for Game 6, a major upset was within the Oilers' grasp, and the fans were ready. Local radio personality Chris Sheets suggested on the air that perhaps Oilers fans should start throwing steaks on the ice. A few passionate fans ran with that idea, and there were even a few arrests made because of the thrown steaks.

The Oilers trailed 2–0 after 40 minutes. In the dressing room, Captain Jason Smith settled the guys down. They talked about being a team, how everyone was important. This was their game and their fans. And barely three minutes into the third period, Fernando Pisani found a way to beat Red Wing goalie Manny Legace. Then, at 6:40, he scored again to tie it up. The period was like a hard-fought tennis match. Johan Franzen put the Wings ahead 3–2, and then young Ales Hemsky crashed the net and scored a gritty goal to make it 3–3. The clock ticked down. With a little over a minute left, Samsonov was behind Detroit's net. He fired a pass to Hemsky, who nailed a one-timer to roof the puck over Legace's shoulder. The fans nearly blew the roof off the arena. The players hugged. The Oilers had won their first playoff series since 1998, when in another upset they had beaten Colorado.

Next up for the Oilers were the San Jose Sharks, whose offence was led by 56-goal scorer Jonathan Cheechoo, Patrick Marleau and scoring champion Joe Thornton. In Game 1, Spacek managed to open the scoring, but the hometown Sharks forechecked aggressively, played a very physical game and outshot the Oilers 30–16 for a 2–1 victory. In Game 2, Raffi Torres landed an open-ice hit on San Jose winger Milan Michalek, who had assisted on Tom Preissing's goal that made it 1–0 Sharks. Michalek went down hard. He didn't return to play for the rest of the game. Still, Thornton scored late in the second to make it 2–1, which stood as the final score.

When the team hit the ice for Game 3, the true-blue Edmonton fans greeted them with volume, energizing the team. Racing up and down the ice, hitting whoever needed to be hit and firing the puck, the Oilers outshot the Sharks 15–2 in the first period. But the score was only 1–0, from a goal by Bergeron. One-goal leads rarely hold up in playoff hockey, even if a team is being outplayed. At one point, Pronger had the puck and needed to clear it. Feisty Ryan Smyth was ready for action and started moving at the precise moment that Pronger wound up to fire the puck out of the Edmonton zone. Smyth looked at Pronger just as he released the puck, but it was too late. As soon as the puck hit Smyth's face, blood squirted from his mouth as he fell, and three teeth landed on the cold ice. Smyth was rushed to the bench as arena maintenance took to the ice to pick up Smyth's teeth and clear away the mess. As he left the ice, Smyth accidently hit a female usher, who ended up falling to the ground, although he didn't know it at the time.

Always a fighter, Smyth returned in the third period, minus a few teeth. The Sharks had a 2–1 lead until the 13-minute mark, when Torres initiated a rush. He sped down the right wing and fired a wrist shot that beat Sharks goalie Vesa Toskala, tying the score. In overtime, Roloson showed that he was more than worth that first-round pick, making an incredible save on a shot by Cheechoo off a perfect pass from Thornton. Roloson

slid across the crease and nabbed the puck out of midair for the biggest save of the 32 he made that night. Toskala was even busier at his end of the rink, and the game went to a third overtime period. The players kept pushing and the fans kept cheering. Finally, 102 minutes and 24 seconds after the opening faceoff, Smyth set up Horcoff, who just shoved the puck under Toskala's pad for a greasy, hard-fought goal. The Oilers raised their arms in victory.

After the game, Smyth discovered that the usher he had accidently knocked over had broken her arm. Of course, he was devastated, and in Game 4 he arranged for her to come down to the bench so that he could sign her cast.

In that fourth game, the Oilers let San Jose take an early 2–0 lead. They battled back, but late in the second period the Sharks were still ahead 3–2. After serving a minor penalty, Samsonov jumped onto the ice. The puck was moving towards Toskala, who came out of his crease to steal it. But Samsonov saw it, picked it up and fired a backhand to tie the score. With the crowd on their side, the Oilers poured it on in the third period, and won 6–3. That was the final score in Game 5 as well, as the Oilers scored three power-play goals and a shorty.

Back in Edmonton three nights later, anthem singer Paul Lorieau was nervous. The crowd in San Jose had booed the Canadian anthem before Game 5, and he half-expected the Edmonton fans to return the favour during "The Star-Spangled Banner." But they didn't. At first, he had a hard time starting the anthem because the crowd was chanting,

"Let's go, Oilers!" But once he got underway, they sang right along with him. And when it came time for "O Canada," Lorieau heard them singing their hearts out, so after just a few bars, he stopped singing and held the mic in the air, letting the fans carry the tune as if they were a choir. The television microphones picked up the singing, and the broadcasters commented that they'd never heard an anthem sung like that before.

Michael Peca and Shawn Horcoff provided all the offence the Oilers needed, while Roloson stole the show, earning the first playoff shutout of his career, as the Oilers won 2–0 and eliminated the

Sharks. The last time the Oilers had played in a conference final was in 1992. Maybe this extra-passionate singing helped the team advance for the first time in over a decade.

Next up for the Oilers were the Mighty Ducks, and for the third time, the eighth-seeded Oilers opened a series on the road, this time at Arrowhead Pond. Roloson again came through, stopping 31 of 32 shots as Edmonton won 3–1. Unfortunately, a flu bug hit the club, and Torres and Bergeron were scratched for Game 2. Nevertheless, the Oilers came away with another 3–1 win, giving them a 2–0 series lead.

Shawn Horcoff in scoring position as Ryan Smyth battles beside the net. Horcoff earned 19 points to come second in scoring in Oilers playoff action, and Smyth had 16 points for a fifth place finish.

Back in Edmonton, fans put flags on their cars, made signs, and wore hats and jerseys. The Ducks badly needed the win and they were edgy, picking at members of the Oilers before faceoffs and after whistles. Toby Petersen, a reserve drawn into the lineup to replace Torres, scored the only goal of the first period. After a scoreless second period, Peca, Staios and Pronger extended the Oiler lead to 4–0. But the Ducks refused to give up, scoring three unanswered goals on Roloson to pull within one. Despite being outshot 38–22, the Oilers held on to win 5–4. By now, the flu bug had fully caught up with the team and they couldn't complete the sweep, dropping a 6–3 decision in Game 4. But Edmonton took Game 5 by a 2–1 margin and won the series. For the first time since 1990, the Oilers were presented with the Clarence Campbell Bowl, symbolic of the Western Conference championship.

For away games, fans had been heading down to Whyte Avenue to watch the games in bars and pubs. Up until now, the energy had been positive and people went down just to soak it all in. But on this night, May 27, an estimated 30,000 fans took to the streets of Edmonton. They lit bonfires, smashed store windows and climbed up streetlights. Many were intoxicated and out of control. The noise could be heard clear across the Saskatchewan River. The police filled up their wagons and hauled fans off to the drunk tank, and took photographs of those being destructive. The pictures were posted on the police service's website, which led to many of the inebriated fans being charged.

In the finals, the Oilers were to meet the Carolina Hurricanes, the Southeast Division champions and the number-two seed in the Eastern Conference. The Hurricanes were one of the highest-scoring teams in the NHL this season, led by Eric Staal's 45 goals and 100 points. Rod Brind'Amour, Erik Cole, Matt Cullen, Cory Stillman and Justin Williams were among the forwards who promised to give Dwayne Roloson a hard time.

Fans were upset when Dwayne Roloson was injured in game 1 of the Stanley Cup Finals. He had become an Oilers hero.

With the heroics of young Ales Hemsky (6 goals, 11 assists in playoffs), the Oilers went to game seven against the Hurricanes in the Stanley Cup Finals.

Late in Game 1, with the score tied 4–4, Roloson went down hard when his net was crashed. He was escorted to the bench by head trainer Barrie Stafford, and Ty Conklin got the call to head to the crease. He only let in one goal, but it was Brind'Amour's game-winner, scored with 32 seconds in regulation time. With Roloson out for the rest of the series, Jussi Markkanen took his place for Game 2. This game was not a pretty one for the Oilers; they lost 5-0.

Down but not beaten, it was an energetic Oiler squad that took the ice at Rexall Place for Game 3—the first Stanley Cup final game to be played in Edmonton since May 22, 1990. Markkanen made 24 saves and Ryan Smyth scored at 17:45 of the third period to give the home team a 2–1 win. But the Hurricanes regained the upper hand, taking Game 4 by a 2–1 margin, and now the Oilers were facing elimination.

The Oilers had plenty of fight left, battling Carolina to a 3–3 draw after 60 minutes. Three and a half minutes into overtime, Pisani, who was having the series of his life, scored his 12th goal of the postseason to give the Oilers the win. When the Oilers shut down Carolina 4–0 in Game 6 to even the series, no one could believe what had happened. One more win, and they would be Stanley Cup champions—*and* the first team since the 1942 Toronto Maple Leafs to come back from a 3-1 deficit in the final.

The Oilers were determined, but the Hurricanes skated hard in Game 7, scoring the first two goals. Pisani scored his 14th of the playoffs at 1:03 of the third period to bring Edmonton within one, but it wasn't enough. When Justin Williams of the Hurricanes scored into the empty net to seal the deal, the Oilers' shoulders slumped. It had been a hard-fought run to the Cup, but a loss cuts deep, no matter how hard and honest the effort.

It was a Cinderella story, right up to the last few minutes.

2006–2007

OILERS WANT A NEW RINK

By 2006, Rexall Place was showing its age. In the dressing room, Fernando Pisani got ready for games beside a bucket. The ceiling above his stall leaked, and "stuff" dripped down from the kitchen. Pisani would squeeze himself to one side of his bench to avoid whatever it was that came down.

Cal Nichols knew that without a new arena, it was just a matter of time before the Oilers would have to move cities. "We needed the arena," Saville later stated. "That was the bottom line." Nichols had been impressed by some of the newer facilities, which offered more comfortable suites and updated food services. To hang on to season-ticket holders and suite holders, the Oilers needed to offer something fresh.

The goal was to have this new arena built in the downtown area, which would help revitalize a dying core. One potential site was just over Jasper Avenue, behind the Hardware Grill on 97th Street, possibly extending to 95th Street (better known as The Quarters). Other areas under discussion were near the West Edmonton Mall, by the City Centre Airport or even northeast of Rexall Place.

David Staples wrote an article for the *Edmonton Journal* that ran under the headline "Revenue Drives Push for New Arena." Another headline in the *Journal* read, in large capital letters, "Oilers Want New Rink," with the sub-heading "Team's Long-Term Plan Includes Replacing Rexall Place, Built In 1974."

But a new arena would remain a dream until a plan was in place to pay for it. Most of the shareholders didn't want to kick in any more of their own money to fund such a huge project. The question remained: Who would pay for this new city structure?

It was around this time that Darryl Katz, who had paid to have the arena named Rexall Place, was asking about how he could buy the team. According to EIG shareholder Bruce Saville, Katz had put out his first feeler around 2005. Katz was a long time Oilers fan, and had been since the day Bill Hunter and the WHA had come to town, but he had other reasons for wanting to buy the Oilers. Much of his motivation for a new arena was to transform and revitalize the city (especially the downtown core) that he loved so much. Having lived through the WHA years and the dynasty years, Katz was proud of his city, and he was discreetly letting people know that he had interest in buying the team. As a successful businessman, he knew the legalities, the stipulations, the business side of the deal—and the roadblocks to buying. None of the owners wanted to sell their share because they wanted to keep the team in the community.

Katz remained undeterred. It wouldn't be long before he was back with a formal offer.

CHRIS PRONGER'S EXIT

After coming so close to a sixth Stanley Cup championship, the Oilers ended the 2005–06 season on the highest of high notes, but they went straight into a low as soon as the off-season began. After one year and a trip to the Stanley Cup final, Chris Pronger wanted out of Edmonton. Speculation as to the reason why were spread all over the media, the gossip turning into tabloid sensationalism. Did he not like the city? Did he butt heads with a teammate? Was he leaving for family reasons? General manager Kevin Lowe knew Pronger was unhappy in Edmonton. In fact, the two had spoken as early as December. "Everything seemed fine," said Lowe, "until I got a call from his agent in early December saying Chris was unhappy and would be looking for a trade at the conclusion of the season. After our historic run to the Stanley Cup finals, I assumed Pronger would negotiate a new deal with us, but instead, through his agent, he reiterated his request to be traded." Everyone was confused by the Pronger trade, including Lowe. "So now, in the heady atmosphere of the Oilers wonderful play-off run, I was put in a position where I had to trade our biggest star and arguably the player most responsible for our success. Instead of facing the normal challenges of getting better for another run the next season, I was suddenly forced into a position of trading away an impact player that would be literally impossible to replace. That scenario obviously did not play well with our passionate fans." Lowe knew it didn't do a team any good to hold on to a player who was so obviously unhappy, so on July 3 he reluctantly dealt Pronger to Anaheim for winger Joffrey Lupul, defenceman Ladislav Smid, a first-round pick in 2007 and a second-round pick in 2008. If the Ducks made it to the Stanley Cup final in 2007, the Oilers also got Anaheim's first-round pick in 2008. There was no tearful goodbye from Pronger. Edmonton was left with a lot of angry fans and an unenthusiastic GM. "I don't know if I've ever had a more stressful time in trying to piece all of this together on the heels of an incredible playoff run," said Kevin Lowe to the press. "It was the last thing we wanted to do."

In just his second NHL season, Lupul had scored 28 goals in the regular season, along with nine in 16 playoff games. Smid, a ninth-overall pick in 2004, was seen as having tons of potential—the *Hockey News* had rated him as the 10th-best hockey prospect in the world.

In the News

On February 2, 2007, the Edmonton Investors Group was the recipient of the 2007 Northern Lights Award of Distinction. Awarded by the Edmonton Chamber of Commerce at the annual Chamber Ball, the theme of the night was "The House of Copper and Blues." To celebrate, the Oilers Fanboni was driven into the event, which was a highlight.

A number of players were lost to free agency. Jaroslav Spacek signed with Buffalo, Michael Peca with Toronto, Georges Laraque with Phoenix, Sergei Samsonov with Montreal, Radek Dvorak with St. Louis and Ty Conklin with Columbus. Dick Tarnstrom signed with Lugano in Switzerland, while Rem Murray, whom the Oilers signed during the stretch run in 2005–06, opted to try his luck with HIFK Helsinki in Finland.

Lowe managed to attract a few significant free agents to fill the gaps left by these departures. Thirty-year-old Petr Sykora, who had spent the previous season with the New York Rangers, was an established goal scorer who would help the Oiler power play. Defenceman Daniel Tjarnqvist had logged three seasons with the Atlanta Thrashers and a fourth with the Minnesota Wild. Unfortunately, an injury would keep him out of all but 37 games in 2006–07. Marty Reasoner, whom the Oilers had sent to Boston at the 2006 trading deadline, was back for a second tour in Edmonton. He would provide depth at centre, playing primarily in a checking role.

Without a first-round pick in the 2006 draft, the Oilers had to wait until the middle of the second round to make a selection. With the 45th pick, they chose Jeff Petry, a Michigan-born defenceman with the Des Moines Buccaneers of the United States Hockey League. After another year of junior, he attended Michigan State University, so it would be the middle of the 2010–11 season before he made his Oiler debut. Drafted in the third round, 75th overall, Theo Peckham was a big, tough defenceman with the Owen Sound Attack of the Ontario Hockey League who would spend parts of six seasons with Edmonton.

AN EMOTIONAL DAY FOR TWO ALBERTA BOYS

With so much turnover on the roster, a letdown was inevitable. Although the Oilers won six of their first eight games and led the Northwest Division with a 16–10–2 record a third of the way into the schedule, the club lost steam in December, and struggled to recover.

For Oiler fans, the most severe blow of the season came on February 27. After 12 years of grit, determination and sweat, fan favourite Ryan Smyth was traded. The Banff-born winger had given everything he had and then some. He had also represented Canada at the World Junior Championships, the World Championships (seven times, including five as team captain) and the Olympics (twice, winning a gold medal in 2002). But with his contract due to expire at the end of the season, Oiler management struggled to reach an agreement with his agent, Don Meehan. Smyth was at home when his mother-in-law came up the stairs and said she had heard on the television that he had been traded. Ryan immediately phoned Meehan, and it was confirmed. Just hours earlier, Smyth had been certain a deal had been made to keep him in Edmonton. Instead, he was being sent to the New York Islanders, and would leave for Long Island the next day. In return, the Oilers got centremen Robert Nilsson and Ryan O'Marra, and a first-round pick

February 27 was a big day for Mark Messier, when his banner was raised to the rafters in Edmonton. It was also a big year—in November 2007 he was inducted into the Hockey Hall of Fame.

Honouring Number 11

Mark Messier was inducted into the Hockey Hall of Fame on November 11, 2007, the sixth Edmonton Oiler to enter the Hall. He began his speech by holding up a wad of tissues and saying, "Just in case." Much of his speech was about the friends and people he met along the way in his career. He recognized Glen Sather and how his vision and mentoring had allowed him to grow up and mature as an individual and a player. He also smiled as he mentioned Wayne Gretzky, who taught the team how to treat the media, sell the game, and be professional.

in 2007. Nilsson had been the Isles' 15th-overall pick in 2003, while they had selected O'Marra 15th in 2005. This trade also freed up some cap space for the Oilers.

Smyth decided not to talk to the media right after he got the news. The Oilers had a game that night, and the evening had been set aside for Mark Messier, whose Number 11 jersey was being retired. The only statement Smyth made was, "I want this to be a great night for Mark Messier. For what he's done for this city. For what he's done for the run of five Stanley Cups."

Messier's banner was raised in front of a sold-out crowd. He skated around the ice in full gear, holding the Stanley Cup, bringing back memories for so many fans. He saluted, and the cheers were deafening. Messier placed the Stanley Cup on a table at centre ice and stood in front of the fans. Tears fell down his face as he told them, "One of the reasons that made it so special to play here is that I was born and raised here." His voice shook with emotion. "To be honoured in this way, standing down here, is a humbling

experience." His three-year-old son Douglas Paul, wearing a Messier jersey, stared up at his dad, and Mark leaned over and picked him up. Although there were a few murmurs about Smyth's trade rumbling through the crowd, the moment still belonged to Messier and all that he had done to win five Stanley Cups with the Edmonton Oilers.

It wasn't until the next morning that the trade news sunk in. Smyth packed his bags and headed to the airport. "I woke up from my nap and I was pretty shocked," said Steve Staios. "I never expected it to happen. It's just tough to lose a teammate you've had that long."

When Smyth walked through the airport, bags slung over his shoulder, with his wife and children beside him, he choked back tears. It had been an emotional 24 hours for Edmonton, first celebrating Messier, and now losing Smyth. Once again, almost two decades after the Gretzky trade, the heart and soul of their team was leaving the fold.

After the Smyth trade, the Oilers lost 16 of their final 18 games. They ended the season with a record of 32–43–7, good for only 71 points and 12th place in the Western Conference. Despite appearing in only 53 games, Smyth's stats still led the club, with 31 goals. His 53 points were also a team high, a lead he shared with two others: Ales Hemsky, who missed 18 games, but whose 40 assists led the club; and Petr Sykora, who played in all 82 games and scored 22 goals.

KATZ MAKES A FORMAL OFFER

In March 2007, Daryl Katz met with NHL commissioner Gary Bettman, in hopes of gathering information about how he might buy the Edmonton Oilers. Katz wanted to know how a sale could be accomplished and he felt it was important to find out what the NHL's board of directors was looking for in a potential owner. He also knew that a new arena would not only help the economic development in the downtown core—prompting the construction of hotels and supporting restaurants and stores—but it was the key to the Oilers' long-term viability in Edmonton. If Edmonton had the best building in the NHL, the team would be able to attract players, which would enhance its bottom line.

In May, Katz met with a few members of the EIG board and let them know he'd be willing to pay a fair price for the team.

Under Alberta law, for a corporation to sell its assets, the deal needed the approval of owners of at least two-thirds of the shares. Board chair Cal Nichols told the *Edmonton Journal* that among the directors alone there were enough partners (that is, they owned

more than a third of the shares between them) opposed to Katz's offer to respond with a resounding no. The team wasn't up for sale. Nichols said the Oilers needed to "stay with the current ownership group because they were a representation of the fans. They were community, and Edmontonians deserved to have their hockey team owned by a community-minded group rather than just one owner."

Meanwhile, the city was pondering the arena question. It had received a report from a leading architectural firm that estimated it would cost as much as $250 million to overhaul Rexall Place and bring it up to current NHL standards. At that price, renovating the old arena didn't seem viable and a new building was a better investment. On April 4, Edmonton mayor Stephen Mandel met with a committee of business and community leaders, including the EIG and Northlands, and asked them to study "the potential of constructing a new sports and entertainment facility" in the city. The committee concluded that Edmonton not only needed a new sports and entertainment facility, but this building needed to be in the downtown core, as part of a district that would combine offices, residential and public spaces with cafés, tourist amenities and pubs, and feature "architecture as art."

The arena was projected to cost $450 million, not counting land, and would be financed through a combination of private and public money. Still, there were the same questions. Who would own the team? Who would be able to pay for the new arena?

2007–2008

KATZ RAISES THE STAKES

Daryl Katz wasn't going to go away that easily. In mid-June, while the players' thoughts were far from the rink, he decided to up his ante. Still operating informally, Katz put another offer before the board—again, for 100 percent of the franchise. Cal Nichols of EIG dismissed it as "a number on a piece of paper," adding: "It may have been on two pages, but an offer had to have all the conditions and subject-to's. [What Katz submitted] was largely hypothetical and conjecture."

On August 8, 2007, a headline in the *Edmonton Journal* said, "Oilers Not For Sale, Period." The *Edmonton Sun* chimed in with "No! Oilers Owners Reject Billionaire Katz's Offer To Buy Team. No! They Won't Sell To Anyone Else, Either." The stories were published in response to Katz raising his offer a second time. Numbers of what Katz was willing to pay circulated through media outlets, many quoting different amounts. Behind closed doors, no matter what the dollar value, he was being denied. "Clearly, I'm disappointed that the ownership

group has elected not to proceed with a sale, but I accept their decision and wish them well," Katz said. "As an Oilers fan and the franchise's largest corporate sponsor, I will continue to be a major supporter of the team."

Finally, on December 14, Cal Nichols stood in front of the media at Rexall Place and announced that he was personally supporting the sale of the team. Edmonton needed a new arena, and he was convinced that the only way to have it built was taking Katz's offer, which had been raised yet again. As with any sale of this magnitude, there were other terms to negotiate and private negotiations that were not to be made public. Some members of the EIG had wanted to sell and others hadn't, but in the end they knew the arena wasn't going to get built with the EIG as owners. It was inevitable the team would have to be moved if there wasn't a new arena. It just wasn't feasible to keep the current financial model for the team. They were the second-smallest media market and oldest facility in the NHL, plus the Oilers didn't have the benefit of the non-hockey revenues generated from the building, as

Northlands was still controlling those kinds of revenues in Edmonton.

Katz had gone to shareholder Bruce Saville, asking what he needed to do to purchase the team. Saville responded that "he needed to have Cal Nichols convinced that it would be the best thing for the community." For Daryl Katz, Edmonton was his hometown and the Oilers were his hometown team, so there was common ground. Everyone wanted what they felt was best for Edmonton.

"In some ways, this was like a lot of other deals I've done," says Katz. "Each side digs in and makes its case for what they think the asset is worth, and how all the other terms will be settled. But on another level, it was like nothing else I've done or expect to do again—and that's because of the emotion we all had wrapped up in the Oilers and the city we all love. The key to making it all happen was Cal Nichols. Cal was the guy who pulled the EIG together in the first place, and he was the key to paving the way for a smooth transition to our ownership."

THE REBUILD CONTINUES

While Katz and the Edmonton Investors Group wrangled over the future of the club, general manager Kevin Lowe and his coaches and scouts focused on the task of improving a team that had gone from the Stanley Cup final to missing the playoffs in the space of a season. They went to Columbus for the NHL Entry Draft armed with three first-round picks. With the sixth-overall pick, they chose Sam Gagner, a hockey-smart playmaking centre who had scored 35 goals and 118 points in 53 games with the London Knights of the OHL in 2006–07. In training camp, the 18-year-old Gagner proved himself and earned a spot on the team. Averaging just under 16 minutes of playing time, Gagner popped in 13 goals and had 36 assists, his 49 points ranking him fifth on the team in scoring.

The other two first-rounders didn't quite pan out. Defenceman Alex Plante, selected 15th, played in only 10 games with Edmonton over three seasons. Centre Riley Nash, born in Consort, Alberta, but raised in British Columbia, was the 21st-overall pick. He had piled up the points with Salmon Arm of the British Columbia Hockey League in 2006–07. He chose to attend Cornell University, and Edmonton would trade him to Carolina in 2010.

On July 1, Joffrey Lupul and Jason Smith were dealt to the Flyers for defenceman Joni Pitkanen, winger Geoff Sanderson and a third-round pick in 2009. After Chris Pronger was traded, the Oiler blue line was never quite the same. A fourth-overall pick in 2002, Pitkanen brought size as well as speed and the ability to rush the puck.

Smith's departure meant the Oilers needed a new captain, and veteran winger Ethan Moreau was given the C.

During the summer, there was a contentious battle of GMs over left winger Dustin Penner. He had notched 29 regular season goals for Anaheim the previous year on their way to winning the Stanley Cup. Penner became an RFA in the spring and Kevin Lowe put forth a five-year, $21.25 million offer sheet, which the Ducks couldn't match because

of their already extended salary cap. Ducks GM Brian Burke went on a media rampage about how the Oilers had poached Penner. "Edmonton has offered a mostly inflated salary for a player, and I think it's an act of desperation for a general manager who is fighting to keep his job," said Burke. Lowe shot back with his own comments. "If he [Burke] wants to debate what our offer sheet did to them or to the salaries, any time," Lowe said in an interview with Edmonton sports station Team 1260. He continued, "I'm sick and tired of it. I know everybody is. I know our peers are like, 'Well, that's Burkie.' The guy is an absolute media junkie and I guess he's achieving what he wants because he gets his name in the headlines. But the reality is, I hate the fact that my name is linked to this." The feud appeared in hockey news across North America. Ultimately, Burke had no choice but to take the draft picks that Lowe dealt him. Since then, an unmatched offer sheet hasn't caused an NHL player to change teams.

Also arriving in Edmonton was Sheldon Souray, a big defenceman. A 26-goal scorer with Montreal in 2006–07, Souray will always be remembered for his many fights. Early in 2007-08, Souray injured his shoulder in a fight and was sidelined for most of the season.

Goalie Mathieu Garon, a former Los Angeles King, would play 47 games for the Oilers, enjoying perhaps the best season of his hockey career.

On February 1, Edmonton acquired Curtis Glencross in a trade with Columbus. Although he wasn't playing huge minutes, he scored nine goals in just 26 games and smoked anyone who got in his way.

YOUTH MOVEMENT

This year's team took a step forward, finishing with a 41-35-6 record and 88 points—an improvement of nine wins and 17 points over the previous season. Although they missed out on the post-season by three points, there were some positives to take away from the season. Youngsters Andrew Cogliano, Sam Gagner and Robert Nilsson made up a line that generated some sparks partway through the season. Cogliano set an NHL record by scoring overtime winners in three consecutive games (March 13 at Colorado, March 15 at Phoenix, and March 16 at San Jose). In his rookie season, the 20-year-old scored 18 goals and 45 points, good for fifth on the team. Right behind him was Nilsson, 23, who scored 10 goals and had 41 points. Gagner had 13 goals and 49 points in his rookie year. Ales Hemsky, who led the club with 71 points, including 20 goals, was already in his fifth NHL season despite being just 24. At 29, Shawn Horcoff was one of the Oilers' veterans. After 53 games, he was leading the team in scoring with 50 points, but a shoulder injury at the all-star game sidelined him for the rest of the season. Dustin Penner led the team with 23 goals and was fourth in points with 47. Of the ten highest-scoring Oilers, nine were 25 or younger.

With new ownership and a core of young, talented players, Oiler fans seemed to have something to hang their hopes on.

Ethan Moreau accepts the captaincy from Head Coach Craig MacTavish.

2008-2009

DRAFTING A FUTURE ALL-STAR

The Oilers had to give up a first-round pick when they signed Dustin Penner as a restricted free agent. Fortunately, they still had the pick they'd obtained in the Chris Pronger trade. When their turn came around, 22nd overall, they called on Jordan Eberle, the leading scorer (42 goals and 75 points) on the Regina Pats of the WHL. After training camp, Eberle was sent back to the Pats, where he would play another two years. Long time Oilers scout Lorne Davis had his eye on Eberle for years. Davis was considered a "bird dog" for the Oilers, and before he passed away on December 20, 2007, he knew the kid was going to be good. Little did Oilers fans know that on January 3, 2009, after the Oilers drafted him, that Eberle would make a name for himself before his first NHL game. In the dying seconds of a game against Russia at the 2009 IIHF World Junior Championships in Ottawa, Eberle stole a smothered puck and went from forehand to backhand, slapping it past Vadim Zhelobnyuk. This skillful goal forced overtime, where Canada defeated Russia in the shootout, earning Canada a fifth straight gold medal. A year later, his reputation grew when he scored twice in the final three minutes of regulation time in the gold-medal game against Team USA. Although the Americans ended up winning 6–5 in overtime, Eberle was named tournament MVP. His trophy case filled up a little more when he was named the Canadian Hockey League Player of the Year for the 2009–10 season.

UNDER NEW MANAGEMENT

The 2008 draft was Kevin Lowe's last as general manager. On July 31, he was promoted to president of hockey operations, and Steve Tambellini succeeded him as GM. As a player, Tambellini had broken into the NHL with the New York Islanders in 1978–79 and was a member of their Stanley Cup championship teams in 1980 and 1981. He also saw time with the Colorado Rockies, New Jersey Devils, Calgary Flames and Vancouver Canucks. He arrived in Edmonton after working as the Canucks' assistant GM. Tambellini had also been director of player personnel

Jason Strudwick played nearly two seasons with the team. Here he shows the famous Oilers work ethic.

for the Canadian Olympic team in 2002, helping the gold medal return to Canada after a 50-year drought.

OFF-SEASON TRADES

On June 29, Jarret Stoll and defenceman Matt Greene went to the Los Angeles Kings for puck-rushing blueliner Lubomir Visnovsky. Unfortunately, Visnovsky injured his shoulder in February and only played 50 games for the Oilers that season.

Canada Day saw Joni Pitkanen traded to Carolina for Erik Cole, a winger with size and speed, a penchant for giving out hits, proven goal-scoring ability and a Stanley Cup ring. Oddly, the Oilers would trade him back to Carolina before the

season was over. The same day, Raffi Torres was sent to Columbus for centreman Gilbert Brule, a sixth-overall pick by the Blue Jackets in 2005. Born in Edmonton but raised in North Vancouver, 21-year-old Brule was touted as having great hands and tons of potential. The Oilers hoped he would develop as a goal scorer.

Another Edmonton native, Jason Strudwick, was signed as a free agent on July 10. He was a solid stay-at-home defenceman who could block shots and throw a hard hit when needed. As the regular season approached, the Oilers picked up tough guy Steve MacIntyre off waivers from the Florida Panthers. On November 11, during a fight with Eric Godard of the Pittsburgh Penguins, he suffered a fractured

Anderson Comes Home

On November 10, 2008, Glenn Anderson was inducted into the NHL Hockey Hall of Fame, an honour that many Oiler fans felt was long overdue. On January 18, 2009, the Oilers retired his Number 9 jersey prior to a game against Wayne Gretzky's Phoenix Coyotes. Jumping off the bench, where he'd taken his place amidst the 2008–09 team, Anderson skated around the ice in full gear before picking up a puck and blasting it into the net. A play-by-play announcer kept pace with him, and when he fired the puck into the spotlighted net, the classic line could be heard over the sound system: "He shoots . . . he scores!" As they had done so many times, Edmonton fans erupted. Anderson took to the podium to thank many people, including his "brothers" Mark Messier and Wayne Gretzky. He also thanked Cal Nichols and Daryl Katz. When it came time to thank his mother, who couldn't travel to the event, he teared up, saying, "I know you're watching it on television." Anderson also spoke about how putting on the Oilers jersey was "like coming home. Home is where the heart is, and that's where my heart is, right here."

A moment between
Andrew Cogliano and
Dwayne Roloson in a
record setting year for
the netminder.

orbital bone. After missing 26 games,
he returned in January and raised havoc
on the ice.

ROLI SETS A RECORD

The season opened with the Oilers using
a three-goalie system—Dwayne Roloson,
Mathieu Garon and Jeff Drouin-
Deslauriers. Eventually, Roloson became
the starter, playing in 60 games—at 39,
becoming the oldest goalie to appear in
60 games or more in one season. With
Roloson firmly in the Number 1 spot,
Garon was sent to Pittsburgh in January
for centre Ryan Stone, goalie Dany
Sabourin and a fourth-round pick.

But Roloson's efforts weren't enough,
and for the third year in a row, the Oilers
failed to make the playoffs. The team
finished 38–35–9 with 85 points, leaving
them in 11th place in the Western
Conference and six points shy of that
coveted playoff spot. Ales Hemsky led
the way with 66 points, and he and
defenceman Sheldon Souray shared the
lead in goals with 23.

Ethan Moreau was the second Oiler
to be awarded the King Clancy Trophy.
(Kevin Lowe received it in 1990.) Moreau
was recognized for his dedication to the
Edmonton Oilers Foundation, specifi-
cally for working with the Inner City
High School project, helping raise funds
to build a new facility for its 150 stu-
dents. Moreau also volunteered for the
Cystic Fibrosis Foundation, Canadian
Cancer Foundation and the United Way.
He often visited the Stollery Children's
Hospital and led the charge in the dress-
ing room for the Caps for Cancer and
For Puck Surprise programs.

2009–2010

MACT MOVES ON

On April 15, 2009, Steve Tambellini held a press conference at which he announced that head coach Craig MacTavish had been dismissed. After Tambellini's first year as the general manager, he concluded that the team needed size and toughness. He wouldn't put up with an "unemotional game" and wanted a team that was hard to play against. In short, he wanted intensity from every player.

To get that intensity back, the Oilers hired veteran coach Pat Quinn, known for his no-nonsense approach and experience. Quinn, also known as "the Big Irishman," had been a defenceman with the Toronto Maple Leafs, Vancouver Canucks and Atlanta Flames. After retiring, he became an assistant coach with the Philadelphia Flyers, and he took over as head coach late in 1978–79. The following season, he led the Flyers to a 35-game unbeaten streak, and although they lost to the New York Islanders in the Stanley Cup final, he won the Jack Adams Award as coach of the year. He won the award a second time in 1991–92,

with the Vancouver Canucks, and was a finalist in 1998–99, while coaching the Leafs. He also coached for Hockey Canada, taking the Canadian men's Olympic team to a gold medal in 2002. Additionally, Quinn had an excellent reputation for being able to coach young players, having guided Canada to gold medals at the IIHF World Under-18 Championship in 2008 and the World Junior Championship in 2009.

A NEW DRAFT TRADITION

The Oilers had the 10th pick in the NHL Entry Draft, and their selection was a player who had been projected to go much higher: Swedish forward Magnus Paajarvi-Svensson. He was a speedy player with good acceleration and a strong wrist shot. The Oilers also liked his hockey sense and ability to pass the puck. When he was called to the stage at the Bell Centre in Montreal, Daryl Katz's young son, Harrison, also went up to give Paajarvi-Svensson his Oilers jersey. This was the start of an Oiler tradition. Paajarvi-Svensson played in Sweden for the 2009–10 season, a move that allowed

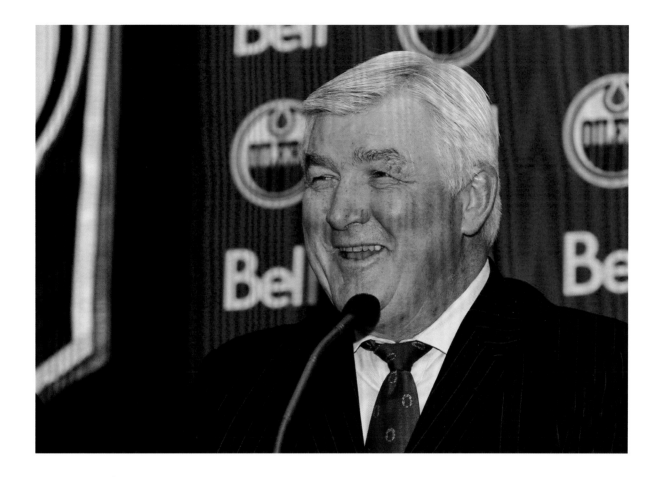

The big Irishman,
Pat Quinn, was hired by
General Manager
Steve Tambellini, pushing
MacT out the door.

him to mature physically and mentally, getting him ready for the big league.

NET LOSSES AND GAINS

The New York Islanders were looking for a goalie when free-agent season opened. Their starter, Rick DiPietro, had suffered a knee injury that limited him to just five games in 2008–09, and it was uncertain when he would return. So, on July 1, they signed Dwayne Roloson to a two-year contract. Fans were sad to see Roloson go, as he had stood on his head during the Oilers' run to the Stanley Cup final in 2006.

Without missing a beat, Edmonton signed Nikolai Khabibulin when he became an unrestricted free agent. Khabibulin had been the Number 1 goalie for Chicago for the past four seasons, and had been the starter for Tampa Bay when they won the Stanley Cup in 2003–04. Prior to the 2008–09 season, the Blackhawks had put Khabibulin on waivers. When no one picked him up, including Russia's Kontinental Hockey League (KHL), the Hawks put him back in the lineup. He played well, racking up the fourth-best goals against average in the league and ranking sixth in save percentage, and

Chicago reached the Western Conference final. But when the season was over, he became an unrestricted free agent. The Oilers were glad to have him.

Among the team's new forwards, there was a familiar face. Mike Comrie signed as a free agent on September 10.

A YEAR NOT TO REMEMBER

Comrie's return was a rare highlight of the 2009–10 season. In a preseason game against the Florida Panthers, he assisted on all four Edmonton goals in a 4–0 victory and dropped the gloves with Eric Himelfarb, prompting the Rexall Place fans to chant his name in appreciation. He looked good early in the season, putting up six points in his first seven games. Unfortunately, mononucleosis would keep Comrie out of the lineup for two and a half months. He ended the year with 13 goals and 21 points in 43 games.

Despite the change of coach and net-minders, the Oilers had a tough season. Opening the schedule at home against Calgary, the Oilers fell behind 3–1 before battling back to tie it up on goals by Gilbert Brule and Sam Gagner. With less than a minute in regulation time, it appeared that overtime was on the way—until Khabibulin left his crease to play a loose puck. Instead of clearing it out of the Oiler zone, he directed the puck onto the stick of Flames winger David Moss, who fired it into the empty net. In January, the Russian netminder had a herniated disk, putting him out for the season. Jeff Drouin-Deslauriers ended up making the majority of the starts in Edmonton's goal.

Nikolai Khabibulin comes in to fill the void left by Dwayne Roloson.

The Oilers' hopes for the season were also dealt a deadly blow when Ales Hemsky sat out 60 games, primarily because of a shoulder injury. He still managed 22 points in the 22 games he did play. Many other Oilers spent time on the injured reserve list: Ryan Stone, 54 games; Marc Pouliot and Sheldon Souray, 44 each; Fernando Pisani, 39; Ladislav Smid, 30; Steve Staios, 22; Gilbert Brule and Sam Gagner, 14 each.

On March 3, the team's top-scoring defenceman, Lubomir Visnovsky (32 points in 57 games), was traded to Anaheim for defenceman Ryan Whitney and a sixth-round pick. Whitney, the fifth-overall pick in the 2002 draft, brought offensive upside to the table. He also was six years younger than Visnovsky. Whitney put up 11 points in 19 games over the balance of the season. Plagued by an injury, he under-went surgery in May to help realign the bones in his right foot.

This might have been the Oilers worst season. They finished with just 62 points and a 27-47-8 record, coming last in the NHL. Dustin Penner led the scoring with 32 goals and 63 points. Following Penner was Sam Gagner with 15 goals and 41 points, Gilbert Brule with 17 goals and 37 points, and Shawn Horcoff with 13 goals and 26 points. Horcoff, whose points were his lowest totals since 2002–03, said of this season "It was tough to lose so much. We would go into arenas knowing he were going to lose, but wondering by how much."

This last place finish, however, did give them the first draft pick for the 2010 NHL Entry Draft.

2010-2011

RENNEY TAKES THE REINS

After such a dismal season, Pat Quinn was relieved of his coaching duties on June 22 and was reassigned to an advisory role in the front office. One of his assistants, Tom Renney, was promoted to head coach. Another of Quinn's assistant coaches, Wayne Fleming, left the Oilers at the end of July to join the staff of the Tampa Bay Lightning.

Renney was no stranger to the NHL. Before coming to Edmonton he had been head coach of the Vancouver Canucks and the New York Rangers, and had led Team Canada to a silver medal in the 1994 Winter Olympics. His coaching career had begun with the Kamloops Blazers of the WHL, where he won the Memorial Cup in 2002. His hockey knowledge was extensive, and he was known as a strong technical coach.

Things were changing quickly. Tom Renney moved from assistant coach to head coach as Pat Quinn coached just one year.

A young, fast Taylor Hall puts out the Flames.

Former captain Kelly Buchberger, who had been an assistant coach with the Oilers since 2008, was kept on. He was joined by former Oiler defenceman Steve Smith.

There was a change in the farm system, as well. Since 2007, the Oilers had been affiliated with the Springfield Falcons of the American Hockey League. At the same time, the organization owned an AHL franchise that hadn't played since the NHL lockout season of 2004–05, when it operated as the Edmonton Road Runners. The decision was made this year to reactivate the team in a new home, Oklahoma City, and under a new

name, the Barons. Todd Nelson was named as head coach. He had been a coach with several minor-league teams since 2001–02, and for the past two seasons he had been an assistant coach with the Atlanta Thrashers.

THE FIRST FIRST PICK

On April 13, the NHL held its annual draft lottery. That night, vice-president Bill Daly stood before television cameras and opened a series of envelopes to reveal which teams would receive the first five picks in the June entry draft. The New York Islanders got the fifth

slot, the fourth went to the Columbus Blue Jackets, and the Florida Panthers were awarded the third pick. That left two teams in the running for the coveted Number 1 pick: Edmonton and Boston. Daly opened the final envelope and pulled out a card marked with the Edmonton Oilers logo. For the first time since they joined the NHL in 1979, the Oilers had the first-overall pick.

Which future star would general manager Steve Tambellini select on June 25 in Los Angeles? He wasn't giving anything away, but the consensus was that his choice would be between Plymouth Whalers centre Tyler Seguin and Windsor Spitfires left winger Taylor Hall. The two forwards had tied for the

Ontario Hockey League lead in points with 106 in 2009–10.

On the night of the draft, fans in Edmonton congregated at Rexall Place for what was coined "The Draft Party." The actual draft event was being shown live on the Jumbotron. Fans were either on Team Hall or Team Seguin, and billboards around Edmonton featured photos of both. The speculation continued right up until Tambellini took the stage and called out Hall's name. Back in Edmonton, the cheering began (Team Hall outnumbered the Seguin fans). Hall was fast, highly skilled, and made an impact every time he stepped on the ice. He helped his team win back-to-back Memorial Cups in 2009 and 2010,

The Oilers were trying to rebuild and had some exciting young players to promote as the next stars. From left to right: Taylor Hall, Jordan Eberle, and Magnus Paajarvi.

winning the tournament MVP award both years. The Oilers were hoping he might be able to jump straight into the NHL and make an impact.

A FIFTH UNHAPPY SEASON

At times, players came and went at such a pace that it seemed as if the Oiler dressing room had a revolving door. Management was trying to regroup and rebuild, looking for some solid wood amidst the splintered ground. Lost to free agency were Mike Comrie, Robert Nilsson, Fernando Pisani, Marc Pouliot and Ryan Potulny. Riley Nash, a first-round pick in 2007, was traded to Carolina. Patrick O'Sullivan was traded to Phoenix for defenceman Jim Vandermeer. Jeff Drouin-Deslauriers, the goalie who held down the fort during Nikolai Khabibulin's absence the previous season, was demoted to Oklahoma City. And team captain Ethan Moreau was claimed off waivers by Columbus. With the loss of Moreau, the captaincy went to Shawn Horcoff.

Defenceman Kurtis Foster was signed as a free agent on July 1. The 28-year-old had spent 2009–10 with Tampa Bay, where he had 42 points in 71 games. In March 2008, while playing for Minnesota, he had been hit from behind and crashed into the end boards, badly breaking his left leg. Eleven months of rehab had enabled him to return to the NHL.

The Oilers' first pick in the 2009 draft, Magnus Paajarvi-Svensson, cracked the lineup. He would leave the "Svensson" off the nameplate on the back of his jersey. Along with Jordan Eberle, Taylor Hall and Sam Gagner, he was considered one of the players around whom the team would rebuild. They were put together in photo shoots for marketing tools, their faces plastered on billboards all over Edmonton.

Young gun Jordan Eberle gets past T.J. Brodie to score on Miikka Kiprusoff.

Despite having some speedy forwards, the Oilers lacked depth on the blue line. At 38, Khabibulin was not the goaltender of the future. He and 24-year-old Devan Dubnyk often alternated in goal. By the season's end, Dubnyk had played in 35 games to Khabibulin's 47.

Again, some key players spent long stretches on the injured reserve list. Ryan Whitney was off to a promising start, with 27 points in 35 games, but in a game against the Buffalo Sabres on December 28, he stepped in a rut on the ice and had to leave the game. Surgery was needed for a popped out tendon, and his season was over. Gilbert Brule sat out 38 games, Shawn Horcoff missed 33. Ales Hemsky, who had missed so much time a year before, was on the sidelines for 32 games. Even the younger players had their time up in the press box. Hall, Eberle and Gagner missed 15, 13 and 12 games,

respectively. Khabibulin was out of action for 11 games. At the other end of the scale, iron-man Andrew Cogliano played in all 82 games. In his first four NHL seasons, he had a perfect attendance record.

The Oilers scored the third-fewest goals in the NHL. Eberle led with 43 points, while Hall, Gagner and Hemsky tied for second with 42. Paajarvi had 34, good for seventh on the team. Hall earned the club-high 22 goals, followed by Dustin Penner with 21. The Oilers finished with a 25–45–12 record, for only 62 points.

Could the team have been successful if not for all the injuries? How much longer would the rebuild take? Could Eberle, Hall and Paajarvi really be the key to future success? Did the team need to add a few veterans to round out the roster? The questions mounted as for the first time in franchise history, they had gone five years without making the playoffs.

The Oilers made history in December 2010 by becoming the first Canadian NHL team to have cheerleaders. The Octane cheerleaders were controversial with Oilers fans. In August 2016, the Oilers announced that the cheerleaders were no more.

A Special Night for Rod Phillips

Beginning in 1974 and spanning 37 years, Rod Phillips was the radio play-by-play voice of the Edmonton Oilers. On March 29, 2011, he called his last game—the Oilers hosting the Los Angeles Kings. Before the game, Phillips walked onto the ice, as he'd been asked, thinking that general manager Kevin Lowe was going to present him with a plaque or some similar commemorative gift. He didn't see the banner until it was right in front of him. He was shocked that the Oilers would do something like this for him. As it was raised, he looked at the number. He'd never been a pro player himself, and this wasn't a hockey number: 3,542, the exact number of games Phillips had called in his career. Phillips had been through five Stanley Cups, the parades, the excitement and the anguish. He'd called it all.

2011–2012

ANOTHER LOTTERY WIN

On April 12, 2011, NHL executive Bill Daly again opened an envelope to reveal that the Edmonton Oilers had received the first pick in the upcoming entry draft. This year, there wasn't as much intrigue about their preferred player. An 18-year-old centre from Burnaby, British Columbia, had caught their attention. He had won a scoring title when he played in the British Columbia Major Midget League with the Vancouver North West Giants, and he had also been named tournament MVP at the Mac's Midget AAA World Invitational Tournament in Calgary. At the time he was drafted by the Oilers, Ryan Nugent-Hopkins was playing in the WHL for the Red Deer Rebels. He had won the Western League's rookie of the year award in 2009–10 and had been runner-up for the CHL rookie of the year award. Popular in the dressing room because of his positive attitude and humility, during training camp Nugent-Hopkins displayed an unbelievable backhand shot, a good forehand, and fantastic skating with strong edge control. Like Taylor Hall before him, he was destined to play for the Oilers immediately.

Edmonton had another pick in the first round, acquired in February when Dustin Penner was traded to Los Angeles. Selecting 19th, the Oilers drafted defenceman Oscar Klefbom. He was valued for his size, skating ability and offensive skill, including a hard shot. He had also shown that he could play physically, an asset that would aid with his transition to the NHL game. He would play two more seasons in Sweden with Farjestad BK before coming to North America.

NUMBER 94 RETURNS

In an effort to add a veteran presence to a dressing room with its share of young-sters, the Oilers brought back a familiar face. Ryan Smyth wanted to return to Edmonton, the place he and his family called home. Of the trade, Tambellini said, "You need people that are respect-ful of these young players. You need people that are encouraging as far as their development. You need people that want to share in their success. There's extreme passion there in Ryan Smyth."

The young Oilers needed some leadership so Ryan Smyth returned to Edmonton. Players skated through the oil derrick before every game, but this tradition ended in 2016.

There were other trades in preparation for the new season.

On July 1, Kurtis Foster was sent to Anaheim for 36-year-old defenceman Andy Sutton. On the 12th, Steve Tambellini did another deal with the Ducks, trading Andrew Cogliano for a second-round draft pick.

Also in July, Sheldon Souray and Jim Vandermeer left as free agents. Edmonton signed Eric Belanger, a 34-year-old centre who had 40 points with Phoenix a year before. Defenceman Cam Barker had been a third-overall pick in 2004. And Ben Eager was a 27-year-old tough guy who had split 2010–11 between Atlanta and San Jose, spending 120 minutes in the penalty box. The Oilers were trying to balance the team with youngsters and veterans.

FLASHES OF BRILLIANCE

Edmonton fans were getting frustrated with the word "rebuilding." They wanted to see results. The Oilers had added some potential stars, but the process of making a winning team seemed to be going on too long. As the string of losing seasons grew longer, management felt the pressure to shuffle the lineup in hopes of finding the right combination of youth and experience, talented players and grinders, scoring ability and defensive responsibility. As the year progressed and the team struggled to win games, more roster moves were made. One that generated a lot of ink and air time was the trade of Tom Gilbert to Minnesota for Nick Schultz.

A fixture on the Oiler blue line since 2006–07, Gilbert had drawn good and

Even flying through the air, Taylor Hall still has his eyes locked on the puck in this game against the Canucks.

bad attention, but many thought he was Edmonton's best defenceman. He got off to a good start in 2011–12, but in a game in Chicago on January 2, the Blackhawks' Daniel Carcillo shoved him hard into the boards as he chased a loose puck behind the Edmonton net. After taking a month to recover from the knee injury he suffered, his return fell flat

three goals, the Rexall Place fans honoured him by throwing hats on the ice. For his fourth goal, a shoe was thrown.

This amazing 8–4 win against Chicago provided a glimpse of the talent and potential of this team, but on the whole it was another challenging season. For the sixth year in a row, the Oilers missed the postseason. Their team

> *"It was really fun for our fans to see something like that tonight. Sam was having the time of his life and so were his linemates and the entire team."*
>
> — *Oilers coach Tom Renney*

and his ice time was cut. The Oilers felt they had to make a one-for-one trade for another defenceman, although Gilbert was more of a two-way player while Schultz was a stay-at-home blueliner who didn't rack up many points.

A highlight of the season was Sam Gagner's eight-point game (four goals and four assists) on February 2 against Chicago. Every time the puck landed on Gagner's stick, he either scored or set up a scoring chance, playing a role in all eight goals Edmonton scored that evening. When he was done, he was the first player to record so many points in an NHL game since April 25, 1989, when Mario Lemieux scored five goals and assisted on three. That night, he was awarded all three stars, and suddenly he was seeing his name lumped in with Wayne Gretzky and Paul Coffey. After

offence moved up from 28th in the league to 20th, while they improved from 28th to 23rd in goals against. The end result was a 32–40–10 record and 74 points—better than the previous season, but not by enough. Only the Columbus Blue Jackets, with 65 points, were lower in the overall standings.

Second-year pro Jordan Eberle broke through, leading the team with 34 goals and 76 points. He was second in the voting for the Lady Byng Trophy, runner-up to Florida Panthers defenceman Brian Campbell. Taylor Hall had 27 goals and 53 points despite missing 21 games. And rookie Ryan Nugent-Hopkins proved himself with 18 goals and 52 points, coming third in scoring even though a shoulder injury limited him to 62 games. Gagner had 18 goals and 47 points, while veteran Ryan

Smyth tallied 46 points, including 17 goals. The goalie duties were split fairly evenly between 25-year-old Devan Dubnyk, who won 20 games and had a solid .914 save percentage in his 47 appearances, and the 39-year-old Khabibulin, who made 40 appearances.

Despite the lack of playoff action, the younger players provided some hope for Edmonton hockey fans. The Oilers had a strong start to the season with a 9-3-2 record, though that fell to 23-37-8 by the end. Ralph Krueger ran a successful power play, 3rd in the league, and young gun Ryan Nugent-Hopkins finished 2nd in voting for the Rookie of the Year Calder Cup Trophy. Things were looking up.

On February 2, 2012, Sam Gagner made history and gave the Oilers a boost with an 8-point night.

ARENA WRANGLING

Many city council meetings were held to discuss the new arena district. On April 6, 2011, Edmonton City Council voted to approve an "Agreement Framework" for the proposed new arena, under which the city would negotiate with the Katz Group on such details as financing of the arena and public structure, maintenance and operating costs, and the city's ability to book events in the building. Counsellors approved the resulting agreement on May 18.

On October 12, the Katz Group and the city of Edmonton flew to New York for a meeting with NHL Commissioner Gary Bettman. The cost of the arena was coming in higher than expected, and the province of Alberta was not going to contribute. The city of Edmonton decided that changes to the financial framework were needed, and once done they would present at another board meeting on October 25-26 in a special City Council meeting and public hearing. As it was public, media was involved. It looked as if the framework was in place and the arena and district were finally going through.

The team salutes the fans, thanking them for their support.

2012–2013

A NEW COACH

On May 17, general manager Steve Tambellini announced that the Oilers were not renewing Tom Renney's contract. The team had not made the playoffs under Renney's two seasons as head coach, and Tambellini was candid about the decision: "We were entering a new phase and needed a change."

The move triggered the usual speculation about who would be next in line to try to make this team into a winner. Among the names bandied about was that of Brent Sutter, the longtime NHL player (and two-time Stanley Cup champion), who had recently been dismissed as head coach of the Calgary Flames and returned to his cattle ranch in Alberta. But on June 27, Tambellini and Kevin Lowe, the Oilers' president of hockey operations, decided to promote from within.

Ralph Krueger was born and raised in Manitoba, but had carved out a career as a player and coach in Germany. He had also coached in Austria, winning five national championships, and was behind the bench for the Swiss national team at multiple international tournaments. In 2010, the Oilers had hired him as an assistant coach, and Tambellini and Lowe hoped his infectious energy would ignite a spark of enthusiasm among the young talent.

ANOTHER NUMBER 1 PICK

For the third year in a row, the lottery balls fell in the Oilers' favour, giving them the Number 1 pick in the NHL Entry Draft. Only once before had a team received the first pick three years running (the Quebec Nordiques). This year, they went for a young Russian who had made an impressive debut in North America with the Sarnia Sting of the OHL. In 65 games in 2010–11, Nail Yakupov scored 101 points, with 49 goals. The following season, he played 42 games and had 69 points. The NHL's Central Scouting Bureau rated him the Number 1 skater in North America. The Oilers liked his explosive power, his skill with the puck in front of the net and his offensive talent, and they thought he could become a top-line forward.

Ralph Krueger behind the bench as the new head coach, replacing Tom Renney.

GETTING THE JUMP ON JUSTIN

One of the most sought-after free agents of 2012 was collegiate defenceman Justin Schultz. Drafted by the Anaheim Ducks in 2008, Schultz played another year of Junior A before enrolling at the University of Wisconsin, where he was twice named an All-American. At the end of his third year he "de-registered," which gave the Ducks 30 days to sign him before he became an unrestricted free agent. Twenty-six teams wanted him, but he signed with Edmonton for a two-year entry-level contract. His decision may have been helped when he got phone calls from Wayne Gretzky and Paul Coffey, singing the Oilers' praises.

Ever since Chris Pronger's departure, the Oilers had been lacking a defence-man who could quarterback the power play. Schultz was skilled and could move the puck, plus he was fast and could shoot. The Oilers had landed him before the official start of free-agent season on July 1. General manager Steve Tambellini was pumped by the signing. "I was convinced, and so was the hockey world, that it was a great way to start the free-agent period," he said.

SEATTLE AND SORRY

A deal is a deal. At least, until it isn't.

From the time the arena framework had been disclosed to the public, there had been numerous meetings to discuss design, engineering, excavation, architecture, PCL Construction, community benefits, and, of course, budget. As time ticked by the costs seemed to be growing. There were still discussions about certain agenda items that fell into a grey area of who should pay. On September 11, 2012, the city of Edmonton wanted to hold an in camera meeting with the Katz Group, but they declined this invitation. The Katz Group didn't want the public involved yet, as there were still so many ongoing negotiations. They sent a letter outlining the number of things that had changed since the New York meeting in 2011, and why the current framework was not going to work for the Oilers. This caused a stall in the negotiations and Mayor

Justin Schultz sees a little daylight and attempts to shoot around Detroit's Henrik Zetterberg.

KATZ GROUP

Daryl A. Katz
Chairman

September 29, 2012

To the People of Edmonton, Northern Alberta and Oilers Fans Everywhere,

I owe you an explanation.

I was upset when certain confidential information was leaked and by comments that I thought were unfair and called my integrity into question. I reacted by trying to send a message to City leaders that they should not take my support for a new arena for granted.

In doing so, I took for granted your support and your love of the Oilers.

That was wrong, and I apologize.

The best I can say is that I did it because I'm fighting for a deal that will enable the team to stay in Edmonton – and not because I want them to be anywhere else.

That's why I bought the Oilers in the first place. Because I want the NHL to be sustainable in Edmonton for the long-term, and because I saw the city's need for a new arena as an opportunity to transform our city for the better.

In hindsight, I have underestimated the degree to which it would be up to us to make the case for public funding. As I think you all know by now, public communications is not in my nature. Chalk that up as a personal shortcoming.

The simple fact is that the Oilers need Edmonton, and Edmonton needs the Oilers. Each is an integral part of the fabric and identity of the other.

We are continuing to work with City Administration to forge a win-win partnership that will benefit our city and that we can all be proud of.

I hope we can count on your support.

Sincerely,

[signature]

Daryl Katz

1702 Bell Tower, 10104 - 103 Avenue, Edmonton, AB Canada T5J 0H8 Tel: (780) 990-0505 Fax: (780) 425-6160

Mandel set a drop-dead date of October 17, 2012, to have the issues resolved.

Arena talks had been going on for four years. The Oilers lease with Northlands was due in less than two years, and ground needed to be broken soon if a new arena was going to be built in time.

Behind closed doors, negotiations were still taking place. When a leak of the dollar figures and demands from the Katz Group trickled out to the public, the situation intensified. The city councillors felt that the Oilers were making too many demands, and Katz in turn felt the councillors were not going to deliver on a promise they had made earlier to help subsidize arena operating costs. Oilers owner Daryl Katz was getting frustrated with the city and the lack of action, and more than once he had made mention that perhaps the team could be moved. But he had never actually done anything to indicate he might sell.

Then suddenly Seattle was an option.

In late September, Katz, Kevin Lowe, Wayne Gretzky and Pat LaForge made a trip to the coastal city of Seattle. Fans found out about the excursion and the news hit the Edmonton papers and air-waves on September 24, with a backlash from fans that no one predicted. The reaction was angry, even hostile (especially on social media), toward the Katz Group, saying they were greedy and the "second coming of Pocklington." In a CBC sports article, Katz Group lawyer Bob Black said, "Nonetheless, and as the city of Edmonton is aware, the Katz Group has been listening to proposals from a number of potential NHL markets for some time. After more than four years of trying to secure an arena deal with less than 24 months remaining on the Oilers' lease at Rexall Place, this is only prudent and should come as no surprise."

However, Daryl Katz himself was shocked at the backlash from fans. He said, "It was my hometown and I wanted to make a difference in the development of the city." On Saturday, September 29, he took out full-page ads in the newspapers in Edmonton to say he was sorry for taking their loyalty for granted.

At the October 17 meeting of the city council, a motion was passed to "cease all negotiations and ongoing City work related to the October 26, 2011, framework." The Katz Group's refusal to attend this council meeting had led many to conclude they weren't interested in continuing with negotiations.

The public responded with a flurry of angry Twitter messages as well as comments on other social media outlets. Most blamed the Katz Group for not compromising; others suggested that they bring in Gary Bettman and put him in a room with Katz and the mayor. Some suggested that the planned Winter Garden, a combination pedestrian bridge and grand entrance, be renamed the "Bridge to Nowhere." Two factions were forming: those who desperately wanted to see a new arena built and those who wondered if it was worthwhile even continuing.

The standoff lasted until December 12. On that date, the Katz Group—accompanied by Patrick LaForge of the Oilers and architect Michael Shugarman— made a presentation to the council and answered questions. It withdrew its demand for an operating subsidy and a requirement that the city rent space in an office building it was constructing. The estimated cost of the project had grown, but the council agreed that the design process would start up again. Time was ticking. City staff were directed to work with the Katz Group to appoint a mediator, in part to keep the talks from slowing down or breaking down altogether. The mediator would also appoint a financial analyst to evaluate the two sides' assumptions about the costs and benefits of the arena. Staff were also expected to work separately with the Katz Group to work out non-financial issues. There was also talk of finding ways to rein in the costs of the project.

The arena project seemed to be back on track and heading in the right direction, although there was a lot of ground to be made up.

SEASON INTERRUPTED

Everywhere an Oiler fan turned in 2012, it seemed there was talk of broken-down negotiations. The NHL's current collective bargaining agreement was due to expire in September, and this time it looked as though the players were preparing for a fight. In December 2010 they had hired Donald Fehr as executive director of the NHL Players' Association. He had done the same job for the baseball players' union.

The league made its first offer on July 14.

The Oilers organized an outdoor inter-squad shinny game for fans on January 13, 2013, at Hawrelak Park. Ryan Nugent-Hopkins watches and gets ready for his next shift for the blue team.

Offers and counteroffers were exchanged, statements and counter-allegations were made, but still there was no deal on September 15, when the NHL announced it was locking out the players for the third time in 18 years.

Finally, on January 6, after 113 days, a new collective bargaining agreement was in place. Including the preseason, a total of 628 games had been lost to cancellation. As they had done in 1995, the teams hurried to get ready to play a 48-game schedule.

CHANGING GMS IN MIDSTREAM

The Oilers started off well, winning four of their seven games in January, but they slipped in February, coming away with just four wins in 12 games. The short schedule didn't allow much room to recover, and the hole got deeper in a hurry when the month of March began with a five-game losing streak that virtually eliminated them from the play-offs. This didn't sit well with Kevin Lowe. On April 15, with seven games still left in the regular season, he held a

Remembering Wayne Fleming

After leaving the Oilers as their assistant coach, Wayne Fleming joined the Tampa Bay Lightning coaching staff. While in Tampa, he kept getting headaches, some of which made him violently ill. After he underwent an MRI, it was discovered that Wayne had a brain tumour. Tampa Bay sent Fleming to the best doctors for treatment. After an eight-hour surgery, most of the tumour was removed, but not all of it. Unfortunately for the hockey world, Wayne Fleming passed away on March 25, 2013, less than two years after he left Edmonton.

Nail Yakupov celebrates a goal on January 24, 2013, by sliding all the way to centre ice. The "Yakapov Slide" became a controversial topic.

press conference to announce that general manager Steve Tambellini was being let go. "Steve is a very good man who worked hard for the Oilers, and I want to thank him for his contributions to the hockey team over that last five years," he said.

Craig MacTavish, who had been brought back to the Oilers the previous summer as senior vice-president of hockey operations, was named as Tambellini's successor. Scott Howson was hired to fill MacTavish's former position. He had been the Oilers' assistant general manager between 2002 and 2007 before becoming GM of the Columbus Blue Jackets.

"Despite improvement over the course of the season, the fact of the matter is we are not where we want to be right now, nor where we should be," Lowe said. "Because careers are short, and opportunities for achievement don't come along very often, we feel strongly that it's important that we make some changes right now."

The management changes made little difference in the short run. The Oilers ended up with a 19–22–7 record, leaving them 12th in the Western Conference, out of the playoffs. The good news was that the team's youngsters were taking the lead on offence. Taylor Hall led the club with 50 points, including 16 goals, in 45 games. Even though he seemed like a veteran by now, Sam Gagner was still just 23 and had 14 goals and 38 points. Eberle came in third with 16 goals and 37 points. Draft pick Nail Yakupov had a great rookie season, scoring a team-high 17 goals and accumulating 31 points. Free agent Justin Schultz, who was also just 22, had eight goals from the blue line and 27 points.

Another year of not making the playoffs was eating at the management staff. They met when the season was over to discuss further changes. This was the eighth year in a row where the Oilers were having an early summer. The rebuild was taking longer than anyone wanted it to.

2013–2014

SHORT STINT

After just one lockout-shortened season, head coach Ralph Krueger was let go. The news came as a shock to Krueger, who had just been in Finland and Sweden for the IIHF World Championship, where he had spent time with Oilers management. General Manager Craig MacTavish acknowledged the decision wasn't fair to Krueger, but that their hockey philosophy didn't completely align, and that made the change necessary. The Oilers had their sights set on Dallas Eakins, head coach of the Toronto Maple Leafs' AHL farm team, and the window of availability was narrow. When they hired him, MacTavish praised Eakins for his ability to keep a cool head under pressure.

DRAFTING FOR SIZE AND SKILL

With the seventh pick in the draft, the Oilers chose Darnell Nurse, a defence-man with size who played a tough, physical game and had some offensive skill. The Oilers were still looking for a player capable of filling the blueline void left by Chris Pronger in 2006. Nurse was rated fourth among North American skaters, and the hope was that with some training and time, he would add bulk and become an imposing figure who could play top minutes. The Oilers knew he might not grace the roster right away, but believed he would be an asset when he matured. In 2012–13, as an alternate captain with the Sault Ste. Marie Greyhounds, he had helped them reach the OHL playoffs, which they had missed for two seasons.

In the third round, 88th overall, Edmonton selected Russian winger Anton Slepyshev. The Oilers liked his speed and great hands, but knew he might have to work on toughness, so he remained in Russia's KHL for a few years. He represented Russia at the World Under-18 Championship in 2011 and 2012, as well as at the 2013 World Junior Championship.

BIG CHANGES

On July 4, longtime Oiler Shawn Horcoff was traded to the Dallas Stars for defence-man Philip Larsen, an average-sized,

Defenseman Andrew Ference became the 13th Oilers captain. He came to Edmonton with Stanley Cup experience, having won with the Bruins in 2011.

skilled defenceman with offensive talent. Illness and injuries would limit him to 30 games. The Oilers also signed Edmonton-born defenceman Andrew Ference, who had won a Stanley Cup with the Boston Bruins in 2011, to a four-year deal. The 34-year-old was named the 14th captain of the Oilers, taking over from Horcoff.

Magnus Paajarvi's contract expired on July 1, and rather than re-sign him, the Oilers traded him to St. Louis, along with a second-round draft pick, for winger David Perron. Perron had already enjoyed a couple of 20-goal seasons, and in his first year with Edmonton he would score 28.

The team lost a couple of netminders to free agency—Yann Danis signed with Philadelphia, while Nikolai Khabibulin returned to Chicago—and gained a couple: Jason LaBarbera from Phoenix and Richard Bachman from the Dallas Stars. But as the season neared the quarter mark, the Oilers still felt they could use some goaltending depth, so on November 8 they signed Ilya Bryzgalov, who had been a runner-up for the Vezina Trophy in 2009–10. Ladislav Smid and Olivier Roy were sent to the Calgary Flames for a couple of minor-league prospects, forward Roman Horak and goaltender Laurent Brossoit.

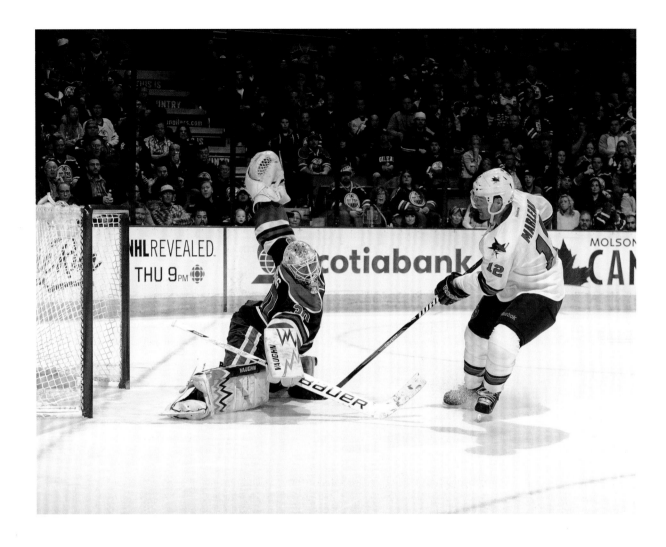

On the eve of the new season, rookie enforcer Luke Gazdic was picked up on waivers from the Dallas Stars. Although he was better known for his physical play than his scoring touch, he would become one of the few players in NHL history to score a goal on his first-ever NHL shift.

Two weeks into the new year, on January 15, goaltender Devan Dubnyk was traded to Nashville for Matt Hendricks. Feisty, tough and a great character, Hendricks fit right in with his new teammates. When he wasn't doing his job as a grinder, he was putting together music playlists for the dressing room. Dubnyk's place in goal was taken by Ben Scrivens, acquired the same day in a trade with Los Angeles. The goaltending picture still hadn't settled as the trade deadline approached and Bryzgalov was sent to Minnesota on March 4, while Viktor Fasth was acquired from Anaheim. The next day, Ales Hemsky was traded to Ottawa, while Nick Schultz was sent to Columbus, both in exchange for draft picks.

On January 29, 2014, Ben Scrivens stopped all 59 shots the San Jose Sharks threw his way, setting an NHL record. Here's one of them—a particularly tough stop against Patrick Marleau.

OIL COUNTRY GETS RESTLESS

If fans were looking for the Oilers' fortunes to change, this wasn't the year. The Oilers ended with a 29-44-9 record and a dismal 67 points—leaving them in last place in the Western Conference and 28th in the league. Throughout the season, fans started throwing jerseys on the ice to show their frustration with a team that was continually losing. The first occurrence was in December, when the Oilers lost 6-0 to St. Louis and a fan tossed an Ales Hemsky jersey on the ice. On January 25, another fan threw a jersey after a game the Oilers lost by a goal to Phoenix. This time, head coach Dallas Eakins called the fan out—the first time in team history a coach had reproached a fan. On March 22, after the Oilers were smoked 8-1 by the Calgary Flames, another jersey was tossed on the ice. Scrivens picked it up with his stick and threw it back into the crowd.

In all, six different goalies defended the Oiler net this year—more than in any season since 1979-80, when the team also went through six goaltenders. Before he was traded, Dubnyk played 32 games. Scrivens took over as the Number 1 goalie and logged 21 games. Bryzgalov played 20, Fasth and LaBarbera each made seven appearances, Bachman played three times.

The leading scorer was Taylor Hall, with 80 points, his best season as an Oiler. Eberle's 65 points were second on the team, while Perron's 57 were third. Nugent-Hopkins had 56 points, including 19 goals, and Gagner had 10 goals and 37 points. The highest-scoring defenceman, even after he was traded in February, was Justin Schultz, with 11 goals and 33 points.

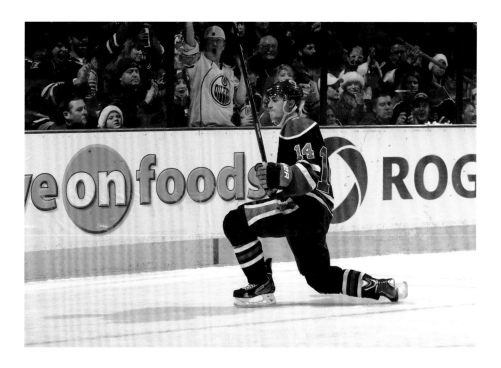

Jordan Eberle was known for his goal scoring ability, and was a top scorer for the Oilers in the 2013–14 season.

Ryan Smyth Retires

On April 11, 2014, Ryan Smyth held a press conference at Rexall Place to announce that he would play the last game of his 19-season career the following night against the Vancouver Canucks. For the first and only time in his career as an Oiler, he wore the C stitched onto his Number 94 jersey. It was a special tribute to all he'd done with the team. One of Smyth's records was the fastest hat trick scored by an Oiler, at two minutes and one second on October 12, 2006, beating Wayne Gretzky's previous record. At the start of this final game, Smyth's son, Alex, stood on the blue line with him during the national anthem.

BREAKING GROUND

Ground was finally broken on March 4, 2014, for Rogers Place, a new, modern arena to replace Rexall Place. Edmonton-based PCL had received the contract to build the arena, which was projected to be completed in time for the beginning of the 2016–17 NHL season. The Winter Garden, once derided as the "Bridge to Nowhere," was now a gathering place called Ford Hall. The 18,347-seat arena would boast wide concourses, 3,100 club seats, 900 loge seats and the biggest Jumbotron in the NHL. Hotels, condominiums and other amenities were also planned for the district, revitalizing the downtown core. Restaurant owners around the area were excited.

Oilers owner Daryl Katz gives Edmonton Mayor Don Iveson an Oiler Jersey for the opening of the new arena. The '16 on the back signifies the year the building will open.

2014-2015

HOCKEY BUILDER HIRED

With a new arena on the way, Daryl Katz felt the time was right to reorganize his sports-related business. At the end of the 2013–14 season, Rexall Sports was renamed as Oilers Entertainment Group (OEG). In addition to the Katz Group's sports and entertainment properties, which included the Oilers, the junior Edmonton Oil Kings and Oiler farm teams in Oklahoma City and Bakersfield, California, OEG would manage Rogers Place.

Katz retained the title of chairman of OEG. Kevin Lowe was appointed vice-chair, while retaining his title as president of hockey operations. Team president Patrick LaForge was named OEG's president and chief operating officer. And there was a new face in the executive suite.

Katz had met Bob Nicholson at the

Young Harrison Katz (in the Oilers jersey to the right) continues his tradition of welcoming draft picks, here when Leon Draisaitl was drafted.

Northlands Coliseum opened in 1974, and was subsequently known as the Edmonton Coliseum, Skyreach Centre, and Rexall Place. However, for the Oilers to stay in Edmonton, a new arena was necessary. In the summer of 2016, prior to the opening of Rogers Place, the name returned to Northlands Coliseum.

2010 Winter Olympics in Vancouver, when Nicholson was president of Hockey Canada. A mutual respect had formed between the two. Nicholson was a builder, having taken Hockey Canada from a small organization with 30 employees to one with a multimillion-dollar budget. Katz had talked to Nicholson that year about joining the Oiler management team in some capacity, but Nicholson wanted to stay with Hockey Canada through one more Winter Olympics. After Canada won Olympic gold medals in 2014 in Sochi, Russia, in both men's and women's hockey, Nicholson decided to retire from Hockey Canada after 25 years with the organization.

It wasn't long after his retirement, however, that Katz pursued Nicholson again, asking him to come to the Oilers as well as have a hand in the arena project. He had witnessed the atmosphere in Edmonton during the World Junior Championship, held in Edmonton and Calgary in 2012. Fans had filled Rexall Place to watch those games. He knew the challenges that came with launching and managing a new arena would be massive, but he saw something special in the way people in the city worked so diligently for charity organizations, and the pride that they had in their city and their teams, including football and hockey. If any city could handle a project like the new arena district, it was Edmonton. He was also pleased to be working alongside Lowe, who had been part of the 2002, 2006, 2010 and 2014 Olympic management teams. He agreed to come on board and was named vice-chair of OEG, responsible for business operations. A press conference was held in mid-June, at which Nicholson assured Edmonton fans, "There are a lot of things that are going well in this organization. I'm not coming here to rip things apart."

DRAISAITL DRAFTED

The Oilers had the third-overall pick in 2014, and it was German-born Leon Draisaitl whose name they called on draft day. Draisaitl was a big forward who played with a maturity that made him look poised and almost calm. In his second year with the Prince Albert Raiders, he had ranked fourth in the WHL (tied with Sam Reinhart of the Kootenay Ice, drafted second by Buffalo), with 105 points (38 goals and 67 assists). His long reach was often compared to that of Mario Lemieux. Coming out of training camp, he was deemed ready for the NHL, and he played in the Oilers' first 37 games of the season. In early January, however, he was returned to junior. Finishing out the year with the Kelowna Rockets, he had 53 points in 32 games and helped the team reach the Memorial Cup final, where they lost in overtime to the Oshawa Generals. Draisaitl was named the MVP of the tournament.

GAGNER GONE

Looking for some help on the blue line, the Oilers sent a fifth-round draft pick to Columbus for impending free agent Nikita Nikitin, and then signed him to a two-year contract. The gamble didn't pay off, as Nikitin played in only 53 games over the next two seasons.

Although he was just 24, Sam Gagner was already a veteran and the longest-serving Oiler on the team. On June 29, just before a no-trade clause in his contract was due to kick in, he was traded to

the Tampa Bay Lightning for 28-year-old winger Teddy Purcell. The Oilers were trying to make changes, put some puzzle pieces together. They needed more forwards with defensive skills and Gagner still had value on the market.

On July 1, free agents Mark Fayne, Benoit Pouliot and Keith Aulie were signed. Fayne, signed to a four-year deal, had played the past four years with the New Jersey Devils and was seen as a shut-down defenceman. Pouliot, who had been to the Stanley Cup final with the New York Rangers in 2014, was signed for five years. Though he was joining his fifth team in as many seasons, he was seen as a big winger who played a physical style and was willing to crash the net. Aulie, a defenceman who had played for Toronto and Tampa Bay, received a one-year deal.

REUNION OF THE 1984 TEAM

Thirty years can pass in the blink of an eye, or so it seemed to the Oilers who won Edmonton's first Stanley Cup championship in 1984. To kick off the 2014–15 season, the Edmonton Oilers organized a massive event at Rexall Place to celebrate the anniversary. Wayne Gretzky led the charge, making phone calls to invite former players. When Paul Coffey got his call from Gretzky, memories flooded back from when the Great One was his captain. Mark Messier was just as happy with his call, offering up a joke that he hadn't graduated from high school, so he would make this his high school reunion.

The reunion was scheduled for October 10, the night after the Oilers' home opener, and would be a fundraiser

The laughs were plenty, as were the tears, when the 1984 team had their 30-year reunion at Rexall Place.

for a new pediatric ambulatory clinic at the Stollery Children's Hospital. When the first 12,000 tickets went on sale, they were bought up within an hour. Once the arena seating was reconfigured, 2,000 more tickets were released and they too were snapped up. Net proceeds, including Ticketmaster's service charges, went to the Edmonton Oilers

The schedule for the players, who had arrived from all over the world, started with a casual dinner at the beautiful home of Daryl Katz. There, in an intimate gathering, the players reminisced about the good old days together. They also got to tour the new Stollery facility.

Then came the evening the fans were waiting for. They were going to see their

> "What an inspiring visit, what an inspiring tour." —Mark Messier

Community Foundation, which in turn directed the funding to the hospital's new wing. All of the players were pleased with this connection; many of those players from 1984 were married now, with children of their own.

heroes on stage as they chatted candidly and laughed while telling stories about the team and winning the Stanley Cups. The cheering was loud and appreciative. When former Oilers owner Peter Pocklington stood in front

Peter Pocklington got emotional when he received a standing ovation at the 2014 reunion. "I was shocked," he said.

of the crowd, fans gave him a standing ovation. It had been years since he'd been anywhere near Oilers fans. Tears streamed down his face. "It was a shock," he said, "What a homecoming." Mark Messier also shared a few tears. Being back on Edmonton ice seemed to have that effect on him.

The only member of the 1984 team who wasn't able to make the event was Kevin McClelland, the hero of the Islanders series who scored the lone Oilers goal in Game 1. Personal issues prevented him from travelling to Edmonton, but a crew was sent to videotape him so that he could be there in spirit and on the big screen.

STUCK IN 28TH PLACE

Draisaitl made his NHL debut in the home opener and scored his first goal on October 24, while Darnell Nurse made his first appearance in an NHL game on October 14. But the magic of the 1984 team reunion didn't rub off on the current edition of the squad. They opened the season with a five-game losing streak. After rebounding with four wins in a row, they lost 24 of their next 27. They hit a particularly low point on November 11, when they lost a home game to the Chicago Blackhawks 7–1. Fans lined up and booed the Oilers as they made their way from the ice to the dressing room. Many of the players had their heads hung low.

In mid-December, head coach Dallas Eakins was fired. General manager Craig MacTavish announced he was taking over, and would be joined behind the bench by Todd Nelson, who was coaching the Oilers' AHL affiliate, the Oklahoma City Barons. This was Nelson's first NHL job, and after a breaking-in period, MacTavish stepped away and let Nelson coach the last 46 games.

There wasn't much that Nelson could have done to save the season. The Oilers were out of playoff contention by Christmas, and finished with 62 points.

Remembering Pat Quinn

After battling liver disease, Pat Quinn died in Vancouver on November 23, 2014. The hockey world was saddened by the loss of "the Big Irishman" who had dedicated his life to hockey, especially to coaching. Pat Quinn loved people and was always available to sign an autograph or pose for a photo with a fan. Even though he'd only coached in Edmonton briefly, he was respected and admired by all. The hockey world had been blessed by Quinn, and Vancouver renamed a section of Abbott Street that ran past their home rink as Pat Quinn Way.

Leon Draisaitl's first goal souvenirs—the puck and game score sheet from October 24, 2014. The Oilers won 6-3 against Carolina, with Draisaitl's contribution coming in the third period.

2015–2016

WE HAVE A WINNER

Some draft years see a lot of buzz generated around a top prospect. This was an unusual one, because there were *two* such players available. Connor McDavid, from Newmarket, Ontario, was a scoring phenom for the Erie Otters who skated like he had rockets on his blades. American Jack Eichel had amassed 71 points in 40 games with Boston University, and was a well-rounded player.

This season saw the draft lottery tweaked slightly. With the third-fewest points in the 2014–15 season, Edmonton had an 11.5 percent chance at moving up to the Number 1 position.

The results were revealed on television on April 18. After about five minutes, only three envelopes were left, meaning that only three teams—the Oilers, Arizona Coyotes and Buffalo Sabres— were still in the running. Bill Daly opened the envelope labelled with the number three, and it contained an Oiler logo set against a gold background instead of the usual white. "We have a winner," he announced. "The first-over-all pick in the 2015 NHL draft belongs to the Edmonton Oilers."

Fans, media and even the Oiler management were shocked. The team would be drafting first overall for the fourth time in six years.

CLEANING HOUSE IN THE FRONT OFFICE

Two days after they won the draft lottery, the Oilers held a press conference to introduce OEG vice-chair Bob Nicholson as the company's chief executive officer. Asked what had changed as far as the organization was concerned, he responded, "Now, everyone in the organization reports directly to myself," adding that he was going to be more hands-on in every aspect.

Nicholson didn't take long to revamp the team's management structure. On April 24, Peter Chiarelli, whom Nicholson had hired to work with the 2014 Canadian Olympic team, was made the Oilers' general manager and president of hockey operations. Chiarelli had spent nine years with the Boston Bruins, leading them to a Stanley Cup championship in 2011 and an appearance in the final in 2013.

Superstar and first overall pick in the 2015 NHL Entry Draft, Connor McDavid, suits up for Edmonton in the fall of 2015, at the age of 18.

Harrison Katz welcomes the Oilers first overall draft, Connor McDavid.

The move meant that Patrick LaForge, longtime club president, would be moving on. Craig MacTavish was assigned the title of senior vice-president of hockey operations. Kevin Lowe became vice-chairman and he would work with Nicholson to further the growth of OEG. Nicholson summed up the reorganization this way: "We have to get this organization in a winning mode."

Next to do was hire a new head coach. Forty-eight hours after he coached Team Canada to a gold medal at the World Championship in Prague, Czech Republic, Todd McLellan was named the 14th head coach in Edmonton Oilers history. McLellan was coming off a seven-year run as head coach of the San Jose Sharks that included two trips to the Western Conference final. Jordan Eberle and Taylor Hall, who were second

and third in scoring on Team Canada, were happy with the decision because they had flourished under McLellan at the worlds. McLellan brought his own assistant coaches with him: Jay Woodcroft, who would handle the forwards, and Jim Johnson, who would work with defence-men. Goalie coach Ian Herbers, (who had played 22 games for the Oilers in the 1993–94 season), was hired on July 15, as another cog in the coaching wheel. With all-new management and staff in place, the Oilers were starting with a clean slate.

Chiarelli wasted no time getting to work on retooling the Oilers roster. On June 26, at the NHL Entry Draft in Sunrise, Florida, he picked Connor McDavid with the first-overall pick. McDavid had incredible speed—especially in his first three steps—hockey sense, and a gift for passing the puck tape-to-tape.

The Oilers bench took on a completely new look in 2015. From right to left: Jay Woodcroft (assistant coach), Todd McLellan (head coach), Ian Herbers (assistant coach), Jim Johnson (assistant coach), and Brad Harrison (assistant equipment manager).

He was the third player to receive exceptional status from Hockey Canada to play in the CHL, at the age of 15. During his OHL career with the Erie Otters, McDavid took home many awards, including the Emms Family Award as the top rookie in the OHL in 2012–13. In his second year, he won the William Hanley Trophy for most sportsmanlike player, the Bobby Smith Trophy for OHL scholastic player of the year, and the CHL Scholastic Player of the Year Award. In his 2014–15 season, his hardware included the Red Tilson Trophy for Most Outstanding Player and the Bobby Smith Trophy for Scholastic Player of the Year. McDavid was touted as the next NHL franchise player.

Chiarelli dealt the 16th and 33rd picks to the New York Islanders for defenceman Griffin Reinhart. A fourth-overall pick in 2012, Reinhart had captained the Edmonton Oil Kings to a Memorial Cup championship. The Oilers hoped he would provide some toughness on the blue line. The next day, Chiarelli nabbed goaltender Cam Talbot from the New York Rangers for draft picks and Eric Gryba from the Ottawa Senators for forward Travis Ewanyk and a fourth-round pick.

On that New York team, Talbot had proven he was "Calm Talbot," a cool and collected goalie with quick reflexes. But he was destined to play second fiddle to Rangers starter Henrik Lundqvist and looked forward to being the Number 1 guy in Edmonton. Gryba was a defence-man who could squeeze opponents along the boards and literally knock them off their feet in open ice.

Free-agent acquisitions included defenceman Andrej Sekera and centre Mark Letestu. A smart player, the Slovakian Sekera was good at reading the play, could fire off crisp passes and was a strong skater. Letestu, a native of tiny Elk Point, Alberta (population 1,462), was happy to be playing in his home province. A faceoff specialist and a good positional player, Letestu would play on the fourth line and benefit the power play with his ability to direct the play.

From the outset, Chiarelli wasn't afraid to be criticized. He sent Leon Draisaitl down to the minors—the Bakersfield Condors were now their AHL farm team. He kept some players on the roster that people didn't agree with. He told the media, "Everyone thinks the roster is written in stone and it's not. We still have to see. Play changes, 10-game segments, 20-game segments; we still have to see what we have here."

Chiarelli was proving to be aggressive, but not impulsive.

CONNOR'S COLLARBONE CRASH

The excitement and anticipation over drafting Connor McDavid had built to a fever pitch. When McDavid arrived in Edmonton, the media looked to him for comments and fans lined up to greet him. He became a hero before he even stepped on the ice.

There seemed to be a little light trying to shine through the gloom of the "decade of darkness," as the Oilers' 10-year playoff drought had been dubbed. Young McDavid stepped on the ice and showed his incredible speed and stickhandling ability, recording 12 points in his first dozen NHL games. The league named him its rookie of the month for October. But then, on November 3, his streak was put on hold. McDavid picked up the puck and raced toward the net with Flyers defenceman Brandon Manning shadowing him.

McDavid looked as if he might have an angle to shoot, but then he caught an edge and crashed into the boards. He got up and skated slowly to the bench, holding his shoulder. Since the period was almost over, he insisted on sitting on the bench until the buzzer went. His face paled. Finally, when it was time to head to the dressing room, he stood and almost passed out. The trainers helped him walk the tunnel. An x-ray showed a broken collarbone—McDavid would be out until February. He had been heading towards a Calder Trophy, but it wasn't to be. In his 37 game absence, the Oilers only won 13 games.

In his first game back, on February 2 against the Columbus Blue Jackets, McDavid made his presence felt by scoring an amazing goal. Using his explosive speed, he split the defence and raced to the net, putting the puck in on a snap shot to the top shelf. He also added two assists in the Oilers' 5–1 win. Nine days later, against Toronto, he scored twice and assisted on the Oilers' other three goals in a 5–2 victory. Clearly, he was back in top form, as evidenced by the rookie-of-the-month honours he earned again in February and March.

BEEFING UP THE FORWARD LINES

The turnover in the front office, the arrival of a once-in-a-lifetime superstar, and the impending move to a new arena sent expectations off the charts. Still, while the disruptions were for the better, the team struggled. General manager Peter Chiarelli, only months into the job, took a methodical approach, as if

Talent oozes from these young players. They have extraordinary scoring skill and potential. Here they celebrate with one another and the fans.

playing a game of chess. Size and toughness were among the needs he hoped to fill, and just after the Christmas trading freeze was lifted, he made his move, acquiring winger Zack Kassian from Montreal for goalie Ben Scrivens.

Acquired in the off-season from Vancouver, Kassian had not played a game for Montreal because he had been

suspended for substance abuse and spent time in a rehab centre. But he had played for Buffalo and Vancouver. While with the Canucks, in a game against the Oilers, Kassian high-sticked Sam Gagner in the mouth, which caused Gagner to lose four teeth and left him with a broken jaw. A metal plate and screws had to be inserted to help mend the damage. Kassian was one of those players, like Ken Linseman, whom you'd rather have playing for you than against. Chiarelli had a hunch about Kassian, and the big winger knew he was getting a second chance at being an NHL hockey player. He showed up in Edmonton willing to work.

Another positive move was made on February 29, when Edmonton acquired winger Patrick Maroon from Anaheim for minor-league defenceman (and former Oil King) Martin Gernat and a fourth-round pick in 2016. Maroon wasted no time showing that he could be an asset, scoring two goals and adding two assists in his first four games as an Oiler. He ended the season with eight goals and six assists in just 16 games—a leap from his performance as a Duck: four goals and nine assists in 56 games. Big and strong, he was the kind of physical forward that the Oilers needed.

With the second-youngest roster in the NHL, this year's team posted a record of 31–43–8 for a total of 70 points. Despite an eight-point improvement over 2014–15, they dropped from 28th place to 29th. Even after missing 37 games, Connor McDavid was nominated for the Calder Memorial Trophy. (Artemi Panarin of the Chicago Blackhawks won.) Taylor Hall led the club with 26 goals and 65 points, Jordan Eberle scored 25 goals, and in his first full season, Leon Draisaitl had 51 points.

Still, fans had reason to hope. They could look forward to Peter Chiarelli's roster moves over the summer, and to a season of games at the brand-new Rogers Place.

FAREWELL TO THE OLD BARN

This was to be the Oilers' last season in Rexall Place. Throughout the year at home games, former players were honoured in an "Once an Oiler, Always an Oiler" highlight. The player was announced and the spotlight zoomed across the arena to where he was standing among the fans. With the player would be a longtime season-ticket holder, who would receive a signed jersey from him.

The farewell game at Rexall Place took place on April 6, against the Vancouver Canucks. After 42 years (including the WHA years), the Oilers would be moving to a new home. The ceremony to say goodbye to the rink was, in true Oilers fashion, a class act. Over 150 alumni were on hand, including Hall of Famers Wayne Gretzky, Mark Messier, Paul Coffey, Grant Fuhr, Jari Kurri, Glen Sather and Glenn Anderson, and they stepped onto the ice, waving to the fans. A four-minute tribute video showcased the team's history, including all those Stanley Cups and the Cinderella run of 2006. One of the most emotional moments of the evening occurred when Joey Moss, who had been a dressing-room attendant for 37 years, proudly carried the flag. He performed his part with such dignity that he sent the fans into a cheering frenzy.

The night was magical, and despite the Oilers' low position in the standings, Edmonton celebrated. After another tough season when wins were scarce, the Oilers won that night, beating the Canucks 6–2.

Glen Sather

On December 11, 2015, before a home game against the New York Rangers, the time came to raise a banner in honour of Glen Sather. This ceremony took on a different feel than those that had come before. Players getting their numbers retired would skate around the ice and wave to the fans. For this event, a spotlight followed Sather as he started at the top of the arena and walked down the stairs, shaking the hands of fans, some of whom had been coming to watch the Oilers play for years. The walk was touching and Glen called the effect "dynamic." The fans responded, standing and cheering for the man who was behind the five Stanley Cup championships. Once at ice level, Sather made his way onto the ice and towards the podium, where he was joined by his family and the others whose banners were waiting for his: Mark Messier, Grant Fuhr, Jari Kurri, Paul Coffey, Glenn Anderson, Al Hamilton and Rod Phillips. Wayne Gretzky was away for a family event, but a video of him played on the Jumbotron as Glen made his way down the steps. In Sather's speech, he talked about his love of Edmonton, the city and the fans. Instead of a player number, Sather's banner featured an image of five Stanley Cups.

2016–2017

PULLING FOR PULJUJARVI

In 2015, the Oilers had beaten the odds in the draft lottery, moving up from the third slot to the first-overall pick. This year, with the second-worst record in the league, their chance of winning the draw was a little bit better at 13.5 percent. But the ping pong balls didn't fall their way, and they actually dropped two spots to the fourth pick.

The Maple Leafs took to the podium first and drafted Auston Matthews. With the second pick, Winnipeg selected Patrick Laine. And then Columbus passed on Jesse Puljujarvi to choose the top-ranked North American skater, Pierre-Luc Dubois. The Oilers hadn't expected Puljujarvi to be available when their turn came. Whispering among themselves, they changed plans. General manager Peter Chiarelli approached the microphone and called out Puljujarvi's name. The right winger had size, skating ability and good puck sense, and he had been named the MVP of the World Junior Championship. Puljujarvi was known as a player who would ride the stationary bike until he dropped—a hard worker who'd fit in well with the new Oilers squad.

TRADING NUMBER 1 PICKS

Every spring, NHL teams pursue undrafted college players in the hope that they'll uncover a late-blooming star. The Oiler GM thought he had found another such player in Drake Caggiula of the University of North Dakota, whom he signed on May 7. Caggiula was crafty and skilled and had a good jump on his first three steps, making him a player who could buzz around the ice, wreaking havoc.

On June 29, Chiarelli made what was quite possibly the boldest trade of the year when he swapped Taylor Hall to the New Jersey Devils for Adam Larsson. Twitter exploded as disgruntled Oilers fans vented their frustration. Hall was a favourite for many, a goal scorer and an incredibly fast skater, and many thought Edmonton had come out on the short end of the deal. But the Oilers needed a defenceman, and Larsson, a right-hand shot, was a good puck mover, efficient, stable, and able to play big minutes.

"Orange Crush" was the theme for the post-season. After a ten-year playoff drought, fans show love and renewed excitement for their young, talented Oilers.

He'd been the Devils' fourth-overall pick in 2011 and became their first defence-man since Scott Niedermayer in 1991–92 to play as an 18-year-old. He'd played four seasons with the Devils.

Hall let his fans know how much he had loved playing for Edmonton, even though they hadn't seen playoff action since he suited up with the team. Hall spoke on a conference call and said, "I was there for six seasons, so you develop a relationship with the team, with the city, with the fans." Further along in the call, Hall added, "I feel like I've been a good soldier for six years. I prepared as best I could, and I did as much I felt I could on the ice. At the end of the day,

they felt that they wanted to go in a different direction, which is fine." Hall had worked hard for the Oilers, playing in 381 games and recording 328 points. Twice (in 2012–13 and 2013–14), he finished among the top 10 NHL scorers.

As free-agent season opened on July 1, Chiarelli announced that the Oilers had signed Milan Lucic, one of the best available this year, to an impressive seven-year, $42 million deal. Lucic, from Burnaby, British Columbia, had been in talks with many NHL general managers. He chose the Oilers as his new team mainly because "of the Connor McDavid factor." Lucic had seen what had happened in Pittsburgh

Following tough guys Dave Semenko and Georges Laraque, Milan Lucic takes up #27. Here he stands before the brand new Rogers Place as it nears completion.

with Sidney Crosby. Players wanted to come to Pittsburgh because of him, and the team won Stanley Cups. Lucic said he would wear Number 27, his old junior number and the one that Dave Semenko and Georges Laraque had worn for Edmonton. A strong power forward, Lucic would bring size and toughness to the Oilers, along with some goal scoring.

On the eve of the season, on October 7, Chiarelli traded another first-overall pick: Nail Yakupov, the first player chosen in 2012, was sent to the St. Louis Blues for a third-round pick that would turn into a second-rounder if Yakupov managed to score 15 goals in the coming season. The move allowed Chiarelli to sign rugged, shot-blocking defenceman Kris Russell.

ROGERS PLACE OPENS

On September 8, a ribbon-cutting ceremony took place at the new Rogers Place. The day was filled with emotion, as it represented for many people the culmination of a lot of hard work. The ceremony kicked off with a celebration of Indigenous artist Alex Janvier, whose 14-metre-wide tile mosaic graces the floor in Ford Hall. It was described as a natural beauty that would instil tranquility and promote community. Mayor Don Iveson took the stage and thanked his predecessor, Stephen Mandel, for all the work he had done to make the arena happen. Iveson felt that the arena "would change Edmonton forever." Ross Grieve from PCL, the construction firm in charge of the project, noted that he was thankful for the safety of all individuals involved in working on a project of such magnitude. Daryl Katz recalled how, when he walked through the building a year ago, while it was still under construction, the experience brought tears to his eyes. Ian O'Donnell said a few words for the Downtown Business Association, as did Guy Laurence from Rogers Communications, which had purchased the naming rights. Premier of Alberta Rachel Notley couldn't attend, but she sent her minister of economic development and trade, Edmonton's own Deron Bilous. The final speaker of the day was Wayne Gretzky, who said that the arena complemented Edmonton as a "classy and friendly" city. The afternoon ended with a colourful Indigenous dance team performing to the beat of their drums.

HUNTER THE MASCOT

After 38 years, the Edmonton Oilers decided it was finally time to have a mascot. They researched Canadian animals—in particular, Alberta animals. The lynx was the one they decided to model their mascot after.

The mascot was named after Wild Bill Hunter, the man behind the WHA Edmonton Oilers, and he wore an Oilers jersey with Number 72 on the back, to represent the year the WHA franchise was born.

Hunter was introduced on September 26, 2016, the night Rogers Place made its NHL debut for a preseason game between the Oilers and Calgary Flames. Social media lit up, saying he was terrifying, looked too mean, had menacing eyes and fangs, and that he should be "roadkill." But the Oilers disagreed, and so did children. Before creating Hunter, the Oilers organization had asked 2,200 kids from kindergarten to Grade 9 to give their opinions, and they loved Hunter. And, like all superheroes, Hunter has a backstory.

During the winter of 2013 I heard many shinny players talking about a new, world-class building that my beloved Oilers were going to play in.

Hunter the Mascot became controversial when he was touted as being "too mean looking." But kids voted for him, and that's all that counts.

I was ecstatic, and knew right then and there that this was my chance to get in on the action. On the night before the first shovel hit the ground, I packed up my stuff and made my way to 104 Avenue and 104 Street, where I built a secret den under the construction site, watching and waiting for this magnificent building to be completed. Just as the finishing touches were being made to the building, I revealed myself to the Oilers. Like my lynx family and friends, I only come out at night to hunt, and on one of those nights I actually came across a bunch of kids playing hockey on an outdoor rink. One look at the game and I was hooked. The speed, the skill, the fun! I began climbing up the banks of the River Valley every night during the winter, catching shinny games with everyone wearing their Edmonton Oilers jerseys, both old and new! It didn't take me long to become a hardcore Oilers fan. Just as the finishing touches were being made to the building, I revealed myself to the Oilers. After their initial shock of a lynx living in a secret den below Rogers Place, they quickly realized how huge a fan I was, and how committed I was to the team.

Like many in Edmonton, Hunter the Lynx never misses a home game—dancing, cheering and taking photos with the fans.

A NEW CAPTAIN

At just 19 years old, and in his second year in the NHL, Connor McDavid was made the Edmonton Oilers' 15th captain. The announcement was made on October 5 after a team practice at Rogers Place. McDavid emerged from the Oilers' new dressing room flanked by his alternate captains, Jordan Eberle, Milan Lucic and Ryan Nugent-Hopkins. As sliding doors decorated with the Oilers logo opened up, and the players walked out in jeans and jerseys, the media was on hand to snap photos and talk to the Oilers' leadership group. McDavid was not only the youngest Oilers captain ever, he was the youngest captain in the history of the NHL.

OPENING NIGHT AT ROGERS PLACE

On October 12, the Oilers staged the grand opening of Rogers Place. Prior to their 2016–17 home opener against their provincial rivals, the Calgary Flames, Wayne Gretzky and his family gathered in front of the arena to unveil his statue, which had been moved from Rexall Place, and Mark Messier was on hand to sign autographs. Inside the rink, draped over the back of every seat, were orange, white or blue T-shirts, strategically placed to form the Oilers logo when viewed from above. The effect was stunning. Before the opening faceoff, the arena lights dimmed. A spotlight followed Gretzky and Messier as they skated onto the ice, wearing white jerseys, holding up their sticks. The atmosphere was more in keeping with a

Opening night at Rogers Place was more like a rock concert than a hockey game. Mark Messier and Wayne Gretzky pass the torch to a new captain.

concert than a sporting event—the noise was deafening.

Then Gretzky and Messier left a puck at centre ice. It was supposed to remain there for the rest of the opening program so that the current captain, Connor McDavid, could pick it up. Unfortunately, the Flames players had used the puck during the warm-ups. After the warm-ups were over, the lights went down again and the Oilers were called out one by one. When it was McDavid's turn, he skated to centre ice and saw that the puck

he was meant to pick up was nowhere in sight. He stayed cool, waving his stick to the fans, who roared their appreciation. No one cheering knew or cared that there had been a hiccup. It didn't matter. The torch had been passed.

Less than two minutes into the game, Patrick Maroon became the first player to score in the new arena. Fans celebrated the event, sending noise to every inch of the rafters. Calgary, however, responded just 36 seconds later. Both Tyler Pitlick and Zack Kassian rallied for the Oilers, and they went to the dressing room for the first intermission with a 3–1 lead. Fans flocked onto the concourse, taking in the wide hallways and new concession stands. The atmosphere was almost euphoric.

The second period took a turn when Calgary scored a pair of shorthanded goals to tie the game. And then McDavid took charge. At 12:17, he nailed one to the back of the net to give the Oilers a 4–3 lead. Then, at 14:33, he took off on a breakaway. Calgary's Dennis Wideman, unable to catch him, hooked McDavid to the ice. The ref signalled for a penalty shot. McDavid didn't disappoint, beating Flames goalie Brian Elliott with a fine display of stickhandling. The Oilers went to the dressing room with a two-goal lead. Nine minutes into the third period, with Flames rookie Sam Bennett in the penalty box, young gun Jesse Puljujarvi scored his first NHL goal to make it 6–3. His smile was almost as broad as the ice surface. The Flames tried to mount a comeback with another goal, but Jordan Eberle sealed the game with the Oilers' seventh. It was a solid win, a great way to usher in the new arena, with a score that was reminiscent of the team's glory days.

A SOLID SEASON

As the Oilers' 2016–17 season picked up speed, it became clear that the 7–4 victory over Calgary wasn't a fluke. The team truly seemed to be on a better footing. They were still a young group— fifth-youngest in the league—and with so many new faces on board, they were still getting to know each other. But they were able to shake off a 6–2 blowout at the hands of the Buffalo Sabres on home ice, in which an ugly goal went in from centre ice, and win their next five. October saw a 7-2-0 run, putting them up in the standings. A 5–8–2 run in November pulled them back towards the middle of the pack, but unlike the previous 10 seasons, this time they regrouped. From December through April, they won 35 of 58 games, en route to a 47-29-9 record and 103 points— their highest win and point totals since 1986–87. In their final 14 games, they managed to go 12-2-0. The Oilers finished second in the Pacific Division, just two points behind Anaheim, and ranked fourth in the Western Conference and eighth in the NHL.

Along the way, Todd McLellan and his coaching staff stayed calm, knowing they were dealing with some inexperienced players. Instead of benching them for mistakes, they let them play through, only coming down on someone if he failed to learn from those errors and committed them over and over. With 100 points for the season, Connor McDavid won the Art Ross Trophy—the first Edmonton player in 30 years to lead the NHL scoring race. He had plenty of help from his teammates: Leon Draisaitl had 29 goals and 77 points, Jordan Eberle contributed 20 goals and 51 points, Milan Lucic played a big role with 23 goals and 50 points, and Ryan Nugent-Hopkins followed closely with 18 goals and 43 points. Patrick Maroon contributed 27 goals. Oscar Klefbom was the highest-scoring defenceman, with 38 points. Cam Talbot showed his worth by playing in 73 regular-season games, securing 42 wins. His seven shutouts tied him for third in the league. Youngster Laurent Brossoit didn't play often, making only eight appearances, but he made them count, posting a 1.99 goals against average and a .928 save percentage.

Compared to recent years, the Oiler lineup was the picture of stability this season. Deals during the regular season were few, although Chiarelli did pick up five-foot, seven-inch centreman David Desharnais from Montreal for little-used defenceman Brandon Davidson on February 28. Desharnais might be one of the smaller players currently playing in the NHL, but Chiarelli had shown a preference for players who "play big." Desharnais had also shown he could be an offensive threat.

A LONG-AWAITED PLAYOFF RUN

After missing out on 10 consecutive postseasons, the Oilers had finally landed an invite to the big dance. Their first-round opponents were coach Todd McLellan's former team, the San Jose Sharks. This would be a match up of the hungry young Oilers and the oldest roster in the NHL. Forwards Patrick Marleau and Joe Thornton made their NHL debuts in 1997—the same year Connor McDavid was born! But the Oilers were a good match for the Sharks—they had won three of the five regular-season meetings between the teams.

For the first time since the 1991 conference final, Game 1 of a playoff series was being played in Edmonton. Fans showed up in droves, and those who weren't lucky enough to score a ticket secured a spot in the adjacent Ford Hall, where the game was shown on a giant screen. From time to time, the television cameras scanned the crowd, while bands played before and after the game. "Orange Crush" became the theme of the series, and merchandise flew off the shelves: T-shirts, hats, pom-poms—and, of course, jerseys. For the first two games of the series, the Rogers Place stands were a sea of orange.

Nerves might have got the best of the Oilers in Game 1. After all, many of the players had never been in an NHL playoff game before. And every time McDavid stepped on the ice, he was swarmed by big veterans who muscled him off the puck. Even so, the Oilers took a 2–0 lead into the first intermission. But Joel Ward got one back on a second-period power play, defenceman Paul Martin tied it in the third, and Melker Karlsson's marker at 3:22 of overtime gave the Sharks the win. Cam Talbot did his best, stopping 41 of 44 shots.

Opening-night jitters were nowhere to be seen in Game 2. After a scoreless second period, Zack Kassian picked up a loose puck on the penalty kill and barrelled down the ice, snapping it past San Jose goalie Martin Jones for a short-handed goal. Kassian had the game of his life, adding two incredible hits. The rest of the game belonged to the goaltenders until, with the Oilers again playing a man short at 10:31 of the third

period, Connor McDavid wheeled down the left side and flicked it into to the net. Talbot had an easier night, called upon to make just 16 saves as he recorded the shutout.

Game 3 in San Jose was another defensive battle. Talbot earned another shutout, stopping 23 shots, while Kassian scored the lone goal to give Edmonton the win. It had been a tight series so far, and with the Oilers holding a 2–1 edge going into Game 4, there was a lot of excitement back home. But the Sharks had their share of offensive weapons, and they were in full display on April 18 as they handed the Oilers a 7–0 shellacking. Talbot shook his head as he headed to the dressing room. With such a young team, the media pondered what might happen in Game 5. Could the Oilers recover from such a lopsided score? Putting the loss in perspective,

Captain McDavid said of the series, "It's 2–2 and we have to win two of three."

Back in Edmonton two nights later, the crowd greeted the Oilers as champions, putting the loss behind them. The game started off on a good note for the Oilers as Patrick Maroon beat Martin Jones at 5:28 of the first period. The fans were on their feet, waving the orange pom-poms that had been placed on their seats prior to the game. Some fans were dressed up in orange wigs and crazy costumes. Ford Hall was jam-packed as well. But the Sharks rallied and scored two goals before the end of the first period. At 8:38 of the second period, David Schlemko made it 3–1 for the visitors.

The hospitality ended there. At 18:33 of the second, Mark Letestu nailed the puck into the back of the net and the crowd erupted. Trailing by a single goal

Captain Connor McDavid leads the team to the playoffs for the first time in a decade.

and pouring shot after shot on Jones—Edmonton would outshoot San Jose 48–30—it took until 17:33 of the third before defenceman Oscar Klefbom tied it up. The seconds ticked off the clock, and Oiler fans prepared for a bonus as the game headed into overtime. The extra period was almost over when Desharnais scooted over the blue line and passed to Andrej Sekera, who gave it to Draisaitl in the corner. Desharnais kept his legs moving and flew towards the net, where Draisaitl fed him a perfect pass. Desharnais one-timed it, scoring his first overtime playoff goal.

The Oilers took Game 6 by a score of 3–1, with goals coming from Draisaitl, Anton Slepyshev and McDavid. That night in Edmonton, a sold-out crowd gathered at Rogers Place, paying five dollars apiece—with the funds going to charity—to watch their team win the series on the super-sized Jumbotron. These events came to be known as Watch Parties. The atmosphere, even though the team was out of town, was electric. Fans even did the wave.

For the second round of the playoffs, Edmonton travelled to Anaheim. Adam Larsson and Mark Letestu each scored two goals, while Draisaitl—who had already racked up three assists—scored into an empty net with 1:05 on the clock to cap a 5–3 victory. As the game ended, fans attending that night's Watch Party poured out of Rogers Place, cheering, "We want the Cup!"

In Game 2, Talbot was remarkable, making 39 saves. Sekera and Maroon scored to give the visiting Oilers a 2–1 victory. Feeling a bit lucky to have stolen a game from the Ducks, the Oilers headed back to home ice with a 2–0 series lead.

Fans were in a frenzy as they showed up for Game 3. But first the anthems had to be sung. Canadian country star Brett Kissel stepped up to the microphone to sing "The Star-Spangled Banner." Strumming the opening chord on a guitar, he sang the first note, but realized that no sound was coming from the public-address system. He stepped back for a moment, then tried again. The glitch didn't affect the television audio feed, so viewers at home were initially puzzled by the false starts. When Kissel realized he couldn't be heard, he took the microphone out of the stand and waved it like a conductor's baton. The crowd responded by belting out the American anthem, loud and clear without any prompting or lyrics being flashed on the Jumbotron. When the time came for Robert Clark, the Oilers' official anthem singer, to perform "O Canada," he followed Kissel's lead, directing 18,347 voices in an impromptu a cappella rendition.

The arena was buzzing with energy, but the mood quickly deflated when Rickard Rakell of the Ducks scored 25 seconds after the opening faceoff. The Oilers were trailing 3–0 when, with 40 seconds to go in the first period, Patrick Maroon put one in. The goal raised the fans' spirits, and the Oilers came out for the second period with fire in their bellies. They skated hard, and it paid off when Slepyshev wired home a shot. Next up, McDavid put in a pretty goal, spinning in a tight circle and rifling the puck over goalie John Gibson's left elbow, tying the game. Anaheim snatched back the lead just 28 seconds later, and pulled ahead by two at 4:56 of the third period on a controversial goal by Jakob Silfverberg, a borderline offside that was allowed to stand. The Ducks took the game 6–3, but the Oilers still led the series 2–1. After the game Todd McLellan was asked about the questionable goal. "That wasn't the backbreaker. The backbreaker was the [one] 25 seconds in."

Game 4 brought even more controversy. It started well enough, with the Oilers scoring twice to get the fans on their feet. Milan Lucic opened the scoring at 15:38 of the first period. Two minutes later, Leon Draisaitl picked up a turnover and rushed down the ice with McDavid at his side. Draisaitl passed to McDavid, who passed back, but it caught a lucky bounce and the puck landed back on McDavid's stick. He roofed it, top corner. The Oilers went to the dressing room with a 2–0 lead. But the Ducks weren't going to let this sit; Anaheim star Ryan Getzlaf scored a minute and a half into the second period. Coach McLellan challenged the goal, alleging that Getzlaf's linemate Corey Perry had interfered with goaltender Cam Talbot. When the referee announced that the challenge had been overturned and the goal would stand, the fans went into an uproar, chanting, "Ref, you suck!"

Getzlaf was on fire. He assisted on Rakell's goal at 5:33 of the period, and then popped in his second of the game at 14:25, sending the Ducks to the dressing room with a 3–2 lead after a period in which they'd outshot the Oilers 21–5. Late in the third period, Talbot was pulled from the net for a sixth attacker, and the Oilers kept the puck in the Anaheim end, making crisp passes. During a scramble in front of the net, Drake Caggiula fell to his knees while scooping the puck up and shooting it at the net. When it went in, the crowd went ballistic. It was Caggiula's first playoff goal. The game went into overtime, but the crowd barely got a chance to take their seats before Silfverberg scored the winner just 45 seconds into the extra frame.

Back in Anaheim for Game 5, there was no scoring until 15 seconds into the second period, when Draisaitl solved Gibson. At 2:55, with the Oilers on a five-on-three, McDavid added a goal, and Caggiula scored his second of the series at 12:28. Talbot and the Oilers kept Anaheim off the score sheet until 16:44 of the third. Then things went off the rails. Getzlaf scored, and just 35 seconds later, Cam Fowler made it 3–2.

The Ducks' third goal proved to be the most controversial and was discussed afterward by every hockey media outlet in North America. With 15 seconds left in regulation time, there was a scramble in front of the net. Ducks forward Ryan Kesler and Oilers D-man Darnell Nurse both ended up in the crease. While down, Kesler restricted Talbot's pad with his gloved hand, keeping him from moving. Rakell, from his backhand, swiped the puck through Talbot's five-hole. The refs made a quick decision to let the goal stand, but every announcer, after looking at the footage, was confident that Kesler had interfered. The game ended up going into double overtime, but it was Corey Perry of the Ducks who scored the winner, putting Anaheim ahead, three

Fans show their appreciation for Leon Draisaitl's playoff hat trick, on May 7, 2017. It was a five-point night for the forward as the Oilers beat the Ducks 7-1, to tie the series 3-3.

games to two. Later, McLellan and Talbot handled the press with class, saying that they had to forget about the call and move on. But it was a huge disappointment for the fans, leaving many disgruntled with the officials. Even Gary Bettman weighed in, saying he needed to stand by the referee's decision. Some fans were reminded of the Miracle on Manchester in 1982, where the Oilers lost a Game 3 to the Kings—so many goals in so little time.

When they returned to home ice for Game 6, the Oilers set out to wallop the Ducks. After the first period, they led 5–0 on two goals from Draisaitl, two from Letestu and one from Kassian. Draisaitl assisted on Slepyshev's 6–0 marker just 45 seconds into the second period, and completed his hat trick at 15:27. Hats rained onto the ice for what felt like ages. They became a story in themselves, with many people tweeting about the gesture. One tweet in particular, from the Bissell Centre:

Our #homeless neighbours could sure use those #Oilers hats! Tweet @EdmontonOilers to help make it happen! Pls Retweet! #YEG #oilersnation

—Bissell Centre (@BissellCentre) May 8, 2017

The next day, the Edmonton Oilers Community Foundation bagged up a thousand hats and sent them to the Bissell Centre, the Hope Mission and Operation Friendship.

Although the Oilers had shown tenacity with their 7–1 victory in Game 6, they suffered a disappointing loss in Game 7 in Anaheim. Drake Caggiula scored the first goal of the game, but former Oiler Andrew Cogliano tied it in the second period and Nick Ritchie scored the series-clinching marker at 3:21 of the third. The playoff run, such a long time in arriving, had come to an end.

2017-2018

TRADING A VETERAN

On June 22, a little over a month after the Oilers' season came to an end, Jordan Eberle was traded to the New York Islanders for centreman Ryan Strome. Over seven years, Eberle had played 507 games, accumulating 382 points. On being traded by the team that had drafted him in 2008, he said, "It's something I've never gone through before. It's a different experience."

Edmonton Oilers general manager Peter Chiarelli also talked to the media about the trade. "It was a function of a number of different things. One, the chance to acquire a player like Ryan Strome. Two, no secret we have got to clear up some [salary cap] space to sign both Connor [McDavid] and Leon [Draisaitl]. And three, there are times that these deals come about and you have to act on them and we just felt it would improve our team."

Strome had been selected fifth overall by the Islanders in 2011, and he was coming off his fourth NHL season, in which he scored 13 goals and had 30 points in 69 games—not the kind of offence Eberle would produce, but he had size, a decent wrist shot and the ability to play both wing and centre.

Five Canadiens and one Oiler. When Connor McDavid makes a rush, opposing teams swarm him.

Connor McDavid celebrates with Leon Draisaitl after they performed a tic-tac-toe play against St. Louis on December 21, 2017. Lucic and Russell join the celebration.

On July 5, Connor McDavid, flanked by Chiarelli, sat in front of the microphone at a press conference at Rogers Place to announce that he had just signed an eight-year, $100 million extension to his contract, starting with the 2018–19 season. His salary cap hit of $12.5 million per season would be the highest since the cap was introduced in 2005. Chiarelli said the contract could have been "higher in value and shorter in term," but McDavid was about "commitment, partnership and character." Not a bad way to start the next nine years.

The 20-year-old McDavid, who had cleaned up at the NHL Awards banquet—bringing home the Art Ross Trophy as the league's scoring champion, the Hart Trophy as most valuable player, and the Ted Lindsay Award as the players' choice of MVP—was poised and honest when he talked about his family and teammates being so important to his life and success. He also addressed the fans in

Edmonton. "I want to win here," he said. "This is a city that I think has such a rich history. It is so important to bring that back. Got a taste of it last year. We need to bring it back. We actually have some unfinished business."

Expectations were high for the 2017–18 season, but the team struggled from the get go. They would win a game and lose a game, and couldn't find consistency. Finally, near the end of February, they started to click, but didn't make the playoffs.

Connor McDavid finished the season with 108 points, enough to win his second consecutive Art Ross trophy for the player with the highest point total. He is just the second player in history to win back-to-back Art Ross's before turning 22 years old. The other player was Wayne Gretzky.

Remembering Dave Semenko

The day after McDavid signed his contract extension, former Oiler Dave Semenko, also known as "Sammy" and "Cement," was memorialized at Rogers Place. Semenko had passed away on June 29, 2017, after battling pancreatic cancer. The ceremony was carried out in grand fashion, with a stage and seats set up on the floor of Rogers Place. Fans were invited, and they sat in the stands, many wearing jerseys in his honour. Semenko had been the Oilers' enforcer during the dynasty era, a linemate of Wayne Gretzky. And at the time of his death, he had been working as an ambassador for the Oilers organization. Father Mike McCaffery, who officiated at the ceremony, was well known to Oiler fans and the organization. He had conducted the marriage ceremony for Wayne Gretzky and Janet Jones and officiated at Wild Bill Hunter's funeral.

Representatives of the team, including Glen Sather, Wayne Gretzky, Paul Coffey, Al Hamilton, Kevin Lowe and Glenn Anderson, spoke about Semenko's days as a hockey player, as well as his big heart and sense of humour. And yes, there were funny stories about Dave Semenko, a man who was larger than life and always kept the guys loose and laughing. A childhood friend, Randy Donkersloot, spoke about playing minor hockey with Dave. And Dave's brother Brian shared funny family stories. Dave's daughter, Hannah, talked about how her father "protected her." She closed by saying, "Dad, you brought the house down."

Many former teammates were in attendance, and they gathered at the Parlour restaurant in Edmonton after the ceremony. There, they shared more stories under the Edmonton summer evening sun. Once an Oiler, always an Oiler.

The People Who Keep the Machine Well Oiled

EQUIPMENT MANAGERS AND TRAINERS

In the bellies of arenas, running the halls, entering and exiting the players' dressing rooms, you'll find the equipment staff. These unsung heroes keep the skates sharpened, sticks ordered and equipment organized—and just generally do whatever it takes to make the players happy.

In the Edmonton Oilers' 40 years in the National Hockey League, there have only been four equipment managers. All of them have gotten to know the personalities on the team inside and out.

The first was John Blackwell, who was with the WHA Edmonton Oilers. After the team's first NHL season, he was transferred to an administrative role in the front office. Kelly Pruden took over as equipment manager for the 1979–80 and 1980–81 seasons. During training camp in 1980, Barrie Stafford of Banff, Alberta, was on hand as well. He had just graduated from the University of Alberta with a bachelor of science degree, and assistant trainer Lyle Kulchisky, better known as "Sparky," showed him the

ropes, introducing him to players and showing him around. Stafford was sent to Kansas that same year to work with the Wichita Wind, the Oilers' farm team in the Central Hockey League.

Glen Sather had been impressed with Stafford during that training camp, and their Banff connection ran solid, so in 1981, when it was time for Pruden to move on, Stafford was called upon to be the Oilers' head equipment manager. At first, he was nervous, thinking he didn't have enough experience, but as a former player (he played four years for the University of Alberta Golden Bears) and a guy who wasn't afraid of the corners, and with Sparky's help, Stafford dove right in and took control.

Stafford had to learn how to control his hot-headedness—a carry-over from his playing days. A fiery disposition could be an asset on the ice, but it wasn't a quality needed in an equipment manager. Stafford had already been in one fight on the bench, with a player in Wichita. Sometimes, players needed to be told to keep the dressing room tidier

Head Equipment Manager
Jeff Lang adjusts Patrick
Maroon's skate in warm up.

or pack their equipment properly, and doing so in a diplomatic fashion was an art that Stafford wanted to master. Occasionally, he called upon Wayne Gretzky to help him out. He would pull Wayne out of the room and ask him to tell the players to stop being so lazy, to pick up their stuff. When Wayne spoke, the guys generally listened.

Still, things could get tense. Once, after an altercation with Kevin Lowe about a ceiling tile issue, Stafford and Lowe went at it in the dressing room, having a full-blown physical fight. But it was stopped, and there were no lasting hard feelings.

Barrie Stafford remembers the highs, but he was also there for the lows. Going to work when the team was winning was amazing fun, and he looked forward to going to work every day. On the other hand, when the team is losing, spending time at the arena day in and day out doesn't have the same appeal—yet the equipment manager always has to stay upbeat.

Stafford worked his 2,000th game during the 2007–08 season.

Lyle "Sparky" Kulchisky is an Edmonton native and a favourite of the players. He was the Oilers' assistant trainer from 1981 until 2008. Sparky got his start as a trainer when he was still in junior high school. His father would give him money to go to the Oil Kings games at the Edmonton Gardens, and young Sparky figured out that if he went in through the same entrance as the players, he could pocket the money and still watch the game. Once, he was trailing Reggie Leach, who was playing for the Flin Flon Bombers. Reggie turned to Sparky and asked if he would be the stick boy for the visiting side. Sparky didn't hesitate to agree. Now he was getting into the game for free, and in addition to the money his father had given him, he got a little bit extra from the Bombers. For the rest of his school years, Sparky showed up and worked the visitors' side at Oil Kings games. By that time, the WHA team had arrived in Edmonton and John Blackwell, the team equipment manager, had asked Sparky if he would handle the visitors' side for Oiler home games.

Sparky was in awe. Here he was, in the presence of players he had only seen on television: Bill Flett, Dave Dryden, Colin Campbell. Sparky even remembers the move to Northlands Coliseum. On opening night against the Cleveland Crusaders in 1974, the players had to dress at the Gardens and be bused to the new arena because their dressing rooms weren't ready. Bare light bulbs hung from the ceiling and plywood was still on the floor. When the game was over, the players were bused back to the Gardens to shower.

During the last WHA season, 1978–79, Sparky claims that "I didn't really watch the Oilers that year, because I watched Gretzky."

When the Oilers joined the NHL, Sparky moved right along with them. At this time, he was responsible for transporting the team's equipment to the airport when they embarked on road trips. He was known for his sense of humour. When Andy Moog attended his first Oilers training camp, he showed up at the motel that he had been told to go to. It certainly wasn't a Hilton, or even a Holiday Inn. At the front desk, he was told he wasn't registered. So Andy got in his car and found a residential street where he could pull over and sleep for the night. The next morning, after his ice session, he talked to Sparky, telling him why he'd spent the night in his car. Sparky said, "Kid, don't say another word. I will take care of this." Sparky

left, and returned with a blanket and pillow. He handed them to Andy and said, "It's going to be cold out there tonight." Of course, Moog's room situation got straightened out.

When the Oilers were performing a serious housecleaning as part of their rebuilding efforts in 2009–10 it extended to the dressing room staff. Stafford and Kulchisky had done so much for the organization, but it was time for something fresh behind the scenes. In 2012, Barrie Stafford was inducted to the Hockey Hall of Fame under the Trainers category. Today, he runs the Alumni Association for the Oilers.

Jeff Lang was hired as head equipment manager. In 2002, Lang had left his job as Hockey Canada's equipment manager and moved up Highway 2 from Calgary to Edmonton to assist Stafford and head trainer Ken Lowe. Lang, better known as "Langer" to the players, had been though the Cinderella Cup run of 2005–06 and would be there through the playoff drought that followed. He found that he had to stay positive at the arena, but it was tough being in the city and always losing. His children started playing hockey during those dark days, and whenever Lang went to the rink to watch their games or practices, he heard many opinions about the Oilers. Consequently, he often sat by himself, on the other side of the rink. The move to Rogers Place has coincided with the organization taking on a fresh feel. But Lang knows, like all the equipment managers before him, that his job is to keep smiling, and keep the players in a good mood, no matter what the scoreboard says.

Joey Moss is a celebrity in Edmonton. Being born with Down syndrome hasn't stopped him from succeeding. He started with the Oilers back in the Gretzky era and is still there today.

JOEY MOSS

Joey Moss can sing "O Canada" with passion and gusto and take care of a locker room, and he's been doing that since the 1984–85 season. Born with Down syndrome, Joey started with the Oilers when Wayne Gretzky was just 20 years old. Gretzky was friends with the Moss family and knew him well. After seeing Joey standing day after day outside (no matter the weather) to catch his bus to the bottle depot where he worked, Wayne thought that perhaps there was something he could do for him. Having an aunt who had Down syndrome, Gretzky knew that Joey was capable of doing more. And he believed everyone deserved a chance to show and use their talents. Gretzky went to head

coach Glen Sather and asked if he could give Joey a job. By this time, Joey was 22, and he and Wayne had known each other for five years. Glen was willing to give him a try. Joey started first working with Sparky Kulchinsky, and while they may have got off to a rocky start, with each having to figure the other out, over time they formed a special friendship. And Joey did prove himself, taking his responsibilities seriously. He sweeps the floor in the locker room, fills water bottles, helps with the laundry and hands out towels to the players.

Joey has worked with different trainers over the years, and has outlasted a few of them. When his face is flashed on the Jumbotron, belting out "O Canada" at the start of the game with his hand across his chest in pride, the crowd goes wild.

Past and Future

As part of the NHL's centennial celebration in 2018, over 3.6 million fans voted for the "Greatest NHL Team of All Time." In June, the NHL announced the winning team was the 1984–85 Edmonton Oilers. They were the team of the century.

In February, the 1985 Stanley Cup Championship team had taken to a circular moving stage at Rogers Place in Edmonton for an evening filled with humorous and touching stores that kept fans entertained for well over two hours. It was a sell out. These are Oilers fans, after all. The event was intimate, and the guests of honour were relaxed and candid, but most of all humbled. Every single player got a moment to shine on stage. Music entertained fans in between the talks with songs that had been made up specifically for the Oilers. Former CBC news anchor Peter Mansbridge offered up an exciting play-by-play of the final game in the 1985 Stanley Cup final, the game that gave the Oilers the Cup. Glen Sather, who had coached that

team, faced off against Mike Keenan (coach of that Flyers team) for the story of their coaching strategies during that series. Keenan revealed that he had stolen the Stanley Cup and taken it to the Flyers dressing room. (In those days, the Cup remained with the winning team for the entire year.) Keenan set it up in the middle of the Flyers' room, telling them not to touch until they won it. It didn't pay off. The Oilers defeated the Flyers, winning the Cup again.

Of this team, Mike Keenan said, "Playing the Edmonton Oilers during their Stanley Cup winning years provided a unique opportunity to test your ultimate limits as a team. They were the most talented, most skilled, most confident and most successful team in the NHL. They set the standard of excellence for all teams to be measured."

The net proceeds from the event were marked for the Edmonton Oilers Community Foundation (EOCF), which will create an endowment in the memory of Dave Semenko, who played on that Championship team.

Asked about his years in Edmonton, Mark Messier remembers the importance of teamwork.

It has been many years since my retirement, even more since I left Edmonton as an Oiler, and I still well-up with emotion when asked to speak about my former teammates and experiences with the Oilers. We used to laugh and say the secret to our success was the 3 D's: Dedication, Determination, and Drambuie.

The reality is it was so much more. Our foundation was built on trust, heart, courage, sacrifice, and a brotherhood that was unparalleled in hockey or any other sport for that matter.

Of course, we had incredible talent. And, yes, we had Wayne GRETZKY, but the single most important lesson we learned is that nobody can win by themselves, especially in the game of hockey. Our commitment to each other and the joy we shared in one another's accomplishments were the backbone of our team.

But maybe the greatest key of all was revealed to us as we came to understand that the stage is always big enough for everybody. We won big and we shared it all as much as we could—with each other, with our families, and with our fans.

THE FUTURE

Sometimes a team has to be built around certain players. Glen Sather built his Cup teams around his stars: Wayne Gretzky, Mark Messier, Grant Fuhr, Glenn Anderson, Paul Coffey, Jari Kurri, Kevin Lowe. They are building around their stars now, fitting the puzzle pieces together. It looks like history repeating itself. Time is a factor, and so is learning and maturity. In the NHL of today, it is more challenging than ever to make the playoffs. It can be unpredictable, too. A team that misses the post-season one year can become Stanley Cup contenders the next.

The Edmonton Oilers are again a team trending up. There's never been more reason to hope that the Cup will return. Edmonton fans, and their beloved city, deserve that much.

Here's to the next 40 years!

Bibliography and Works Cited

PERSONAL INTERVIEWS

Glenn Anderson; Bob Black; Darryl Boessenkal; Kelly Buchberger; Paul Coffey; Andy Devlin; Barry Fraser; Brad Gilewich; Wayne Gretzky; Al Hamilton; Ken Hitchcock; Shawn Horcoff; Charlie Huddy; Bev Hunter; Dave Hunter; Curtis Joseph; John Karvellis; Daryl Katz; Mike Keenan; Lyle Kuchinsky; Jari Kurri; Pat Laforge; Jeff Lang; Ron Low; Kevin Lowe; Stew MacDonald; Craig MacTavish; Connor McDavid; Lanny McDonald; Pat McLaughlin; Mark Messier; Don Metz; Andy Moog; Ethan Moreau; Cal Nichols; Bob Nicholson; Fernando Pisani; Peter Pocklington; Dwayne Roloson; Glen Sather; Bruce Saville; Dave Semenko; Tim Shipton; Craig Simpson; Jason Smith; Ryan Smyth; Barrie Stafford; Bob Stauffer; Duane Sutter; Bill Tuele

NEWSPAPERS AND PERIODICALS

Banff Crag and Canyon; *Boston Globe*; *Boyle McCauley News*; *Calgary Herald*; *Calgary Sun*; *Canadian Press*; *Chicago Tribune*; *Dallas Morning News*; *Edmonton Journal*; *Edmonton Sun*; *The Hockey News*; *Los Angeles Times*; *Macleans*; *Montreal Gazette*; *Montreal Star*; *New York Clipper*; *New York Daily News*; *New York Post*; *New York Times*; *Newsday*; *Ottawa Citizen*; *Sports Illustrated*; *St. Albert Gazette*; *Star Weekly*; *Time*; *Toronto Daily News*; *Toronto Globe and Mail*; *Toronto Star*; *Toronto Sun*; *Winnipeg Free Press*; *Winnipeg Sun*; *Vancouver Sun*

ELECTRONIC MEDIA

Bleacherreport; CBC Archives; Fansedge; Greatest Hockey Legends; Hockeybydesign; Hockey Hall of Fame; Hockey DB; Hockey Night in Canada; Hockey Reference; Macleans.ca; NHL.com; Oilersnation; Oilogosphere; Sportsnet.ca; TSN.ca; Youtube

BOOKS

Brunt, Stephen. *Gretzky's Tears: Hockey, Canada and the Day Everything Changed*. Toronto: Vintage, 2010.

Cameron, Steve. *Hockey Hall of Fame Book of Players*. Toronto: Firefly Books, 2013.

Fuhr, Grant and Bruce Dowbiggin. *Grant Fuhr: The Story of a Hockey Legend*. Toronto: Random House, 2014.

Gretzky, Wayne and Kirstie McLellan Day. *99: Stories of the Game*. Toronto: Viking, 2016.

Gretzky, Wayne and John Davidson. *99: My Life in Pictures*. Toronto: Dan Diamond and Associates, 2000.

Klinkenberg, Marty. *The McDavid Effect: Connor McDavid and the New Hope for Hockey*. Toronto: Simon and Schuster, 2016.

Lowe, Kevin and Shirley Fischler and Stan Fischler. *Champions: The making of the Edmonton Oilers*. Toronto: Prentice-Hall Canada, 1988.

McCown, Bob. *McCown's Law: The 100 Greatest Hockey Arguments*. Toronto: Doubleday Canada, 2007.

Nye, J'lyn and Peter Pocklington and Terry McConnel. *I'd Trade Him Again: On Gretzky, Politics and the Pursuit of the Perfect Deal*. Toronto: Fenn Publishing, 2009.

Podnieks, Andrew, ed. *The Complete Hockey Dictionary*. Toronto: Fenn Publishing, 2007.

Robson, Dan. *Quinn: The Life of a Hockey Legend*. Toronto: Viking, 2015.

Schultz Nicholson, Lorna. *The Next Ones: Hockey's Future Stars*. Toronto: Fenn Publishing, 2010.

Spector, Mark. *Battle of Alberta: The Historic Rivalry Between The Edmonton Oilers and Calgary Flames*. Toronto: McClelland and Stewart, 2015.

Weber, Bob. *Wild Bill: Bill Hunter's Legendary 65 Years in Canadian Sport*. Calgary: Johnson Gorman Publishers, 2000.

MISCELLANEOUS

Metz, D.H. and Gord Redel and Mike Beley. *Oil Change. Seasons 1–3*. Edmonton: Aquila Productions, 2010–2012.

McKeown/McGee Films. *Boys on the Bus*, 1987.

Edmonton Oilers Media Guides, 1979–80 through 2017–18.

City Shaping, Summary Report of the Leadership Committee for a New Sports/Entertainment Facility for Edmonton, 2008.

Building Owners and Managers Association (BOMA), Edmonton Arena District. *Working Together to Revitalize Downtown: The Opportunity of a New Downtown Entertainment and Sports District*, 2010.

The City of Edmonton. *Designing a New Arena for Edmonton: A Summary of Views from the Public*, 2012.

City of Edmonton Public Records.

Image Credits

Acknowledgements

The Edmonton Oilers are an incredible organization. I'm honoured to have written their history. Many people helped me put this book together. I was given their time and their stories, and a good book is about the story. Everyone remembers things differently and I've tried to stay true to how they were told to me. Without the players, owners, staff, friends, media, lawyers, and fans, this book could never have been written. In no particular order, these people shared their memories with me.

Ryan Smyth, Jeff Lang, Pat Laforge, Don Metz, Jason Smith, Kevin Lowe, Wayne Gretzky, Al Hamilton, Glen Sather, Bruce Saville, Peter Pocklington, Andy Moog, Karla Moog, Cal Nichols, Fernando Pisani, Bob Stauffer, Kelly Buchberger, Craig MacTavish, Craig Simpson, Daryl Katz, Bob Black, Pat McLaughlin, Steve Tambellini, John Karvellis, Bob Nicholson, Stew MacDonald, Darryl Boessenkal, Brad Gilewich, Dave Semenko, Paul Coffey, Barry Fraser, Barrie Stafford, Lyle Kulchisky, Tim Shipton, Mark Messier, Shawn Horcoff, Connor McDavid, Bill Tuele, Glenn Anderson, Jari Kurri, Ethan Moreau, Shawn Horcoff, Charlie Huddy, Ken Hitchcock, Lanny McDonald, Mike Keenan, Duane Sutter, Dave Hunter, Dwayne Roloson, Ron Low, Tom Renney, Bev Hunter.

Special thanks goes to Wayne Gretzky, Kevin Lowe, Ryan Smyth, Glen Sather, and Connor McDavid (and Jeff Jackson, Orr Group), for providing the introductions. And to Mark Messier for his beautiful ending.

Cal Nichols, what would I have done without your meticulous Oilers binders, but more than that, your time? Thank you for your sound advice and careful review.

The Katz group of John Karvellis, Brad Gilewich, and Bob Black for providing insight and advice into legal matters that had my head swirling. Bob, thanks for loaning me your "Bag of Rocks."

Thanks to Daryl Katz for answering all my questions. Thank you for your love of Edmonton and the Oilers.

Massive thanks to Oilers photographer Andy Devlin for spending two weeks of his time helping me go through photos. He is an amazing photographer, and very patient and kind too.

Huge thanks to Bill Tuele and Bob Stauffer for reading the manuscript in draft form and giving such fabulous corrections. Your attention to detail was incredible.

My editor at Penguin Random House, Justin Stoller, was always available to answer my flurry of panicked emails ever so calmly, and to have coffee whenever I was in Toronto. Just to talk. His meticulous work made a definite difference to the finished product. Lloyd Davis is owed thanks for his copy-editing and his precise hockey stats. And the Penguin Random House design team for making such an eye-catching book.

I'd also like to thank all media outlets, especially those in Edmonton. I relied on well written articles from both the *Edmonton Sun* and the *Edmonton Journal* to guide me through certain years. Jim Matheson and David Staples are two amazing Edmonton writers. Thank you for your words.

My last thanks is to the Edmonton Oilers for allowing me to write this book. And to the Oilers fans, because this is all for you. Enjoy! Keep cheering.

Index

Acton, Keith, 100
Addie, Dave, 171
Alberta Oilers, 6–7, 200, 210
Alexander, Leslie, 169–170
Ali, Muhammad, 16, 57
Allard, Dr. Charles, 7–8, 11–12
Allen, Bobby, 197
Allen, Neal, 171
Ambrosius, Jakab, 171
Anaheim Ducks, 138–139, 144, 176, 204, 218, 222, 226, 233, 235, 243, 252, 257, 266, 282, 290, 293–295
Anderson, Glenn, 24, 41–42, 44, 47, 53, 55–57, 62, 64, 68, 71, 74, 76–78, 84, 88–89, 95–96, 98, 100, 105, 107, 112, 114, 115, 121, 123, 125, 128, 141, 145, 148, 153, 238, 282–283, 298, 304
Anderson, Ron, 6
Arnott, Jason 138–140, 153, 164, 201
Art Ross Trophy, 41, 45, 83, 91–92, 290, 297
Atlanta Flames, 180, 240
Atlanta Thrashers, 179, 197, 228, 245, 252
Aulie, Keith, 272
Avco Cup, 11, 17, 128
Babych, Wayne, 35
Bachman, Richard, 265, 267, 279
Badali, Gus, 14, 35, 37
Bailey, Garnet "Ace," 29, 76, 128, 194
Balsa, Manuel, 171
Barker, Cam, 252
Barrett, Ted, 171
Barrie, Doug, 6
Bean, Edward E., 171
Beauregard, Stephane, 113
Beers, Bob, 140–141
Belanger, Eric, 252
Belfour, Ed, 169, 178, 184, 193
Ben Hatskin Trophy, 25
Bennett, Sam, 290
Bentley, Doug, 77
Berehowsky, Drake, 168, 175
Bergeron, Marc-Andre, 218, 220, 222
Bergman, Thommie, 12
Berube, Craig, 128, 145
Bettman, Gary, 144, 206–207, 209, 212, 231, 255, 260, 295
Beukeboom, Jeff, 59, 123, 128, 141
Bianchin, Wayne, 29
Bilous, Deron, 287
Black, Bob, 259
Blackwell, John, 299, 301
Bobby Smith Trophy, 278
Boivin, Pierre, 207
Bonsignore, Jason, 143–144, 164
Boschman, Laurie, 55
Bossy, Mike, 45, 56–57, 71–72
Boston Bruins, 9, 11, 42, 46, 60, 71–72, 74, 82, 98–100, 104, 114–115, 128, 135, 151, 179, 188, 194, 197, 214, 218, 228, 246, 265, 278

Bourne, Bob, 56, 71, 92
Bourque, Ray, 114
Brackenbury, Curt, 40, 48
Brewer, Eric, 188, 189, 191, 193, 197, 214
Brind'Amour, Rod, 223–224
Brodeur, Martin, 139
Brodie, T.J., 247
Brossoit, Laurent, 265, 291
Brown, Dave, 95, 121, 128
Brown, Ken, 210
Brown, Sean, 151, 197
Brubaker, Jeff, 90
Brule, Gilbert, 237, 243, 248
Bryzgalov, Ilya, 265–267
Buchanan, Gordon, 171
Buchberger, Kelly, 81, 94–95, 112, 131–133, 136, 148–149, 153–155, 157, 159, 167, 173, 178–179, 181, 245
Buffalo Sabres, 9, 22, 26, 89, 91, 128, 130, 135, 139, 214, 228, 248, 272, 277, 280, 290
Burke, Brian, 235
Burnett, George, 145–146, 151
Butler, Bill, 171
Byakin, Ilja, 140
Bub Slug (comic strip), 86
Caggiula, Drake, 284, 294–295
Calder Cup, 145
Calder Memorial Trophy, 32, 104, 106, 139, 254, 280, 282
Calgary Flames, 54–55, 60, 62–64, 84–85, 87, 89, 93, 96, 99, 106, 108, 110–111, 115, 123, 135, 138, 140, 153–155, 177, 197, 199, 236, 243, 245, 247, 256, 265, 267, 287–290
Callighen, Brett, 29, 41
Campbell, Brian, 253
Campbell, Colin, 27, 301
Campedelli, Dom, 90
Canada Cup, 71–72
Canada's Sports Hall of Fame, 200
Cape Breton Oilers, 135, 145, 153
Carcillo, Daniel, 253
Carlin, Brian, 6
Carlyle, Steve, 6
Carolina Hurricanes, 223–224, 233, 237, 247, 275
Carpenter, Bobby, 92
Carroll, Billy, 73, 82
Carson, Jimmy, 106, 109, 111–112
Carter, Anson, 188, 190, 193, 197, 199
Chartraw, Rick, 68
Cheechoo, Jonathan, 218, 220–221
Cheevers, Gerry, 39, 41–42
Chiarelli, Peter, 277–280, 282, 284–286, 291, 296–297
Chimera, Jason, 163

Chipperfield, Ron, 27–28, 32
CHL Scholastic Player of the Year Award, 278
Chretien, Jean, 142
Cierny, Jozef, 139
Ciger, Zdeno, 136, 140–141, 153, 176
Cincinnati Stingers, 21, 24
Clarence Campbell Bowl, 223
Clark, Robert, 293
Clark, Wendel, 97
Clarke, Bobby, 32
Cleary, Daniel, 176, 191–192
Cleveland Crusaders, 6, 8–9, 301
Coffey, Paul, 35, 37–39, 44, 46, 48–49, 56–57, 60, 64–65, 71, 91, 95, 97–98, 103, 122, 127, 131–132, 213, 217, 253, 257, 272, 282, 283, 298, 304
Cogliano, Andrew, 215, 235, 239, 248, 252, 295
Cole, Erik, 223, 237
Colf, Dick, 171
Colorado Avalanche, 147, 159, 166–168, 184, 188, 197, 211, 216, 218, 220, 235
Colorado Rockies, 22, 236
Columbus Blue Jackets, 204, 228, 235, 237, 246–247, 253, 263, 266, 272, 280, 284
Commonwealth Stadium, 206–207
Comrie, Bill, 179
Comrie, Herb, 179
Comrie, Mike, 179, 186–187, 191, 193, 197, 199, 204, 243, 247
Comrie, Paul, 164, 179
Conacher, Brian, 12
Conacher, Pat, 68
Conklin, Ty, 197, 211, 224, 228
Conn Smythe Trophy, 68, 80, 96, 101, 111, 115
Connor, Cam, 29
Corson, Shayne, 135, 137, 140–141, 143, 148–149, 151, 153
Courtnall, Geoff, 98
Crawford, Marc, 168
Crosby, Sidney, 215, 286
Cross, Cory, 199–200, 216
Cullen, Matt, 223
Cumming, James, 148
Czerkawski, Mariusz, 151, 155, 163
Dallas Stars, 146, 155–157, 159, 169, 177–178, 184, 191–193, 200–201, 264–266
Dalton, Michael, 171
Daly, Bill, 245–246, 251, 277
Damphousse, Vincent, 128–132, 135
Danis, Yann, 265
Davidson, Brandon, 291
Davidson, Gary, 6
Davis, Lorne, 236
DeBrusk, Louie, 128, 132–133
Delaney, Gary, 86
Desharnais, David, 291, 293

Detroit Red Wings, 11, 59, 82, 89, 93, 100, 108–109, 111–112, 135, 154, 175, 194, 218–220, 258
de Vries, Greg, 175
Devereaux, Boyd, 184
Dickenson, William. See Hunter, "Wild Bill."
Dionne, Marcel, 32, 41
DiPietro, Rick, 241
Doan, Shane, 147
Donkersloot, Randy, 298
Dowd, Jim, 176, 184
Drake, Clare, 10
Draisaitl, Leon, 271, 274–275, 279, 282, 290, 293–297
Driscoll, Peter, 15
Drouin-Deslauriers, Jeff, 239, 243, 247
Dryden, Dave, 7, 22, 25, 34, 301
Dryden, Ken, 25
Dubnyk, Devan, 248, 254, 266–267
Dubois, Pierre-Luc, 284
Dvorak, Radek, 199–201, 228
Eager, Ben, 252
Eakin, Bruce, 82
Eakins, Dallas, 264, 267, 274
Eberle, Jordan, 236, 246–248, 253, 263, 267, 278, 282, 288, 290, 296
Edmonton Coliseum, 9, 143–144, 174, 271
Edmonton Gardens, 7–8, 27, 201, 300–301
Edmonton Investors Group (EIG), 170–171, 180–181, 205, 225, 227, 231–233
Edmonton Oil Kings, 5–6, 8–11, 29, 179, 194, 215, 300–301
Edmonton Oil Kings (junior), 270, 278, 282
Edmonton Oilers
1972–1979 (WHA years), 5–17, 21, 29–30, 39, 180, 299, 301
1979–1990, 18–117
1990–1997, 118–159
1997–2003, 160–201
2003–2018, 202–304
Stanley Cup championships, 66–72, 80, 96, 100–101, 103–104, 110, 115–116, 127–128, 136, 139, 169, 179, 184, 187, 191, 198, 210
Edmonton Oilers Community Foundation (EOCF), 273, 295, 303
Edwards, Gary, 42
Eichel, Jack, 277
Elko, Ernie, 171
Ellett, Dave, 113
Elliott, Brian, 290
Elofsson, Jonas, 176
Emms Family Award, 278
Esposito, Phil, 41, 45, 90
Essensa, Bob, 154, 166–167, 174
Evans, Daryl, 47
Ewanyk, Travis, 279

Falkenberg, Bob, 6, 87, 91–92, 95, 99, 108, 112, 115, 121–125, 128, 145, 210–211, 282–283, 304
Gage, Joaquin, 191
Gagner, Sam, 233, 235, 243, 247–248, 253, 255, 263, 267, 272, 280
Gare, Danny, 89
Garon, Mathieu, 235, 239
Gazdic, Luke, 266
Gelinas, Martin, 108
Gelinas, Martin, 111–112, 125, 138
Gernat, Martin, 282
Getzlaf, Ryan, 294
Gibson, John, 293–294
Gilbert, Tom, 211, 252–253
Gilchrist, Brent, 135, 137
Gillies, Clark, 56
Glencross, Curtis, 235
Glynn, Brian, 128, 132
Gobuty, Michael, 14
Godard, Eric, 237, 239
Goodenow, Bob, 207, 209, 212
Gordie Howe Trophy, 25
Gordon, Boyd, 279
Gordon, Larry, 12
Granato, Tony, 131
Graves, Adam, 110–112, 128, 141
Graves, Steve, 121
Green, Josh, 188
Green, Ted, 71, 128, 130–131, 138, 140, 163
Greene, Matt, 237
Gregg, Gary, 170–171
Gregg, Randy, 68, 71, 115, 121, 170
Gretzky, Janet (Jones), 182, 298
Gretzky, Paulina, 182
Gretzky, Phyllis, 17, 182
Gretzky, Trevor, 182
Gretzky, Ty, 182
Gretzky, Walter, 14, 17, 103, 182
Gretzky, Wayne
before joining Edmonton Oilers, 13–15, 35
with WHA Edmonton Oilers (1978–1979), 13–14, 16–17
with NHL Edmonton Oilers (1979–1988), 21–23, 29, 31, 35, 37–39, 41, 44–47, 50–51, 54, 56–57, 59–60, 62, 64, 66, 68, 71–72, 74–78, 80, 82–83, 85, 90–92, 95–96, 99–101, 205, 253, 268, 300–302, 304
with LA Kings, 102–108, 111, 113, 125, 127, 130, 131–132, 230
with NY Rangers, 174
post-retirement (1999 onward), 177–178, 182, 194, 198, 206–207, 209, 217, 230, 238, 257, 259, 272, 282–283, 287–288, 290, 298
stats, 17, 32, 35, 41, 45, 46, 54–55, 57, 60, 74, 83, 99, 107, 109, 130
family, 14, 17, 103, 116, 182, 298
Grier, Mike, 151, 156, 168, 191

Grieve, Ross, 286
Gryba, Eric, 278–279
Guerin, Bill, 164–165, 167, 169, 188, 190
Guidolin, Bep, 11
Gund, George, 127
Gund, Gordon, 127
Gustafsson, Bengt-Ake, 22
Hagman, Matti, 37, 41
Hall, Taylor, 245–248, 251–253, 263, 267, 278, 282, 284–285
Hamilton, Al, 7, 9–11, 17, 26–27, 34, 38–39, 283, 298
Hamilton, Don, 171
Hamrlik, Roman, 164, 183, 188
Hannan, Dave, 97
Hanson, Rick, 90
Harker, Derek, 6
Harrison, Brad, 279
Harrison, Jim, 6
Hart Memorial Trophy, 34, 41, 74, 92, 99, 115, 214, 297
Hartford Whalers, 5, 21, 40, 51, 60, 73, 89, 135
Hawerchuk, Dale, 113
Hawgood, Greg, 100, 115
Hecht, Jochen, 195
Hedberg, Anders, 11
Hemsky, Ales, 195, 199, 204, 218, 220, 224, 231, 235, 239, 243, 248, 266–267
Hendricks, Matt, 266
Herbers, Ian, 278–279
Heritage Classic, 202, 205–207, 209
Hextall, Ron, 92, 95–96
Hicks, Doug, 22, 27
Himelfarb, Eric, 243
Hitchcock, Ken, 191–192
Hockey Canada, 240, 271, 278, 301
Hockey Hall of Fame, 116, 169, 182, 198, 210, 213, 228, 230, 238, 282
Hockey Night in Canada, 13
Hodgson, Ron, 171
Hogue, Benoit, 169
Hole, Jim F., 170–171, 173, 187
Holmstrom, Tomas, 219
Horacek, Jan, 195
Horak, Roman, 265
Horcoff, Shawn, 174, 199, 201, 216, 218, 220–222, 235, 243, 247–248, 264–265
Hospodar, Ed, 77
Hossa, Marian, 163
Howe, Gordie, 13, 21
Howson, Scott, 263
Hrkac, Tony, 167
Hrudey, Kelly, 125
Hrynewich, Tim, 81
Huddy, Charlie, 68, 71, 74, 78, 84, 99, 109, 115, 125, 131, 132, 197, 215
Hughes, Pat, 62, 65, 68, 75, 82
Hull Olympiques, 104, 108, 195
Hull, Bobby, 21
Hull, Brett, 178
Hunter (mascot), 287–288
Hunter, Dave, 28, 62, 65, 77–78, 97, 213
Hunter, "Wild Bill," 2, 5–12, 39, 179, 200, 225, 287, 298
Iginla, Jarome, 147
Indianapolis Racers, 13–15, 17, 21, 23–24, 28, 42
Ing, Peter, 128, 131

Isbister, Brad, 199
Iveson, Don, 269, Don, 286
Jack Adams Award, 240
Jackson, Don, 68, 213
Janvier, Alex, 286
Joel, Billy, 42
Johnson, "Badger Bob," 62
Johnson, Jim, 279
Jones, Martin, 291–293
Jones, Terry, 69
Joseph, Chris, 97, 122, 132, 141
Joseph, Curtis, 151, 153–159, 165–168, 174, 176
Joyal, Eddie, 6
Kamensky, Valeri, 167
Kamloops Blazers, 122, 147, 244
Kamppuri, Hannu, 25
Kariya, Paul, 176
Karlsson, Melker, 291
Kassian, Dennis, 6
Kassian, Zack, 280, 282, 289, 291–292, 295
Katz Group, 255, 258–260, 270
Katz, Barry, 205
Katz, Daryl, 204–205, 225–226, 231–233, 238, 240, 259–260, 269–271, 273, 287
Katz, Harrison, 240
Keenan, Mike, 77, 94, 303
Kelly, Steve, 147, 164
Kerr, Tim, 77
Kesler, Ryan, 294
Khabibulin, Nikolai, 241–243, 247–248, 254, 265
Kidd, Trevor, 153
Kilger, Chad, 176
Kinasewich, Ray, 10
King Clancy Memorial Trophy, 115, 239
Kiprusoff, Miikka, 247
Kissel, Brett, 293
Kitchener Rangers, 35
Klefbom, Oscar, 251, 290, 293
Klima, Petr, 110, 112, 114–115, 120–121, 123, 125, 132, 137–138, 175
Knoll, Gerald, 171
Kontos, Chris, 107
Kootenay Ice, 191, 199, 272
Korolyuk, Alexander, 177
Korpikoski, Lauri, 279
Kostovich, Max, 32
Kovalenko, Andrei, 154–157, 183
Kravchuck, Igor, 136, 140–141, 153
Krueger, Ralph, 254, 256–257, 264
Krushelnyski, Mike, 72, 77–78, 104
Krutov, Vladimir, 37
Kuchar, Wally, 171
Kulchinsky, Lyle, "Sparky," 93, 116, 213, 299–302
Kurri, Jari, 37–38, 41–42, 46, 48–51, 55, 62, 64, 66, 72, 74–75, 77–78, 80, 82–83, 91–92, 95, 132, 100, 106, 109, 112–113, 115, 121, 128, 131, 182, 198, 282, 283, 304
LaBarbera, Jason, 265, 267
Lacombe, Normand, 91
LaCouture, Dan, 163
Lady Byng Memorial Trophy, 34, 253
Laflamme, Christian, 176
Lafleur, Guy, 42, 207, 209
LaFontaine, Pat, 59, 65–66
LaForge, Pat, 205–207, 259–260, 270, 278

Laidlaw, Tom, 107
Laine, Patrick, 284
Lamb, Mark, 108–109, 113, 132, 135
Lang, Jeff, 300–301
Lang, Robert, 218–219
Langenbrunner, Jamie, 178–192
Laraque, Georges, 147, 149, 183–184, 191–192, 201, 209, 228, 286
Larmer, Steve, 75, 77, 132
Larsen, Philip, 264
Larsson, Adam, 284–285, 293
Laurence, Guy, 287
Leach, Reggie, 80, 300
Ledyard, Grant, 159
Legace, Manny, 220
Lehtinen, Jere, 201
Lemay, Moe, 82, 90
Lemelin, Rejean, 100
Lemieux, Claude, 167
Lemieux, Mario, 83, 99, 253, 272
Lester B. Pearson Trophy, 115
Letestu, Mark, 279, 292–293, 295
Lidstrom, Nicklas, 220
Lindgren, Lars, 51
Lindgren, Mats, 141, 155, 169, 175
Lindros, Eric, 197
Lindstrom, Willy, 11, 55, 68, 75, 78, 82
Linseman, Ken, 22, 32, 51, 53, 64, 66, 72, 81, 100, 121, 128, 282
Loney, Brent, 51
LoPresti, Pete, 25
Lorieau, Paul, 178, 221
Los Angeles Kings, 32, 35, 47, 54–55, 65, 74, 76, 92, 103–108, 111, 113, 121, 123, 127–128, 130–132, 138, 180, 184, 194, 235, 237, 249, 251, 284–285
Low, Ron, 32, 42, 45, 55, 140, 145–146, 151, 163, 166–168, 173–174, 176, 179
Lowe, Ken, 117, 174, 301
Lowe, Kevin, 23–24, 26, 32, 40, 44, 48, 71, 91, 106–107, 110, 112–113, 115–116, 128–129, 135–136, 141, 154–156, 159, 173–174, 179–181, 184–185, 188, 190–191, 195, 197–198, 200–201, 204–205, 214–216, 226, 228, 233, 235–236, 239, 249, 256, 259, 261, 263, 270–271, 278, 298, 300, 304
Lucic, Milan, 218, 285, 286, 288, 290, 294, 297
Lumley, Dave, 30–31, 64, 66, 68, 73, 84
Lundqvist, Henrik, 279
Luongo, Roberto, 163
Lupul, Joffrey, 226, 233
Lynch, Doug, 214
MacDonald, Blair, 7, 28–29, 32, 34, 41–42
MacGregor, Bruce, 27, 83
MacIntyre, Steve, 237
Maciver, Norm, 131–132
MacLean, John, 193
MacTavish, Craig, 74, 81–82, 106, 111, 113–114, 122, 125, 128, 132, 134–136, 140–141, 143, 145, 181, 188, 193, 197, 199, 201, 214–215, 219–220, 234–235, 240–241, 263–264, 274, 278
Makelki, Larry, 170–171
Maki, Wayne, 128
Maltby, Kirk, 218
Mandel, Stephen, 231, 286, 259

Manning, Brandon, 280
Mansbridge, Peter, 303
Manson, Dave, 128–129, 131–132, 137, 141, 143
Mantha, Moe, 97
Marchant, Todd, 141, 145, 153, 155, 159, 167, 169, 177, 191, 199, 201, 204
Marchment, Bryan, 155, 164
Markkanen, Jussi, 197, 224
Marleau, Patrick, 163, 220, 266, 291
Maroon, Patrick, 282, 289, 290, 292–293, 300
Martin, Paul, 291
Martin, Terry, 73
Matthews, Auston, 284
Matvichuk, Richard, 159
Mayson, Tom, 171
McAmmond, Dean, 136, 153, 155, 166–167, 176
McCaffery, Father Mike, 298
McCammon, Bob, 163
McClelland, Kevin, 60, 62, 65, 77, 94, 109, 274
McDavid, Connor, 276–278, 280, 282, 285, 288–294, 296–298
McDonald, Lanny, 62–63, 85, 87
McFarlane, Todd, 171
McGillis, Dan, 165
McLean, Kirk, 132, 154
McLellan, Todd, 213, 278–279, 290–291, 294–295
McNair, Robert, 170
McNall, Bruce, 103
McSorley, Marty, 81, 94, 104, 111, 131–132, 174–175, 213
McTaggart, Jim, 55
Meehan, Don, 228
Mellanby, Scott, 126–128, 130, 132, 138
Meloche, Gilles, 81
Melton, Tim, 171
Memorial Cup, 5, 9–11, 29, 147, 214–215, 244, 246, 272, 278
Messier, Douglas Paul, 230
Messier, Mark, 21, 23–24, 32, 36–37, 41, 44, 46–48, 53, 55, 62, 64–66, 68, 71, 74, 77–78, 80, 85, 91, 94–95, 98–99, 103, 105–106, 110–116, 123, 128, 141, 153, 182, 205, 208–209, 228–230, 238, 272–274, 282–283, 288–289, 304
Michalek, Milan, 220
Micheletti, Joe, 27
Middlebrook, Lindsay, 55
Mighty Ducks of Anaheim. See Anaheim Ducks.
Mihalcheon, Art, 171
Miller, Paul, 55
Minnesota North Stars, 11, 16, 21, 23, 25, 27, 42, 63–64, 73, 89, 108, 125, 127–128, 135, 165
Minnesota Wild, 216, 228, 247, 252, 266
Mio, Eddie, 15, 22, 25, 42
Mironov, Boris, 141, 153, 166–168, 176
Modano, Mike, 156, 192, 201
Molson Cup, 154
Momesso, Sergio, 131
Montreal Canadiens, 9, 11, 25, 28–29, 35, 42, 44, 73, 99, 135, 154, 207, 209, 228, 235, 280, 291, 296

Moog, Andy, 38–39, 41–42, 44–45, 54–55, 60, 63–66, 74, 84–85, 91–92, 98, 100, 108, 115–116, 156, 159, 301
Moog, Arielle, 63
Moog, Karla, 63, 116
Moores, Billy, 215
Moreau, Ethan, 172–173, 176, 181, 201, 211, 233–235, 239, 247
Morrow, Ken, 56
Moss, David, 243
Moss, Joey, 182, 282, 302
Muckler, John, 71–72, 108–112, 114–115, 128, 130
Muir, Bryan, 164
Mullen, Joe, 84
Muller, Kirk, 193
Muni, Craig, 81, 89, 99
Murdoch, Don, 32
Murphy, Dennis, 6
Murphy, Joe, 110–113, 123, 125, 131–132, 135–136, 153
Murphy, Larry, 35
Murray, Rem, 162–163, 177, 191–193, 197, 228
Murray, Troy, 77
Musil, Frantisek "Frank," 165, 191
Nachbaur, Don, 51
Napier, Mark, 22, 73, 75, 91
Nash, Riley, 233, 247
Nashville Predators, 176, 266
Nedved, Petr, 211
Neely, Cam, 114
Neilson, Roger, 64–65
Nelson, Todd, 245, 274
New Jersey Devils, 55, 100, 123, 136, 139, 236, 272, 284–285
New York Islanders, 44–46, 54–60, 64–66, 71–73, 153, 163, 175, 188, 199, 214, 228, 236, 240–241, 245, 278, 296
New York Rangers, 9, 11, 37, 90, 128, 135–137, 141, 182, 197, 199–200, 206–207, 211, 228, 244, 278–279, 283
NHL All-Star Games, 72, 205–206, 216
NHL player lockouts, 144–145, 191, 212, 214–215, 245, 261, 264
NHL Players' Association, 115, 144, 204, 212, 260
Nicholls, Bernie, 128, 130–132, 136, 141
Nichols, Cal, 147–150, 170–171, 205, 225, 231–233, 238
Nicholson, Bob, 270–271, 277
Niedermayer, Scott, 285
Nieuwendyk, Joe, 159, 178
Niinimaa, Janne, 165, 168, 183, 191, 197, 199
Nikitin, Nikita, 272
Nilsson, Brian, 171
Nilsson, Kent, 89, 95
Nilsson, Robert, 228, 235, 247
Nilsson, Ulf, 11
Norris Trophy, 74, 83, 214
Norris, Jack, 210
Northern Lights Award of Distinction, 227
Northlands Coliseum, 7–9, 14, 27, 37, 59–60, 62, 66, 72, 78, 85, 93, 95–96, 101, 107, 113, 123, 125, 127, 142–143, 147, 167, 169,

173–174, 200, 271, 301
Norton, Jeff, 153
Notley, Rachel, 287
Nugent-Hopkins, Ryan, 251, 253–254, 261, 267, 288, 290
Nurse, Darnell, 264, 274, 294
Oates, Adam, 204–205
Octane cheerleaders, 248
Odgers, Jeff, 168
O'Donnell, Ian, 287
Oilers Entertainment Group (OEG), 270–271, 277–278
Oklahoma City Barons (AHL), 245, 247, 274
Oksiuta, Roman, 136
Olausson, Fredrik, 140–141
Oliver, David, 145, 153
Olympic Games, 24, 37, 98, 175–176, 197, 214, 228, 237, 240, 244, 271
O'Marra, Ryan, 228, 230
Orr, Bobby, 41, 83, 217
Osgood, Chris, 154
O'Sullivan, Patrick, 247
Ottawa Senators, 135, 175, 278–279
Owens, Al, 171
Paajarvi-Svensson, Magnus, 240–241, 246–248, 265
Paine, Dick, 171
Panarin, Artemi, 282
Paterson, Joe, 77
Patey, Doug, 31
Pearson, Scott, 138, 140–141
Peca, Michael, 214, 222, 228
Peckham, Theo, 228
Pederson, Barry, 71
Penner, Dustin, 233, 235–236, 243, 248, 251
Perron, David, 265, 267
Perry, Corey, 204, 294
Petersen, Toby, 222
Petry, Jeff, 228
Philadelphia Flyers, 30, 32, 51, 53, 77–78, 80, 88–90, 94–96, 128, 130, 163, 165, 175, 180, 183, 204, 233, 240, 265, 280, 303
Phillips, Rod, 249, 283
Phoenix Coyotes, 176, 198, 217, 228, 235, 238, 247, 252, 265, 267
Pilous, Rudy, 14
Pisa, Ales, 199
Pisani, Fernando, 201, 218–220, 224–225, 243, 247
Pitkanen, Joni, 233, 237
Pitlick, Tyler, 289
Pittsburgh Penguins, 11, 29, 60, 81–82, 97, 215, 237, 239, 285–286
Plante, Alex, 233
Plante, Jacques, 7–9
Pocklington, Eva, 12
Pocklington, Peter, 11–15, 17–18, 21–22, 44, 68–69, 75, 86–87, 97, 103–105, 115, 127–128, 137, 142–143, 148, 160, 169, 173, 180, 274
Poti, Tom, 177, 197, 191
Potulny, Ryan, 247
Potvin, Denis, 65, 71
Pouliot, Benoit, 272
Pouliot, Marc, 243, 247
Pouzar, Jaroslav, 50
Preissing, Tom, 220
Presidents' Trophy, 159, 169
Price, Pat, 22, 27

Primeau, Kevin, 140, 145
Pronger, Chris, 214–215, 218, 220–222, 226, 233, 236, 258, 264
Pruden, Kelly, 299
Puljujarvi, Jesse, 284, 290
Purcell, Teddy, 272
Quebec Nordiques, 5, 9, 21, 32, 39, 137–138, 147, 188, 256
Quinn, Pat, 132, 240, 241, 244, 275
Rakell, Rickard, 293–294
Ranford, Bill, 98, 106, 108, 111–115, 123, 125, 131–132, 137, 151
Ranheim, Paul, 123
Rasmussen, Gerry, 86
Reasoner, Marty, 195, 200, 218, 228
Red Tilson Trophy, 278
Reddick, Eldon "Pokey," 108, 123
Reid, David, 209
Reinhart, Griffin, 278
Reinhart, Sam, 272
Renney, Tom, 244, 253, 256–257
Rexall Place, 9, 204, 217, 219, 224–225, 231–232, 243, 246, 253, 260, 268–269, 271–273, 282, 288
Ricci, Mike, 177
Rice, Steven, 128, 140
Richard, Maurice "Rocket," 45
Richardson, Luke, 128–129, 131, 163
Riesen, Michel, 163, 195
Rita, Jani, 216
Ritchie, Nick, 295
Roberge, Marcel, 171
Roberge, Roger, 171
Robinson, Larry, 42, 207
Robitaille, Luc, 104, 106, 125, 131
Roenick, Jeremy, 132
Rogers Place, 269–271, 282, 286–289, 291, 293, 297–298, 301, 303
Roloson, Dwayne, 216, 220–224, 239, 241, 243
Roozen, Harold and Cathy, 171
Roulston, Tom, 60
Roussel, Dominic, 191
Roy, Derek, 279
Roy, Olivier, 265
Roy, Patrick, 154, 167–169
Ruotsalainen, Reijo, 90
Russell, Kris, 286, 297
Rychel, Warren, 168
Sabourin, Dany, 239
Saddledome, 55, 60, 72, 123
Sakic, Joe, 166, 167
Salmelainen, Tony, 216
Salo, Tommy, 175–178, 191, 193, 197, 201, 211
Samsonov, Sergei, 218, 220–221, 228
San Jose Sharks, 127, 138, 153–154, 175, 177, 210, 218, 220–222, 235, 252, 266, 278, 291–293
Sanderson, Geoff, 233
Satan, Miroslav, 153, 155
Sather, Anne, 15
Sather, Glen, 11–13, 15–16, 21–31, 33, 37, 39–42, 44–45, 47–48, 51, 53–54, 56, 59, 63–65, 71–73, 76, 78, 81, 83, 86–87, 89, 91, 94, 96–97, 103–104, 107–109, 111, 116, 121, 128, 140–141, 145, 147–148, 151, 153–154, 163–165, 169, 173, 175–176, 179–182,

187–188, 206–207, 230, 282–283, 298–299, 302–304
Sault Ste. Marie Greyhounds, 14, 35, 59, 264
Savard, Denis, 35, 75, 77
Saville, Bruce, 170–171, 187, 225, 233
Schlemko, David, 292
Schultz, Justin, 257–258, 263, 267
Schultz, Nick, 252–253, 266
Scrivens, Ben, 266–267, 280
Seguin, Tyler, 246
Sekera, Andrej, 279–293
Selivanov, Alex, 181
Semenko, Brian, 298
Semenko, Dave, 16–17, 21, 31, 35, 37, 40, 43, 53–54, 57, 75, 78–79, 83–84, 89, 94, 149, 182–184, 213, 286, 298, 304
Semenko, Hannah, 298
Semenov, Anatoli, 122, 125, 135
Sevigny, Richard, 42, 44
Shanahan, Brendan, 215
Sharples, Jeff, 110
Shaw, Brian, 10
Shaw, David, 128
Sheard, Dale, 171
Sherven, Gord, 73
Shields, Steve, 177
Shtalenkov, Mikhail, 176
Shugarman, Michael, 260
Shutt, Steve, 42
Silfverberg, Jakob, 294
Siltanen, Risto, 27, 37–38, 41, 51
Simpson, Craig, 97–100, 106–107, 113, 115, 123, 125, 139, 215
Sinden, Harry, 104, 188
Sjoberg, Lars-Erik, 12
Skalbania, Nelson, 11–15, 21
Skyreach Centre, 9, 174, 177–178, 187, 201, 204, 271
Slepyshev, Anton, 264, 293, 295
Smid, Ladislav, 243, 265
Smith, Billy, 56–57, 64–66
Smith, Geoff, 109, 122
Smith, Jason, 177, 181, 183, 191, 195–197, 201, 218, 220, 233
Smith, Steve, 81–82, 85, 87, 94, 96, 99, 115, 128, 131, 245
Smyth, Alex, 268
Smyth, Ryan, 144, 152–155, 157, 166–167, 177–178, 183–184, 190, 193, 197, 199, 201, 211, 218–222, 224, 228, 230–231, 250–253, 268
Sochatsky, Simon, 171
Souray, Sheldon, 235, 239, 243, 252
Spacek, Jaroslav, 216, 219–220, 228
Springsteen, Bruce, 42
Staal, Eric, 223
Stafford, Barrie, 56, 59, 223, 299–301
Staios, Steve, 195, 197, 201, 206, 219, 222, 230, 243
Stalwick, Rusty, 171
Stanley Cup finals/championships, 9, 22, 30, 44, 53, 57, 58, 60, 65, 66–72, 74–76, 78, 80, 87, 94–96, 100–101, 103–104, 110–111, 115–116, 127–128, 136, 139, 141, 159, 169, 178–180, 184, 187, 191, 198, 205, 210, 214, 223–224, 226, 230, 233, 236–237, 240–241, 249, 256, 265, 272–273, 278, 282–283, 286, 303–304
Staples, David, 225

Stastny, Peter, 214
Stastny, Yan, 214, 218
Stefan, Greg, 93
Stillman, Cory, 223
Stoll, Jarret, 199, 218–219, 237
Stone, Ryan, 239, 243
Strome, Ryan, 296
Strudwick, Jason, 237
Summanen, Raimo, 82, 90
Sutter, Brent, 57, 71, 256
Sutter, Darryl, 77
Sutter, Duane, 56–57
Sutter, Rich, 78
Sutter, Ron, 77–78, 88–89
Sutton, Andy, 252
Sykora, Petr, 228, 231
Takko, Kari, 123
Talbot, Cam, 278–279, 291–295
Tambellini, Steve, 236, 240–241, 246, 251–252, 256, 258, 263
Tampa Bay Lightning, 135–136, 138, 141, 144, 164, 181, 241, 244, 247, 263, 272
Tarnstrom, Dick, 216, 228
Ted Lindsay Award, 297
Thornton, Joe, 163, 220–221, 291
Thornton, Scott, 128, 145, 154
Tikkanen, Esa, 59, 91–92, 98, 100, 107, 109, 113, 115, 123, 125, 132, 136–137, 141
Tjarnqvist, Daniel, 228
Toal, Mike, 32
Tocchet, Rick, 78
Todd, Kevin, 136
Tonelli, John, 71–72
Toronto Maple Leafs, 9, 31–32, 37, 73, 89, 93, 97, 128, 135, 174, 177, 180, 199, 224, 228, 240, 264, 272, 280, 284
Torres, Raffi, 199, 200, 211, 219–220, 222, 237
Toskala, Vesa, 221
Trottier, Bryan, 71
Tugnutt, Ron, 131, 137–138
Turco, Marty, 201
Ulanov, Igor, 191
Unger, Garry, 47
Vachon, Rogie, 132
Vancouver Canucks, 41, 51, 65, 82, 84, 90, 121, 132, 138, 153–154, 163, 177, 197, 218, 236, 240, 244, 252, 268, 280, 282
Van Dorp, Wayne, 91, 97
Vandermeer, Jim, 247, 252
Veitch, Darren, 35
Verbeek, Pat, 156
Vernon, Mike, 99, 115, 123, 154
Vezina Trophy, 99, 154, 265
Visnovsky, Lubomir, 237, 243
Vujtek, Vladimir, 135
Walters, Ron, 6
Ward, Joel, 291
Washington Capitals, 22, 35, 188, 194
Watson, Bryan, 31
Watson, Chuck, 170
Watt, Allan, 205
Weaver, Barry, 171, 174, 205
Weaver, Keith, 171
Weight, Doug, 136–137, 140–141, 150, 153–156, 166–167, 175, 177, 179, 181, 183–184, 190, 193, 195, 197
Weir, Stan, 31

Wesley, Glen, 100
Whitney, Ryan, 243, 248
Wickenheiser, Doug, 35
Wideman, Dennis, 290
William Hanley Trophy, 278
Williams, Jason, 219
Williams, Justin, 223–224
Williams, Tiger, 92
Wilson, Carey, 62
Wilson, Doug, 71
Winchester, Brad, 219
Winnipeg Jets (NHL), 21, 29, 35, 55, 60, 74, 84, 93, 99, 112–113, 138, 141, 143, 151, 154, 164, 176, 284
Winnipeg Jets (WHA), 5, 7, 10–11, 14–15, 17
Woodcroft, Jay, 278–279
Woods, Jim, 171
World Championships, 11, 121, 214, 228, 264, 278
World Junior Championships, 37, 135, 188, 214, 228, 236, 240, 264, 271, 284
Woywitka, Jeff, 204, 214
Yakupov, Nail, 256, 262–263, 286
Yelle, Stephane, 167
York, Mike, 197, 199, 201, 214
Yzerman, Steve, 59, 94
Zanello, Jim, 171
Zelepukin, Valeri, 164
Zetterberg, Henrik, 219–220, 258
Zhelobnyuk, Vadim, 236
Ziegler, John, 22, 115, 121
Zubov, Sergei, 156, 178